Sustainable Tourism Contracts

Sara Landini

Sustainable Tourism Contracts

G. Giappichelli Editore

Sara Landini
Department of Legal Sciences
University of Florence
Florence, Italy

ISBN 978-3-030-83139-4   ISBN 978-3-030-83140-0   (eBook)
https://doi.org/10.1007/978-3-030-83140-0

© Springer Nature Switzerland AG and G. Giappichelli Editore 2021

This work is subject to copyright. All rights are solely and exclusively licensed by the Publisher, whether the whole or part of the material is concerned, specifically the rights of translation, reprinting, reuse of illustrations, recitation, broadcasting, reproduction on microfilms or in any other physical way, and transmission or information storage and retrieval, electronic adaptation, computer software, or by similar or dissimilar methodology now known or hereafter developed.

The use of general descriptive names, registered names, trademarks, service marks, etc. in this publication does not imply, even in the absence of a specific statement, that such names are exempt from the relevant protective laws and regulations and therefore free for general use.

The publisher, the authors, and the editors are safe to assume that the advice and information in this book are believed to be true and accurate at the date of publication. Neither the publisher nor the authors or the editors give a warranty, expressed or implied, with respect to the material contained herein or for any errors or omissions that may have been made. The publisher remains neutral with regard to jurisdictional claims in published maps and institutional affiliations.

This Springer imprint is published by the registered company Springer Nature Switzerland AG.
The registered company address is: Gewerbestrasse 11, 6330 Cham, Switzerland

Preface

Tourism has taken on a significant economic dimension over the course of the twentieth century, at both a European and global scale, and has characterized itself as a specific source of stress for ecosystems.

Among the negative consequences related to tourism activities, there is a possible loss in the social and cultural identity of the host area, an increase in waste production, an increase in the consumption of primary goods and resources (water, energy, etc.), the alteration and destruction of mountains, lakes, coasts, marine ecosystems, a loss of biodiversity, aesthetic and visual impacts, soil and water pollution, congestion and noise pollution, the concentration of benefits in a few large companies and/or foreign countries, an increase in the demand for mobility, illegal and/or child labour and prostitution.

The impact of tourism on the environment can be defined in terms of "environmental and social pressure": greater influx of vehicles, greater presence of people, increased waste production, and increased construction of new accommodation facilities.

We must consider not only the pollution emitted by travel (plane, car, etc.) but also fundamental factors such as the construction and maintenance of hotels, industrial foods in hotels, or souvenirs traditionally bought by tourists, which are instead considered in more recent studies.

The solution can be found in regular interventions aimed at implementing prohibitions and limits. This book aims to provide an overview of the role of private autonomy in the regulation of all forms of tourism and in governing sustainable development. A bottom-up approach is proposed with a shared management of environmental problems that stem, at first, from the bottom, that is, from local businesses that, partly thanks to the inputs and requests from external subjects (intermediary organizations such as trade associations and civil societies), promote the development of strategies and tools for activating environmental management processes that involve the entire territory. In this perspective, the participation of the various actors creates a process that, starting from the local production system and the shared set of its experiences and knowledge of the operators, manages to involve territorial institutions and civil societies.

The book is divided into three parts. The first part is dedicated to private tourism law sources. In this part, we highlight the role of private autonomy in regulating both business-to-consumer contracts and business-to-business contracts. Companies and individuals determine the rules of their relationships within the framework of national law (with specific regard to consumer law) and within international law.

Particular attention is dedicated to the principle of sustainability applied to the tourism sector in terms of the balance between cultural heritage protection and economic development.

The second part is dedicated to business-to-consumer contracts (such as hotel contracts, timeshares, tourist apartment lease; home exchanges), travel packages, and transport contracts. Tourism is a matter of being elsewhere and it implies the use of transport, which can be considered as the necessary precondition of tourism itself. This part will focus on specific contractual conditions that can be introduced into B2C contracts with sustainable goals.

The third part deals with business-to-business contracts and, in particular, contracts that regulate structural formulas like management contracts and franchising contracts. These are types of business governance structures and can be defined as either part of or entire collaborating parties' activities performed in order to achieve a common goal. Cooperation, trust, reliance, mutuality, and the resolution of problems by consent represent the real foundations of the B2B relationship because of the parties' interdependence. This part will consider how the rules of governance of a tourism enterprise, including risk management, can be shaped in a sustainable perspective.

The book's methodology is characterized by strict attention to practice and, in particular, to case law and clauses that are generally included in tourism contracts. A perspective such as this one is fundamental because tourism law, as well as tourism itself, is mainly a product of society.

Particular attention is placed on uniform law processes, among which we can include European Union Law and UNIDROIT. Tourism contracts are generally international contracts. The determination of the applicable national law, according to the rules of international private law, is not a satisfactory solution. The presence of different national laws can cause disparities, uncertainties, and barriers affecting business. These problems can be solved by the harmonization processes in progress and, in particular, through conventions designed to develop a uniform system.

One might ask: why write a book on tourism sustainability in a period in which the pandemic has transformed over-tourism into under-tourism? Because the need for leisure has not ceased, but the ways in which it is implemented have simply changed (e.g., during the Covid pandemic, we had an intensification of local tourism, partly due to the intensification of smart working). There remains the issue of a green tourism industry that turns tourism into a resource for the environment, rather than a threat. Moreover, as we will see, the pandemic has represented a new challenge for sustainability: health sustainability with the need to offer clients certain safety services.

Florence, Italy   Sara Landini
June 2017

Contents

Part I   The Sources of Tourism Law and the Principle of Sustainable Industry

1   An Introduction to Sustainable Tourism 3
  1.1   Definitions of Tourism 3
    1.1.1   Tourism, Movement and Leisure 3
  1.2   The Periods of Tourism 4
    1.2.1   A Brief History of Tourism 4
    1.2.2   ICT and Tourism 6
    1.2.3   Tourism and Virtual Reality 6
    1.2.4   Tourism in the "Society of Uncertainty" 7
  1.3   Peculiarities of Tourism from the Legal Point of View 10
    1.3.1   Tourism Is a Global Phenomenon 10
    1.3.2   Tourism Is a Non-Stop Phenomenon 10
    1.3.3   Tourism Needs to be Sustainable 11
  References 12

2   National and International Law. The Importance of Cooperation .. 13
  2.1   National Political Governance and Tourism 13
    2.1.1   National Tourism Law 13
  2.2   European Law 14
    2.2.1   Tourism in EU Law 14
    2.2.2   The Role of the EU Court of Justice and the
            Importance of Uniformation of Law in Tourism 16
    2.2.3   The Role of European Directives in Tourism Contract
            Law 17
  2.3   International Norms 18
    2.3.1   International Cooperation and Tourism 18
    2.3.2   International Contract Law 19
    2.3.3   UNWTO Towards a Sustainable Tourism 20

ix

	2.4	Consumers' Protection	22
		2.4.1 Consumers' Legal Protection	22
		2.4.2 Customers' Care	23
	References		24

3 Customary Law 25
   3.1 Customary Law and Legal Order 25
      3.1.1 Definitions 25
      3.1.2 General Customary Law and International Customary Law 26
   3.2 Customary Law in Tourism Sector 26
      3.2.1 Some Examples 26
      3.2.2 Customary Law and Sustainable Development 27
   References 27

4 Private Autonomy 29
   4.1 Private Autonomy Across Countries 29
      4.1.1 A Comparative Approach to Contracts 29
      4.1.2 National Contract Law in International Contracts 30
   4.2 Key Points in Writing a Contract 31
      4.2.1 Identification of the Standard of Performance 31
      4.2.2 Dealing the Agreement 31
      4.2.3 Limits to Freedom of Contract 33
   4.3 Judicial Intervention in Contract Matters 33
      4.3.1 Illegal and Unfair Contract 33
      4.3.2 Damages in Case of Breach of Contract 34
   4.4 Tourism Contracts 35
      4.4.1 B2B and B2C Contracts 35
      4.4.2 Sustainable Contracts 35
   References 37

5 The Worldwide Concept of Sustainability and Tourism 39
   5.1 Sustainability and Tourism 39
      5.1.1 The Environmental and Social Impact of Tourism 39
      5.1.2 Concepts of Sustainability 40
      5.1.3 The Concept of Sustainability in UN Actions 41
   5.2 Defining Sustainability in Tourism Sector 42
      5.2.1 The Environmental and Social Impact of Tourism 42
      5.2.2 Is Sustainability an Unfocused Concept? 44
      5.2.3 Measuring Sustainability 45
      5.2.4 Some Examples of Sustainable Tourism 48
   5.3 The Role of Courts and Scholars 51
      5.3.1 Courts, Scholars and Sources of Law 51
      5.3.2 Scholars, Courts and Sustainability 52
   References 53

Contents   xi

Part II   Consumer Contracts and Tourism

6   Consumer Contracts and Sustainability 57
- 6.1   Consumer Contracts and Sustainability 57
  - 6.1.1   Sustainable Consumer 57
  - 6.1.2   Consumer and Tourism 58
  - 6.1.3   Why Do Consumers Need Protection? 60
- 6.2   Standard Contracts and Consumer Autonomy 61
  - 6.2.1   Consumers' Choice 61
  - 6.2.2   Consumers' Protection Against Unfair Terms 62
  - 6.2.3   Many of the Consumers' Rights Remain Unfulfilled ... 64
- 6.3   Consumers' Protection Private Law Remedies 66
  - 6.3.1   Different Remedies 66
  - 6.3.2   Consumers' Protection and Punitive Damages 66
- References 68

7   Hospitality Industry and Contracts 71
- 7.1   Hospitality Industry Market 71
  - 7.1.1   Tradition and Innovation in Hospitality Industry 71
  - 7.1.2   Food&Beverage 74
  - 7.1.3   Sustainable Hospitality 75
- 7.2   The Hotel Accommodation Contract 77
  - 7.2.1   Content of Hotel Contract 77
  - 7.2.2   Green Hotel 78
  - 7.2.3   Breach of Hotel Contract 80
  - 7.2.4   Hotelkeepers' Liability 81
  - 7.2.5   Hotel Contract vs Tourist Lease Contract 83
- 7.3   Tourism in Sharing Economy 84
  - 7.3.1   Timeshare and Tourism 84
  - 7.3.2   Timeshare in EU Directive 85
  - 7.3.3   Home Exchange and Tourism 86
- References 88

8   Travel Contracts and Sustainable Mobility 91
- 8.1   Transport Law 91
  - 8.1.1   Transport Law and Consumers' Protection 91
  - 8.1.2   Transportation Contract 92
- 8.2   European and International Transportation Laws 93
  - 8.2.1   Maritime Transportation Law 93
  - 8.2.2   Air Transport 97
  - 8.2.3   Rail Transport 99
- 8.3   Sustainable Mobility and Tourism 100
  - 8.3.1   Sustainable Mobility 100
  - 8.3.2   Sustainable Transport and Travel 101
- References 102

xii   Contents

9 Mass Travel Contracts 103
    9.1   Inclusive Tour 103
        9.1.1   From Thomas Cook's Idea to Mass Tourism 103
        9.1.2   Regulation of Mass Tourism 104
    9.2   International Law 104
        9.2.1   International Convention on Travel Contracts 104
        9.2.2   General Obligation on the Tour Organizer and
                on the Traveller 105
        9.2.3   General Obligation on the Intermediary 107
    9.3   Travel Packages and European Union Law 107
        9.3.1   The First Directive on Travel Package 107
        9.3.2   The New Directive 108
    9.4   Ruined Holiday 112
        9.4.1   Non-Material Damage in Case of Travel Contracts 112
        9.4.2   Ruined Holiday Damage According to the Directive
                2302/2015 113
        9.4.3   One of the Leading Case on Ruined Holiday Damage .. 115
        9.4.4   Non Material Damage and Green Tourism Services ... 116
    References 116

10 Unfair Commercial Practices 119
    10.1   Martketing Strategies in Tourism Market 119
        10.1.1   Marketing in Brief 119
        10.1.2   DAGMAR Model 121
        10.1.3   Commercial Practices 122
    10.2   Best Commercial Practices 123
        10.2.1   Illegal and Unfair Advertising 123
        10.2.2   Unfair Commercial Practices in EU Law 125
        10.2.3   Unfair Commercial Practices and Unfair Commercial
                Terms 128
        10.2.4   Some Cases 130
        10.2.5   Environmental Claims and Green Claims 136
    References 140

**Part III Tourism Industry Business Contracts and Sustainability
Policies**

11 Tourism Industry Business Contracts 145
    11.1   Tourism Industry Business Contracts 145
        11.1.1   B2B Contracts in Tourism Market 145
        11.1.2   Long Term Contracts and Resilience Clauses 147
        11.1.3   Long Term Contracts and Business Interruption 149
    11.2   Business Contract Law and Competition Law 151
        11.2.1   Unfair Competition, Unfair Terms in Case of B2B
                Contracts 151
        11.2.2   Some Cases 153
    References 156

Contents

xiii

12 Tourism Industry Contracts and Structural Formulas: Management and Ownership 159
  12.1 Business's Legal Structures 159
    12.1.1 Business Ownership, Partnership, Corporation 159
  12.2 Hotel Lease 160
    12.2.1 Contents of Hotel Lease 160
    12.2.2 Lease, Management, Franchising 162
  12.3 Hotel Franchising 163
    12.3.1 Franchising Contents 163
    12.3.2 Green Franchising 166
  12.4 Hotel Management Contract 167
    12.4.1 Contents of Management Contracts 167
    12.4.2 Management Contract as Example of Collaborative Contracting 171
  References 175

13 Conclusions 177
  13.1 Contract as a Source of Tourism Law 177
    13.1.1 Private Autonomy and Regulation of Tourism Activity 177
    13.1.2 The Distinction Between B2B and B2C Contracts 178
  13.2 Tourism Contracts and Levers to Sustainability 179
    13.2.1 Contracts as Levers 179
  13.3 Contracts 2.0 Towards Sustainable Tourism 181
    13.3.1 Smart Contracts 181
    13.3.2 Smart Contracts in Tourism Sector 182
    13.3.3 Smart Contracts and Sustainable Tourism 182
  References 183

Part I
The Sources of Tourism Law and the Principle of Sustainable Industry

Chapter 1
An Introduction to Sustainable Tourism

Contents

1.1	Definitions of Tourism	3
	1.1.1 Tourism, Movement and Leisure	3
1.2	The Periods of Tourism	4
	1.2.1 A Brief History of Tourism	4
	1.2.2 ICT and Tourism	6
	1.2.3 Tourism and Virtual Reality	6
	1.2.4 Tourism in the "Society of Uncertainty"	7
1.3	Peculiarities of Tourism from the Legal Point of View	10
	1.3.1 Tourism Is a Global Phenomenon	10
	1.3.2 Tourism Is a Non-Stop Phenomenon	10
	1.3.3 Tourism Needs to be Sustainable	11
References		12

1.1 Definitions of Tourism

1.1.1 Tourism, Movement and Leisure

Tourism is one of the forms of recreation along with sports, hobbies, and other uses of leisure time.

Different definitions have been proposed. Tourism could be defined as the movement of people away from their normal place of residence. This definition is incomplete. Purpose and distance are also determining factors in the phenomenon of tourism.

The Institute of Tourism in Britain suggests the following definition: "Tourism is the temporary short-term movement of people to destinations outside the places where they normally live and work, and the activities during their stay at these destinations; it includes movement for all purposes, as well as day visits or excursions". According to the International Conference on Leisure Recreation Tourism held in Cardiff in 1981, "tourism may be defined in terms of particular activities

---

© The Author(s), under exclusive license to Springer Nature Switzerland AG 2021
S. Landini, *Sustainable Tourism Contracts*,
https://doi.org/10.1007/978-3-030-83140-0_1

selected by choice and undertaken outside the home environment. Tourism may or may not involve overnight stays away from home".

All of the above definitions are quite general. The concept of tourism can be defined broadly in order to embrace all forms of the phenomenon.

Of course, coming up with a technical definition for the sake of statistical studies is possible, but to define the concept of tourism is a difficult task and one that may not be necessary.

In fact, from the legal point of view, this phenomenon is composed of different situations ruled in different ways and by different sources of law (acts of parliament, customary laws, contracts).

It might be more important to focus our attention on certain peculiarities of tourist products. It has often been said that "Selling holidays is selling dreams". When someone books a hotel room, a journey, or a holiday package, he/she is also buying the temporary use of a particular environment consisting of novel geographical features, cultural benefits, services, atmosphere, hospitality, and other intangible benefits. Therefore, it is correct to say that the product of tourism is largely psychological and that it is an instrument for the development of the personal identity of individuals. Thus, it is right to maintain that tourism it is not only an economic matter.

1.2 The Periods of Tourism

1.2.1 A Brief History of Tourism

The word 'tourism' comes from the word 'tour', which was associated with the idea of a voyage, peregrination, or route. The word 'tourism' did not appear until the early nineteenth century.

Historical studies usually distinguish three principal epochs: the first starts with the railway age (around 1840); the second covers the second industrial revolution (around 1870) that completely changed the way people travelled; the third covers the years between the two world wars, characterized by a significant development in private motor cars, buses, coaches etc.[1]

There is another epoch that we must add to this list, one that started after 1950, and was characterized by mass tourism, an increase in business travel and a significant change in the products offered by tourism. Someone observes: "Although the nineteenth century produced a considerable change in the size and nature of tourism, it was not until well into the twentieth century that "mass" tourism can truly be said to have come about. There were two main periods of growth. (A) First between the two World Wars the European countries in particular underwent a period of social upheaval out of which came higher expectations by the masses of holiday

---

[1] See Lickorish and Jenkins (2016); Furlough and Baranowski (2001); Smith (1998).

1.2 The Periods of Tourism

entitlement, incomes and material living standards...(B) In the 1950s and 1960s pre-war growth was resumed but spread much more widely so that international tourism began to reach mass markets in many countries".[2]

Of course, even before the industrial revolution people used to travel for pilgrimage, business, and official purposes.

For example, the Greeks hosted international visitors during the first Olympic Games, held in 776 BC, and Romans also travelled on holiday as far away as Egypt. In addition, spas were well established during the time of Roman Empire.

From the end of the sixteenth century, individuals travelled for educational purposes in order to learn about foreign countries and their inhabitants.

However, we have to consider that during these periods the concept of tourism was different, because the concept of leisure time was different.

Before the Industrial revolution, foreign travel was part of the education of an aristocratic man. The majority of the population hardly travelled beyond their village.

The contemporary idea of leisure time did not exist, because there was no separation between the working day and holiday.

The industrial revolution brought about changes in the economy and in society. Until the eighteenth century, the most common form of transportation was the horse. In the eighteen century, the increasing demand for travel, the improvement of new forms of transportation, and the development of road systems were associated with an increase in coach services.

The evolution of the railway and road systems deeply affected the type and amount of accommodation used in conjunction with travel. Accommodation for travellers can generally be viewed in two ways: terminal accommodation or transit accommodation. At the destination, accommodation, catering, and entertainment constitute the primary tourist services.

In the second half of the nineteenth century, in the main European and American cities, the management of the larger hotels began to change from single owners and their families to company organisations. Hotel companies and hotel chains came onto the scene with several establishments under the same management and usually the same name.

When journeys consisted of taking several different types of transport, specialist organisers began to assemble the travellers' more complex journeys on their behalf, issuing tickets as agents for the transport companies.

During the time between the two world wars, governments began to recognize the economic importance of tourism, particularly in the balance of payments. Many western countries have established networks of tourist offices and invested massively in advertising and in tourism literature.

---

[2]Holloway (1989 reprint in 2016), p. 22 and p. 33.

1.2.2 ICT and Tourism

Finally, a new era needs to be added: technology and tourism. Internet has provided many advantages to tour operators: better dissemination of commercial communication through websites and social media; more effective product communication; the display of the product on an international market; greater and more efficient access to information, both on the customer side and on the retailer side. The customer can benefit from an enormous amount of information, using it to their advantage, while the retailer can exploit Big Data to their own benefit. As we will see, technology has changed the way that tourism works with the possibility, for example, for the customer to assemble the services of tourist packages independently and to access platforms that allow citizens to exchange travel or accommodation tourist offers.[3]

Technology has introduced new players into the tourism market: meta-searches and online travel agencies (OTAs). OTAs, as the word itself implies, carry out intermediary activities between customer and supplier (hotels, carriers, etc.), like traditional agencies. These are booking portals through which customers, in this case tourists, can compare different hospitality offers for the destination they have chosen, and if satisfied by the search, they can book directly online. On each booking made, a commission that varies from company to company is usually withheld, which is almost never charged to the end customer, but is paid almost entirely by the supplier. The rule that is usually presented in contracts between OTAs and suppliers states that OTAs can sell those products and services at the same prices as their suppliers, usually asking for a fee for each sale made through their channels. The meta-search groups together the prices and rates of many, if not all, OTAs and websites on the network onto a single platform. In this way, customers, or users, are able to focus on a single site, finding almost all of the offers that are available on the web. Their differences with OTAs lie in the marketing strategy. Unlike OTAs, meta-searches do not apply commissions to their affiliates, but charge the costs to the booking sites they promote, which can be expressed in fees per click or in fees for the visibility that the page has collected.

1.2.3 Tourism and Virtual Reality

Another innovation in the tourism market is related to virtual reality.[4]

Virtual reality is a simulated three-dimensional reality and is often very realistic thanks to specific software and hardware. It is a three-dimensional, computer generated environment which can be explored and interacted with by a physical person. He/she becomes part of this virtual world or is immersed within this

---

[3] Xiang and Gretzel (2010), pp. 179–188; Ray (2015), pp. 78–96.
[4] Perry Hobson and Williams (1995), pp.124–135; Steuer (1992), pp. 73–93.

1.2 The Periods of Tourism

environment and whilst there, is able to manipulate objects or perform a series of actions.

Virtual reality can be used, for example, by coaches and players to train more efficiently across a range of sports, as they are able to experience certain situations repeatedly and can improve their performances. Essentially, it's used as an aid to help measure athletic performance and analyse techniques. Virtual reality can help in medical training. Virtual patients are used to allow students to develop skills which can later be applied in the real world.

Even in tourism it can find different applications. Below is a summary of its possible applications:

- marketing of destinations or facilities. With the creation of 360 videos, a potential customer can visit places, accommodation facilities and entertainment venues in advance, so that they can choose their destination with greater awareness.
- didactic videos on the attractions and places they will visit.
- in-room entertainment in hotels. This is more suitable for hotels that aim to offer something other than pay TV in their rooms.

It is difficult to consider virtual reality that is enjoyed at home as a substitute for tourism. The absence of physical movement excludes the presence of a tourist phenomenon.

1.2.4 Tourism in the "Society of Uncertainty"

Another evolution in tourism is determined by the present condition of the "society of uncertainty" that we live in: natural catastrophic events (including pandemics) and human events make it difficult to plan, especially when traveling. We are witnessing more and more last minute and flexible tourist choices (with the possibility of unlimited cancellations) or assistance by insurance coverage that offers reimbursement in the case of travel for the chosen destination becoming impossible.[5]

The insurance contract has always been the main risk transfer tool and can therefore become an effective measure to implement resilience against unexpected events.

Tourism law provides many hypothesis of mandatory insurance: article 7 of Regulation (EEC) No 2407/92 provides mandatory insurance for air carrier; national law usually provides mandatory insurance for travel agency.

Moreover, travellers usually buy optional travel insurance that generally covers medical expenses, financial default of travel suppliers, and other losses incurred while traveling, either within one's own country, or internationally. Temporary travel insurance can usually be arranged at the time of the booking of a single trip

---

[5] Baumann (2007).

to cover exactly the duration of that trip, but is possible also to buy a "multi-trip" policy covering an unlimited number of trips within a set time frame.

The most common risks covered by travel insurance are:

- Medical emergency both in case of accident and sickness;
- Emergency evacuation;
- Repatriation of remains;
- Return of a minor;
- Trip cancellation;
- Trip interruption;
- Accidental death, injury or disablement benefit;
- Overseas funeral expenses;
- Lost, stolen or damaged baggage, personal effects or travel documents;
- Delayed baggage (and emergency replacement of essential items);
- Flight connection was missed due to airline schedule;
- Travel delays due to weather.

Not all risks are covered. Insurance companies will often exclude coverage for ongoing known events to new policies, for specific catastrophic events, such as volcanic activity, pandemics and endemics, acts of war, and terrorism.

Other common exclusions in travel insurance policies include undeclared pre-existing medical conditions, travelling for the purpose of receiving medical treatment, elective surgery or treatment, or injury or illness caused by alcohol, drug use, or reckless behaviour.

Ways of flexibility in tourism offers have been recommended by Eu Commission. On 5 March 2020 the Eu Commission published on the Commission's website a tourism and transport package composed of guidelines and a recommendation to help the travel and transport industry. The EU Commission maintains that the traveller has the right to have the ticket reimbursed when the trip is cancelled due to COVID-19 according to Eu Directive on Package Travel Directive (EU) 2015/2302. On the other hand, the European Commission recommends vouchers as an attractive alternative to reimbursement.

On 13 May 2020, the European Commission published its guidelines and recommendations on how to resume tourism and transport after the pandemic using vouchers and rerouting:

- The voucher should have a minimum validity period of 12 months. The air carrier or travel provider should automatically reimburse the amount after the end of its validity period if the voucher has not been redeemed.
- If the voucher is valid for more than 12 months, the air passenger or traveller should have the right to ask for reimbursement 12 months after the issuance of the voucher concerned.
- The air passenger or traveller should be able to exchange the voucher for all new booking before the expiry date of the voucher, including for trips with departure after this date.

1.2 The Periods of Tourism

- The air passenger or traveller should able to use vouchers for payments for all departures or package travels offered by the air carrier or travel provider.
- The air carrier and the travel provider should be able to offer the same route or package travel under the same service conditions as detailed in the original booking.
- The air carrier or travel provider should consider whether the voucher can be used by other air carriers or travel providers within the same group of companies.
- The air passenger or traveller should be able to use the voucher for new bookings through the same travel agency which booked the original booking.
- Vouchers for transport services should be transferable to another passenger without any additional cost. Vouchers for package travel should also be transferable to another traveller without any additional cost, if the providers of the services included in the package agree to the transfer without any additional cost.
- In order to make vouchers more attractive, air carriers and travel providers could consider issuing vouchers with a higher value than the amount of any payments made for the package travel or transport service originally booked, for example through an additional lump sum or additional service elements.
- Vouchers should indicate their validity period and specify all the rights attached to them. They should be issued on a durable medium; such as email or paper.
- The voucher must be secured against the bankruptcy of the airline or travel provider.

The Commission published a report on the application of the Package Travel Directive on 1 March 2021.

The report moves from the experience gained with the application of the Package Travel Directive since its entry into application in July 2018. It presents preliminary results of the assessment of national measures transposing the Directive. It also assesses the rules in the context of the challenges that have since emerged during the pandemic crisis.

The Commission stressed also on travel insurance. As noted the insurance contracts usually contain exclusions of catastrophic events including pandemic and endemic.

In its report, the Commission noted that these exclusions limit the possibility of travellers to insure themselves against possible losses due to cancellation of a trip caused by a pandemic.

Some travel business stakeholders have suggested that organisers should be allowed to include appropriate personal travel insurance in a package with an opt-in/out option. Within the Package Travel Directive stakeholder group, consumer organisations however stressed that any insurance taken out by the travellers themselves should in no way limit existing travellers' refund rights and the protection under the mandatory insolvency protection.

1.3 Peculiarities of Tourism from the Legal Point of View

1.3.1 Tourism Is a Global Phenomenon

As a result of the above considerations, we can highlight some peculiarities of tourism that are of interest in a legal perspective.

Firstly, tourism is a global phenomenon. Many people choose to travel to learn about different cultures. It is not only cultural travellers that visit historic and culturally significant sites.[6]

For the poorest countries in particular, tourism is one of the greatest economic sources. For that reason, governments and multilateral policies (multiple countries working together on a specific issue) impact on tourist activities. Governments can encourage tourism through regulations, official statements, collaborations, and incentives across multiple governmental bodies. The United Nations World Tourist Organisation (UNWTO intergovernmental organization) serves as a global forum for tourism policy issues, helping developing countries with sustainable tourism policies and providing technical and financial assistance to countries seeking to attract foreign tourists.

1.3.2 Tourism Is a Non-Stop Phenomenon

As we have seen, tourism is also a phenomenon that continuously evolves. It is difficult to regulate it, moreover massive and detailed national laws can become a burden for the tourism industry. Many governments decide against strongly regulating the private law of tourism according to a policy of minimal regulation.

Thus, the main sources of tourism private law are customary law and private autonomy, which are clearly limited by national law (i.e., consumer's protection law, environmental protection law, etc.) and fundamental international principles. In fact, tourism can affect fundamental rights (sex tourism, for example) (4), on the fundamental principle of solidarity and on the principle of hospitality in particular.

Hospitality is not synonymous with aid or charity. It simply means extending a welcome to others, who have rights and who must be guaranteed a status and a stability of existence, according to the fundamental principles of living together.

Moreover, tourism can affect environmental sustainability. Natural attractions might themselves be destroyed by the multitude of tourists visiting them. Governments must raise awareness about the natural environment needing protection from pollution caused by economic activity which allows for the environment to be enjoyed by many people.[7]

---

[6]Zuelow (2011); Chakraborty (2007).

[7]George and Varghese (2007).

1.3.3 Tourism Needs to be Sustainable

Sustainable development is a key concept in United Nations actions. It aims to meet the needs of present generations without impacting on the ability of future generations to meet their own needs. It provides a comprehensive approach bringing together economic, social and environmental considerations in the perspective to mutually reinforce each other.

The UN's 2030 Agenda, adopted by world leaders in 2015, represents the new global sustainable development framework and sets 17 Sustainable Development Goals, that provide concrete objectives for the next 15 years, focussed particularly on: human dignity; regional and global stability; a healthy planet; fair and resilient societies; prosperous economies.

In November 2016, the European Commission outlined its strategic approach towards the implementation of the 2030 Agenda, including the Sustainable Development Goals. Sustainability informs key principles and concept of national and international legislation and it is guide for the entire legal system.

The relationship between environmental quality and tourism success is discussed, focusing on ways to protect the world's tourism destinations for future generations.[8]

Sustainable tourism can be defined as tourism that considers its current and future impact on the environment, society and the economy.

Sustainability is a key word in tourism. It has become a priority to combine the growth of the tourism sector with the preservation of cultural properties: both the so-called cultural property (museums, archaeological sites, etc.), and environmental heritage (natural beauty, parks, etc.).

Sustainable tourism is important because travel shouldn't be harmful. We should travel in a way that can benefit the people and communities we're in, and that mitigates negative impacts of travel on the environment. Sustainable tourism is about showing we care the world. Thanks to sustainability principle tourism has the potential to make the world a better place by bringing economic benefits to poorer destinations, through cultural exchange and understanding and through self-growth.

Sustainable tourism and ecotourism are two possible ways of addressing the many environmental and social problems associated with tourism. The UNEP (United Nations Environment Programme) and the UNWTO list 12 principles of sustainable tourism: economic viability, local prosperity, employment quality, social equity, visitor fulfilment, local control, community well-being, cultural richness, physical integrity, biological diversity, resource efficiency, and environmental purity. UNEP has a long history of contributing toward the development and implementation of environmental law. DELC is the focal Division within UNEP which oversees the many facets of this global legal framework. Hence, the role of DELC within the framework of UNEP is primarily to ensure the progressive development of environmental law across different environmental sectors and levels of governance.

---

[8] Bosselmann (2016).

At a global level, DELC has been pivotal in the facilitation of intergovernmental platforms for the promotion and implementation of multilateral environmental agreements (MEAs) and defining international environmental norms.

As result of these considerations, we must say that private tourism law is mainly composed of rules arising not from institutions, but from what happens in a changing society (customary law and contracts) according to the principles of hospitality and of environmental sustainability.[9]

References

Baumann, Z. (2007). *Liquid society: Living the age of uncertainty*. Polity.

Bosselmann, F. (2016). *Transforming law and governance*. Routledge.

Chakraborty, A. (2007). *Global tourism*. Abebooks.

Furlough, E., & Baranowski, S. (2001). *Being elsewhere: Tourism, consumer culture, and identity in modern Europe*. University of Michigan.

George, B., & Varghese, V. (2007). Human rights in tourism: Conceptualization and Stakeholder perspectives. *EJBO Electronic Journal of Business Ethics and Organization Studies, 12*, 40.

Holloway, J. C. (1989 reprint in 2016). *The business of tourism*. Pearson

Hunter, C., & Green, H. (1995). *Tourism and the environment: a sustainable relationship?* Van Nostrand Reinohod.

Lickorish, J. L., & Jenkins, C. L. (2016). *Introduction to tourism*. Routledge.

Perry Hobson, J. S., & Williams, A. (1995). Virtual reality: A new horizon for the tourism industry. *Journal of Vacation Marketing, 1*(2), 124.

Ray, N. (2015). *Emerging innovative marketing strategies in the tourism industry* (p. 78). IGI Global.

Smith, P. (1998). *History of Tourism: Thomas Cook and the origins of leisure travel*. Routledge.

Steuer, J. (1992). Defining virtual reality: Dimensions determining telepresence. *Journal of Communication, 42*(4), 73.

Xiang, Z., & Gretzel, U. (2010). Role of social media in online travel information search. *Tourism Management, 31*(2), 179.

Zuelow, E. G. E. (2011). *Touring beyond the nation: A transnational approach to European tourism history*. Routledge.

---

[9]Hunter and Green (1995).

Chapter 2
National and International Law. The Importance of Cooperation

Contents

2.1	National Political Governance and Tourism	13
	2.1.1 National Tourism Law	13
2.2	European Law	14
	2.2.1 Tourism in EU Law	14
	2.2.2 The Role of the EU Court of Justice and the Importance of Uniformation of Law in Tourism	16
	2.2.3 The Role of European Directives in Tourism Contract Law	17
2.3	International Norms	18
	2.3.1 International Cooperation and Tourism	18
	2.3.2 International Contract Law	19
	2.3.3 UNWTO Towards a Sustainable Tourism	20
2.4	Consumers' Protection	22
	2.4.1 Consumers' Legal Protection	22
	2.4.2 Customers' Care	23
References		24

2.1 National Political Governance and Tourism

2.1.1 National Tourism Law

As we have mentioned, national legislators define and regulate tourism management in terms of relationships between the state, municipalities and other entities in tourism-related activities.

Governments usually determine state policies in the tourism sector. State institutions then use their powers to execute state policies and to create conditions for the development of tourism.

The aim of tourism law is to: ensure conditions for tourism development and distinguish it as an economic sector of major importance; introduce unified criteria for the provision of tourism services; ensure consumer protection in the tourism sector; determine the rights and obligations of all entities involved in the tourism

---

© The Author(s), under exclusive license to Springer Nature Switzerland AG 2021
S. Landini, *Sustainable Tourism Contracts*,
https://doi.org/10.1007/978-3-030-83140-0_2

sector; regulate control over tourism activities and over the quality of the tourism product.

Tourism law regulates all of the specific business activities, trips, and participations in cultural events, forums and other events carried out in tourism sites and other locations that target the creation, presentation and consumption of goods and services that form the national tourism product.

The following are considered tourism activities: the activities of tour operators and tourism agents; hotel and restaurant activity; the provision of additional tourism services.

The law generally considers tourism sites: accommodation premises like hotels, hostels, villas and tourism complexes; other lodgings such as rest stations, family hotels, apartments, rooms, houses, bungalows and campsites; entertainment spots and restaurants, fast food places, cafés, bars and sweet shops; places used for the provision of information, tour operator and tour agency activities; beaches near the sea, rivers and lakes and beaches near artificial water bodies like dams and swimming pools; ski tracks for the practice of various winter sports, which include alpine skiing, snowboarding and ski running; centers offering additional tourism services like spas, sports and entertainment options; museums, cultural monuments as well as culture institutes; national parks, nature parks, reserves, protected areas and nature landmarks as defined in the protected territory laws; huts, instruction centers, tourism shelters and feeding places inside huts and mountain shelters.

The law considers several types of tourism: vacation; cultural and historic; ecological; health and spa; sport; rural; business and conventional etc.

States execute policies in the tourism sector through: cooperation in the development of the sector and its recognition as an economic activity of major importance; the creation of a legal framework needed for the development of tourism, in accordance to international norms, regulations and practices; the guarantee of financial resources and the administration of marketing and promotional campaigns that popularize national tourism products; the creation of conditions for the development of vacation, cultural and historic, eco, health, spa, sport, rural, conventional and other types of tourism; the management and quality control of tourism; the involvement of international cooperation in the tourism sector.

2.2 European Law

2.2.1 Tourism in EU Law

In European Union member states (as it is well known EU is the political and economic union of 27 member states that are located primarily in Europe), European Directives have had a deep impact on national tourism laws. The European Union law has significantly affected national private law systems, especially regarding the impact of European Directives on private law (such as consumer laws, insurance laws, etc.).

2.2 European Law

As it is well known, a Directive is a legislative act of the European Union that "shall be binding, as to the result to be achieved, upon each Member State to which it is addressed, but shall leave to the national authorities the choice of form and methods" (art. 288 of "The Treaty on the Functioning of the European Union").

We cannot understate the relevance of the Charter of Fundamental Rights of the European Union (known as the Charter of Nice), that illustrates the whole range of civil, political, economic and social rights of European citizens and people resident in the EU. The Charter of Nice is now part of the Lisbon Treaty signed in 2007.

According to Article 51 of the Charter: "The provisions of this Charter are addressed to the institutions and bodies of the Union with due regard for the principle of subsidiarity and to the Member States only when they are implementing Union law. They shall therefore respect the rights, observe the principles, and promote the application there of in accordance with their respective powers". Most of the principles asserted by the Charter have a deep impact on the tourism private law system such as dignity, equality, etc.

Part One of the Treaty on the Functioning of the European Union (TFEU) states that the tourism market falls within those actions designed to 'support, coordinate or supplement the actions of the Member States'.

According to art. 195 "The Union shall complement the action of the Member States in the tourism sector, in particular by promoting the competitiveness of Union undertakings in that sector.

To that end, Union action shall be aimed at: (a) encouraging the creation of a favourable environment for the development of undertakings in this sector; (b) promoting cooperation between the Member States, particularly by the exchange of good practice. The European Parliament and the Council, acting in accordance with the ordinary legislative procedure, shall establish specific measures to complement actions within the Member States to achieve the objectives referred to in this Article, excluding any harmonisation of the laws and regulations of the Member States."

However, the Treaty does not change the nature of the Union's powers in this area.

The first Council Resolution on tourism, dated April 10th, 1984, acknowledged the importance of tourism in European integration and invited the Commission to make proposals.

In April 1999, it published a paper entitled 'Enhancing tourism's potential for employment' [COM (1999)0205].

The Council Resolution of May 21st, 2002 stressed the economic importance of tourism and established that it would increase its recognition at a European level and integrate it into other EU policies.

On this basis, the Commission subsequently implemented many measures and activities. In particular, an annual European Tourism Forum has been held since 2002. Representatives from the tourism industry, EU institutions and EU Member State governments attend this annual forum.

Between 2001 and 2010, the Commission published five reports on its policy guidelines for the development of the tourism sector. The June 2010 report in particular, titled 'Europe, the world's No 1 tourist destination' analyses the relevant factors and obstacles relating to the competitive and sustainable development of tourism: demographic and climate change, shortage of energy and water resources, and even certain examples of force majeure. The main objective is to improve tourism competition, while maintaining its quality and its compatibility with sustainable development.

2.2.2 The Role of the EU Court of Justice and the Importance of Uniformation of Law in Tourism

The subject of uniform laws is of growing importance not only in Europe. It responds to the general demand for efficiency and standardization of the present time.[1]

The mission of the Court of Justice has been to ensure that "the law is observed" "in the interpretation and application" of the Treaties. As part of that mission, the Court of Justice of the European Union: reviews the legality of the acts of the institutions of the European Union, ensures that the Member States comply with obligations under the Treaties, and interprets European Union law at the request of the national courts and tribunals. In these terms the Court of Justice ensures the uniform application and interpretation of EU Law.

In addition, the Court of Justice of the European Communities (CJEC) has significantly affected national private law. The CJEC ensures that the EU legislation is interpreted and applied in the same way in all EU countries. Nevertheless, the judgments of the CJEC have also had an important role in the innovation of national private law. In fact, several CJEC judgments have raised questions about some fundamental dogmas of contract laws, particularly regarding the evolution of consumers' contract law according to European Directives.

There can be another relationship between European Law and Private Law. As Christian Joerges has recently noted, we may wonder whether European law has affected national private law systems or, on the contrary, whether national private law systems of the European Union member States are of any relevance to European integration.[2] We can refer to the Common Core Project involving more than one hundred scholars, mostly from Europe and the United States. They are trying to derive the common core of the European private law from the various legal systems of European Union member states.

Moreover, thanks to public consultations, we can detect new issues in the member states.

---

[1] Zeller (2002), p. 163.
[2] Joerges (1997), pp. 378–406; Von Bar et al. (2009); Grossi (2010).

2.2.3 The Role of European Directives in Tourism Contract Law

With specific regard to European Directives on tourism, it is worth recalling the 1990 Travel Package Directive (90/314/EEC recent update see this chapter, paragraph 7.2) protecting European consumers booking pre-arranged package holidays. It protects European consumers going on holiday and covers pre-arranged package holidays combining at least two of the following: (a) transport, (b) accommodation (c) other tourist services such as sightseeing tours (sold at an inclusive price and when the service covers more than 24 hours or includes an overnight stay).

The Directive provides protection covering: information requirements, liabilities for services, and protection (reimbursement of sums paid or repatriation) in the case of a tour operator or airline going bankrupt. In recent years, the development of the Internet and the emergence of low-cost air carriers have revolutionised holiday planning: an increasing number of EU citizens now put their holidays together themselves.

Thus, the overall proportion of holidaymakers booking traditional package holidays, protected by the Directive, has fallen. The Commission has therefore examined three main options: modernising the current legislation, leaving it as it is, or scrapping it entirely. The Directive (EU) 2015/2302 of the European Parliament and of the Council of November 25th, 2015 on travel package and linked travel, amended Regulation (EC) No 2006/2004 and Directive 2011/83/EU of the European Parliament and of the Council repealing Council Directive 90/314/EEC.

The Commission launched a public consultation on the revision of the Directive of November 2009 that focused on finding possible ways of solving the main limitations of the existing travel package rules. It also aimed to quantify the impact of various possible legislative options.

National law, although it is close to the territorial and cultural problems of the individual country, it fails to grasp the international aspects and the consequences of regulatory gaps at the international level.

As previously mentioned, tourism is a global phenomenon that is strictly associated with the idea of movement. Thus, tourism belongs to a sphere of interstate cooperation and an instrument of international communication. The development of tourism activities imposes states to facilitate tourism formalities, liberalize tourism services, unify and harmonize the legal regulation of tourism activities, protect the environment from adverse influences of international tourism, and ensure tourists' rights, among others. The settlement of these issues can be approached from the legal point of view only through international treaties and thanks to international cooperation.[3]

---

[3] Kala and Abaydeldinov (2016), pp. 714–720.

2.3 International Norms

2.3.1 *International Cooperation and Tourism*

States execute policies in the tourism sector by creating the legal framework needed for the development of tourism, in accordance to **international norms**, and by becoming involved in international cooperation.

First of all, it is important to remember that tourism is founded on the international principle of hospitality. It is well known that Immanuel Kant talked about a cosmopolitan right as a guiding principle to protect people from war and morally founded this cosmopolitan right on the unwritten principle of universal hospitality. Jacques Derrida provided a theoretical framework on hospitality regarding the relationships between people in their everyday lives. In particular, he addressed the proximity of the other as an important part of Levinas's concept: for Derrida, the foundation of ethics is hospitality as the acceptance of the other as different but of equal standing.[4]

The two fundamental international conventions on tourism are the International Convention on Travel Contracts (CCV) signed in Brussels, April 23rd, 1970 and the Convention on the Liability of Hotelkeepers concerning the Property of their Guests signed in Paris on December 17th, 1962.

An international convention (also known as "treaty") is an express agreement under international law entered into by sovereign states and international organisation actors in international law.

The CCV rules on both organised travel contracts and intermediary travel contracts. It provides general obligations for travel organisers, intermediaries and for travellers: Travel Organisers and Intermediaries shall safeguard the rights and interests of the traveller according to general principles of law and good usages in this field. The traveller shall, in particular, furnish all necessary information specifically requested from him and comply with the regulations relating to the journey, sojourn or any other services.

The Convention on the Liability of Hotelkeepers (Paris, 17.XII.1962) sets out a list of provisions under which hotelkeepers are liable for the property of their guests. In particular, the liability of the hotelkeeper is engaged for any damage to, destruction, or loss of property brought to the hotel by any guest who stays at the hotel and has sleeping accommodation put at his/her disposal. This liability is limited (up to the equivalent of 3000 gold francs). However, the liability of hotelkeepers is unlimited where the property has been deposited with them or where they have refused to receive property, which they are bound to receive for safe custody. The Convention provides that Parties can limit, under some conditions, the liability of the hotelkeeper. Specifically, any notice or agreement aiming to exclude or diminish the hotelkeeper's liability given or made before the damage, destruction or loss has occurred shall be null and void.

---

[4] Kant (1795, 1999), pp. 3–29.

2.3 International Norms

Regarding international law and tourism, we must bear in mind that tourism contracts are mainly international contracts that relate to the cross-border dealings of individuals or companies.

2.3.2 International Contract Law

International contract law concerns the legal rules relating to cross-border agreements. When parties coming from different countries enter into a contract, international contract law governs them unless they agree to adopt the laws of one country. The Rome Convention on the Law Applicable to Contractual Obligations has unified the choice of laws rules throughout the Community. This means that all courts within the European Union will apply the same conflict of law rules and therefore, in principle, the substantive applicable law will be the same regardless of the forum. Art 5 of the Rome Convention aims to protect the consumer by determining the proper law of certain consumer contracts.

To this end, Art. 5 limits the parties' choice of the applicable law. The contract will be governed by the law chosen by the parties, but the application of the chosen law shall not have the result of depriving the consumer of the protection afforded to him by the mandatory rules of the place of his habitual residence. In the absence of such a choice the law of the place of the consumer's habitual residence will apply. However, when the chosen court is the court of a non-Member State, the Rome Convention does not apply, and the consumer will consequently not be protected by Art 5. The level of protection afforded to the consumer through the harmonisation of the laws of the Member States can be avoided through the choice of a foreign law as the law applicable to the contract. With regard to European Community law is of particular interest the Eu Directive 93/13 on Consumers Contracts and the Eu Directive 2019/2161 amending Council Directive 93/13/EEC and Directives 98/6/EC, 2005/29/EC and 2011/83/EU of the European Parliament and of the Council as regards the better enforcement and modernization of Union consumer protection rules.[5] International contract law is broadly based on the idea of good faith and fair dealing in contracts including fair negotiations, an obligation to cooperate, and good faith when terminating a contract. It also ensures that unfair contracts or deals are not enforceable. One key element of international contract law is that the parties' nationality does not play any role when applying the law, thereby placing all parties on an equal playing field. Rules of the contracts need to be interpreted by what a reasonable person would consider fair and appropriate given the circumstances. The identification of the law applicable to the contract is established by the parties. It can be chosen either from the national laws of the parties, from the laws of a third state, or even from systems of uniform law. The reference is mainly to the UNIDROIT system that is an intergovernmental organisation whose objective is to harmonize

---

[5] Marques (2017), p. 213.

international private law across countries through uniform rules, international conventions, and soft law (sets of principles and guidelines).

Regarding international cooperation, we must also consider the role of international organisations such as the World Tourism Organisation (UNWTO), the United Nations agency responsible for the promotion of responsible, sustainable, and universally accessible tourism.

2.3.3 UNWTO Towards a Sustainable Tourism

The UNWTO's membership includes 156 countries, 6 Associate Members and over 400 Affiliate Members representing the private sector, educational institutions, tourism associations and local tourism authorities.

The World Tourism Conference 1980 convened in Manila with the World Tourism Organisation, which included the participation of 107 state delegations and 91 observer delegations.

The Declaration of Manila touches upon all aspects of tourism and considers it the responsibility of states to develop and enhance tourism as more than a purely economic activity. It states that "tourism does more harm than good to people and to societies in the Third World". Most importantly, point 18 of the Agreement recognises that "The satisfaction of tourism requirements must not be prejudicial to the social and economic interest of the population in tourist areas, to the environment or, above all, to natural resources which are the fundamental attraction of tourism, and historical and cultural sites".

The General Assembly resolution of November 19th, 1981 concerns the outcome of the conference. In particular the following conclusion: "Recognizing the new dimension and role of tourism as a positive instrument towards the improvement of the quality of life for all peoples, as well as a vital force for peace and international understanding,... urges States to give due attention to the principles of the Manila Declaration while formulating and implementing, as appropriate, their tourism policies, plans and programmes, in accordance with their national priorities and within the framework of the programme of work of the World Tourism Organisation; requests the World Tourism Organisation to continue its efforts towards the future development and promotion of tourism, especially in the developing countries, bearing in mind the implementation of the principles and guidelines contained in the Manila Declaration; requests international, intergovernmental and non-governmental organisations directly or indirectly interested in tourism to extend their assistance, in consultation and co-operation with the World Tourism Organisation, towards the implementation of the Manila Declaration".

The UNWTO promotes tourism by offering leadership and support to the sector in advancing knowledge and tourism policies worldwide. Moreover, the UNWTO encourages the implementation of the Global Code of Ethics for Tourism, which is a comprehensive set of principles designed to maximise the sector's benefits while minimising its potentially negative impact on the environment, cultural heritage and societies across the globe.

The code provides ten principles covering all the economic, social, cultural and environmental components of travel and tourism:

- Tourism shall contribute to mutual understanding and respect between peoples and societies;
- Tourism shall be a vehicle for individual and collective fulfilment;
- Tourism shall be a factor of sustainable development;
- Tourism shall be a user of the cultural heritage of mankind and a contributor to its enhancement;
- Tourism shall be a beneficial activity for host countries and communities;
- Tourism professionals have an obligation to provide tourists with objective and honest information on their places of destination and on the conditions of travel, hospitality and stays; they should ensure that the contractual clauses proposed to their customers are readily understandable as to the nature, price and quality of the services they commit themselves to providing and the financial compensation payable by them in the event of a unilateral breach of contract on their part;
- Right to tourism;
- Liberty of tourist movements;
- Rights of the workers and entrepreneurs in the tourism industry.

The public and private stakeholders in tourism development should cooperate in the implementation of these principles and monitor their effective application.

One of the most recent UNWTO declarations was issued on December 13th, 2019. The World Tourism Organisation and the United Nations Educational, Scientific and Cultural Organisation's (UNESCO) Fourth World Conference on Culture and Tourism spotlights the added value of culture for destinations and focuses on sustainability in the future of cultural tourism.

These recommendations aim at: sensitizing stakeholders to the added value of culture for a destination; enhancing product diversification, socio-economic development and sustainable growth; celebrating cultural diversity and intercultural dialogue; addressing research gaps on how tourism continues to grow, impacting the transmission of cultures; creating community-centred initiatives that gather practitioners and the bearers of traditional knowledge to strengthen systems for transmitting cultures through tourism for future generations; implementing the UNWTO Recommendations on Sustainable Development of Indigenous Tourism, as well as expanding partnerships between communities, destinations and tourism operators, and guiding the responsible behaviour of visitors; establishing management systems that combine up-to-date knowledge, digital solutions and inclusive approaches to enhance the visitor experience as well as respect for communities' needs, adequate interpretation and fair trade; building measurement systems that create an enabling environment for cultural investments; tracking the added value of culture, visitor flows and the distribution of benefits; strengthening strategic frameworks that are destination-specific with a view of enabling innovation, local entrepreneurship, creativity, craftsmanship and community empowerment, notably of women and youth; involving the whole destination in urban planning and destination management through the participation of local communities and the private/public sectors, ensuring the opinions of residents are reflected as the bearers of traditions and cultural expressions rooted in their daily lives; disseminating informative and educational materials that target the tourism sector and visitors; respecting local cultural values and properties; developing human talent and encouraging talent retention given its crucial contribution to sustainability, entrepreneurship, skills matching and overall cultural tourism competitiveness; supporting partnerships between the private and public sectors that employ new technologies in order to build capacity, diversify and increase the attractiveness and competitiveness of the cultural tourism on offer; fostering collaboration between tourism destinations, academia and the private sector to improve education, training and research on creative industries and heritage, thus creating new jobs and forming culturally informed professionals; investing in human capacities and the sustainable development of less visited areas; training on cultural and thematic routes and contributing to intercultural dialogue, international cooperation and peace; utilizing cultural facilities such as museums to further engage both visitors and residents in local cultures and traditions.

These codes and declarations can be classified under "soft law". Soft law is commonly distinguished from "hard law". The term "hard law" indicates that all rules are legally binding. Therefore, "hard law" may be a superfluous term. Every law is hard, but we may use the term "hard law" to distinguish this kind of law from the so-called "soft law".

Soft law is rapidly developing in private law systems. The term "soft-law" refers to a great variety of conduct rules that do not have the same enforcement as the law: declarations of principles, codes of practice, recommendations, guidelines, standards, charters, resolutions, etc. Although all these kinds of rules are not legally binding, there is an expectation that they will be respected and practiced by the community of individuals.[6]

Soft law is important not only as a tool to change international law by gradually becoming hard law but also to remain so, ordering conduct by objectives and values. This solution becomes especially important in those areas where the continuous need to adapt to the changing reality makes standardization through hard law unsuitable.

2.4 Consumers' Protection

2.4.1 Consumers' Legal Protection

Soft law has had a deep impact regarding the protection of consumer interests.

---

[6]Ferrando (2010); Mullerat and Brennan (2010).

2.4 Consumers' Protection

Principles of consumer protection were officially stated in European law in 1975 by the April 14th, 1975 resolution on a preliminary program of the European Economic Community for a consumer protection and information policy. Some authors argue "Many international issues are new and complex. The underlying problems may not be well understood, so states cannot anticipate all possible consequences of a legalized arrangement. One way to deal with such problems is to delegate authority to a central party (for example, a court or international organisation) to implement, interpret, and adapt the agreement as circumstances unfold. This approach avoids the costs of having no agreement, or of having to (re)negotiate continuously, but it typically entails unacceptably high sovereignty costs. Soft legalization provides a number of more attractive alternatives for dealing with uncertainty".[7]

The program included the right to protection of health and safety, the right to financial interest protection, the right to compensation for damages, the right to information and education, and the right of representation. Since then, the Community policy on consumer protection has been increasing. Consumers' interests have been specifically identified in various normative contexts at both national and community levels.

Regardless, it is a matter of fact that the consumers' interests are not only under the protection of hard law. At the present time, we also have to consider the interplay between consumer law and the rules contained in business conduct codes established to enhance customer satisfaction.

Companies make continuous efforts to maintain high customer satisfaction levels. Customer satisfaction is important for the success of firms because it increases purchasing levels and word-of-mouth recommendations. It is also the most reliable indicator of the quality of the service offered to customers.

Business organisations need to find new strategies, in addition to traditional ones, in order to compete. Today, they are responding to these challenges by establishing more collaborative relationships with their customers.

Companies ask their consumers for feedback about their products, services, slogans, logos, etc. They can ask questions verbally or in questionnaire form.

As with any other branches of science, a rigorous approach needs to be taken in designing and executing questionnaire studies.

The results of customer satisfaction questionnaires have also been used to formulate and implement business conduct codes.

2.4.2 Customers' Care

Making rules to meet high quality standards is part of the customer satisfaction process. Companies practice business ethics by adopting codes of conduct (or ethic

---

[7] Abbott and Snidal (2000), pp. 421–456. See also Chinkin (1989), p. 381.

codes). It is important to create good relationships with business partners, both suppliers and customers, in order to benefit from fair business together and to ensure customer satisfaction through high quality products, good pricing, on-time delivery and excellent service.

Of course, all directors, officers and employees must respect and obey applicable laws and regulations. Conduct codes are just one particular type of policy statement. It is a set of principles of conduct within an organisation that guide decision-making. Usually, these codes are binding on directors, officers and employees. In case of violations, sanctions will be applied by the organisation itself.

Business ethics emerged as a specialty in the 1960s, following the "social responsibility" movement. More recently, it has been emerging under the influence of corporate social responsibility on customer satisfaction.

Companies have been writing business conduct codes for decades, but the role of these codes is changing. The focus is shifting away from writing a system of norms to regulate conduct within a company to leveraging a code of values that inspires a good performance among employees, management and executives according to the consumers' interests too.

References

Abbott, K. W., & Snidal, D. (2000). Hard and soft law in international governance. *International Organization, 54*, 421.

Chinkin, C. M. (1989). The challenge of soft law: Development and change in international law. *The International and Comparative Law Quarterly*, 381.

Ferrando, A. C. (2010). *Business ethic and corporate governance*. Pearson.

Grossi, P. (2010). *A history of European law (Making of Europe)*. Hopper (tr), Hoboken.

Joerges, C. (1997). The impact of European integration on private law, reductionist perceptions, true conflicts and a new constitutional perspective. *European Law Journal, 3*(4), 378.

Kala, N., & Abaydeldinov, Y. (2016). International legal aspects of tourism activity: International treaties analysis. *Journal of Advanced Research in Law and Economics, 7*, 714.

Kant, I. (1999, first ed. 1795). Toward perpetual peace. In *Practical Philosophy-Cambridge Edition of the Works of Immanuel Kant* (M.J. Gregor, Trans.) University of Cambridge.

Marques, C. L. (2017). Relations between international law and consumers in the globalized world: Challenges and prospects. In C. L. Marques & D. Wei (Eds.), *Consumer law and socioeconomic development: National and international dimensions* (p. 213). Springer.

Mullerat, R., & Brennan, D. (Eds.). (2010). *Corporate social responsibility*. Alphen aan den Rijn.

Von Bar, C., Clive, E., & Shulte-Nölke, H. (2009). *Principles, definitions and model rules of European law. Draft Common Frame of Reference (DCFR)*. European Law Publishers.

Zeller, B. (2002). The development of uniform laws - a historical perspective. *Pace International Law Review, 14*, 163.

Chapter 3
Customary Law

Contents

3.1 Customary Law and Legal Order 25
    3.1.1 Definitions 25
    3.1.2 General Customary Law and International Customary Law 26
3.2 Customary Law in Tourism Sector 26
    3.2.1 Some Examples 26
    3.2.2 Customary Law and Sustainable Development 27
References 27

3.1 Customary Law and Legal Order

3.1.1 Definitions

Another important source of tourism private law is the customary law that we find when a certain legal practice is practiced, and the relevant actors consider it to be the law. So, *opinio juris* is an essential element of customary law that differs from the mere usages. *Opinio juris* is a shortened form of the Latin phrase "opinio juris sive necessitates", which means "an opinion of law or necessity". It denotes a subjective obligation, a sense that one is bound to the law in question.[1]

Usually, customary law can be applied only when an act refers to customary laws. Moreover, customary law can fill in gaps in the written law.

Customary law has to be distinguished from the conventional customs that lead the parties to an agreement. A conventional custom is a fixed practice that is binding because it has been expressly incorporated, or implied, in a contract. Some European civil codes (such as the Italian civil code, art. 1340) refer to conventional customs as sources of integration for a contract. Conventional customs are binding, not due to any legal authority, but because it has been expressly incorporated, or implied, in a contract between the parties. The conventional customs are not valid and effective by

---

[1] Sender and Wood (2017), pp. 299–330; Walden (1977), p. 344.

© The Author(s), under exclusive license to Springer Nature Switzerland AG 2021
S. Landini, *Sustainable Tourism Contracts*,
https://doi.org/10.1007/978-3-030-83140-0_3

themselves; the terms of the custom need to be accepted and incorporated by the parties into an agreement within the limit to private autonomy.

3.1.2 General Customary Law and International Customary Law

We have to distinguish general customary law from international customary law that concerns those aspects of international law deriving from customs. Along with general principles and treaties, international customs are considered by the international Court of Justice, the United Nations, and its member states to be among the primary sources of international law.[2]

The International Court of Justice (ICJ) is the principal judicial organ of the United Nations (UN). It was established in June 1945 by the Charter of the United Nations and began to work in April 1946. The Court settles, in accordance with international law, legal disputes submitted to it by States and gives advisory opinions on legal questions referred to it by authorized United Nations organs and specialized agencies.

According to art. 38 of the Statutes of the International Court of Justice "The Court, whose function is to decide in accordance with international law such disputes as are submitted to it, shall apply: ...

c. the general principles of law recognized by civilized nations...".

3.2 Customary Law in Tourism Sector

3.2.1 Some Examples

In the tourism sector, customary law plays a relevant role. In terms of customary tourism law, it is important to recall hotel overbooking rules. National courts generally seem to agree that in many instances overbooking is necessary to overcome problems of no-show and late cancellations. They hold hotel overbooking to be a customary justifiable practice to offset losses from no-shows.

Of course, many hotels have adopted a pledge that requires their assistance in securing comparable accommodations, if, for any reason, a room should not be available for a client who holds a valid confirmed reservation. A few countries have enacted legislation that addresses hotel overbookings, such as Florida's law that makes the hotel responsible for "every effort" to find alternate accommodations and up to a $500 fine for each guest turned away because of the overbooking. Other countries, like Italy, have no specific written laws regulating overbooking.

---

[2]Fidler (1996), p. 198; Sender and Wood (2016), pp. 133–159.

Thus, overbooking problems are solved by private autonomy, according to contractual conditions contained in the hotel contract, or by customary law. In Italy customary laws are collected by the Commercial Chambers of the different Italian Provinces. Customary law also has a different position in the hierarchy of sources of law: in Italy and Spain customary law cannot violate law, while in France and Germany it can.[3]

3.2.2 Customary Law and Sustainable Development

Customary law presents a closer relation to the reality of the territory in which it develops and, in this way, it is more malleable and closer to the concrete interests of the stakeholders.

In the same way, it can contribute to sustainable development plans by balancing the opposing interests in practice. It is a fact that customary law has recently experienced a comeback especially in connection with the notion of sustainable development and the increasing influence of non-governmental organisations (NGOs). Some studies demonstrate that it is fruitful (in terms of better sustainability) to move away from state planning and towards local self-government. Some Authors stress on the necessity for resiliency of legal rules in the face of rapid environmental change. Ecosystems are always evolving and short term natural resource management solutions often inappropriate as well as top down legislative solutions. An answer can be found in customary law considering the 'bottom-up' democratic character of customary law systems that is able to adapt the solutions, time by time, to the continuous and rapid changes.[4] As we going to see in the next chapter, similar considerations can be made with regard to private autonomy. In this case it is important to find levers that can move individuals and companies towards sustainable choices.

References

Fidler, D. P. (1996). Challenging the classical concept of custom: Perspectives on the future of customary international law. *German Yearbook of International Law, 39*, 198.
Kischel, U. (2019). *Comparative law*. Oxford University Press.

---

[3] Kischel (2019), pp. 367–369.
[4] Orebech et al. (2006).

Orebech, P., Bosselman, F., Bjarup, J., Callies, D., Chanock, M., & Petersen, H. (2006). *The role of customary law in sustainable development*. Cambridge University Press.

Sender, O., & Wood, M. (2016). The emergence of customary international law: Between theory and practice. In C. Brölmann & Y. Radi (Eds.), *Research handbook on the theory and practice of international lawmaking* (p. 133). Edward Elgar.

Sender, O., & Wood, M. (2017). A mystery no longer? Opinio Juris and other theoretical controversies associated with customary international law. *Israel Law Review, 50*(3), 299.

Walden, R. M. (1977). The subjective element in the formation of customary international law. *Israel Law Review, 12*, 344.

Chapter 4
Private Autonomy

Contents

4.1	Private Autonomy Across Countries	29
	4.1.1 A Comparative Approach to Contracts	29
	4.1.2 National Contract Law in International Contracts	30
4.2	Key Points in Writing a Contract	31
	4.2.1 Identification of the Standard of Performance	31
	4.2.2 Dealing the Agreement	31
	4.2.3 Limits to Freedom of Contract	33
4.3	Judicial Intervention in Contract Matters	33
	4.3.1 Illegal and Unfair Contract	33
	4.3.2 Damages in Case of Breach of Contract	34
4.4	Tourism Contracts	35
	4.4.1 B2B and B2C Contracts	35
	4.4.2 Sustainable Contracts	35
References		37

4.1 Private Autonomy Across Countries

4.1.1 A Comparative Approach to Contracts

One of the modern fundamental principles of private law is that the parties are free to manage their economic relationship according to their private autonomy.[1]

There are different national laws on private law and particularly on contract law. Considering foreign legal models is a process that requires understanding of the foreign legal system in its totality. At the same time, an understanding approach to foreign law by applying the methods of comparative law, is becoming more and

---

[1] Atiyah (1979). The author illustrates how the growth of consumer protection, rent and employment legislation has moved contracts back into smaller confines, based on general notions of fairness. More recently we can remember *The fall and rise of freedom of contract* edited by Buckley (1999). The book is a collection of essays on the topic of the new role of private autonomy in the evolving society where negotiation could be a way to reach common objectives.

© The Author(s), under exclusive license to Springer Nature Switzerland AG 2021
S. Landini, *Sustainable Tourism Contracts*,
https://doi.org/10.1007/978-3-030-83140-0_4

more important in the process of negotiation in case of international contracts with regard to the choice of the law governing the contract. The categories, or families, of law have been developed as a tool to classify legal systems. Various classifications may be proposed; a classical distinction is between systems of Common Law, systems of Civil Law, systems of Islamic law, and socialist systems.

The division between Common Law systems and Civil Law systems is traditionally based on the different sources of law: the judicial precedent and the statutes. With regard to contracts, however, some authors consider more relevant to focus on the different way of interpreting a contract and on the different role that the legal system plays in integrating the contract. This can influence the way contracts are drafted.[2]

From the point of view of international contracts, therefore, the most interesting classification is that between Common Law system and Civil Law system where the presence of principles like good faith leaves a vary discretion to judges in the interpretation and integration of contracts. Moreover, when a contract is drafted on the basis of a model developed under the Common Law system, but it is regulated by the law of a Civil Law system, it becomes important, in the interpretation and execution of the contract, to understand why certain contractual provisions have been inserted or written in that certain way in the original model that was meant to operate under a Common Law system.

4.1.2 National Contract Law in International Contracts

National laws contain general contract principles and regulate specific types of agreements (so-called typical contracts). However, many norms regulating typical contracts can be modified by an agreement between the parties. Moreover, according to the principle of freedom of contract, parties can also make contracts that are not included in those specifically regulated by the law (so-called atypical contracts) if such contracts are directed to the realization of interests worthy of protection according to the legal order.

Parties are bound by the terms of their contract. A contract is legally enforceable if there are mechanisms of enforcement of contractual obligations.

Contracts may be characterised by either informal or formal contract enforcement mechanisms. Scholars link the role of institutions in determining economic performance directly to the quality of a countries' institutions. Self-enforcement constitutes the primary feature of contracts. Informal enforcement mechanisms appear to encourage and support long term relational exchanges, but they can fail to be effective especially in case of impersonal exchanges. However, an alternative paradigm has emerged which finds support for its non-formalist contract enforcement approach in relational contract theory. This paradigm underlines the role of

---

[2]Cordero Moss (2004), p. 35 ff.

4.2 Key Points in Writing a Contract

social norms and networks which effect contract enforcement without a third party enforcement mechanism (formal enforcement).[3]

4.2 Key Points in Writing a Contract

4.2.1 Identification of the Standard of Performance

It is important to identify the **standard of performance** required in relation to each contractual obligation since a failure to perform to the required standard constitutes a breach. In case of a breach of contract, the defaulting party has to pay damage to the other in order to compensate the unrealized interest of the injured party. According to the general rules, damages are meant to place the claimant in the same position as if the contract had been performed. Damages are usually awarded for expectation loss (loss of a bargain) or reliance loss (wasted expenditure). In some cases, the court may award damages which go beyond a strict measure of compensation, such as in case of reputational losses, or in case of so-called nominal damage.[4] Nominal damages are not intended to compensate a loss, but they are awarded simply to sanction the fact that there has been a breach of contract. Nominal damage has an important deterrent function in case of non-economic losses; in this case the proof of the damage can present a problem. A solution could be represented by the introduction of penalties into the contract. Nominal damage and penalties are relevant in the presence of green clauses where, in case of a breach, it is possible to have no losses or to have losses that are difficult to prove (such as reputational losses). For example, in case of a breach of a clause in a franchising contract providing duties on the franchisee regarding limits to gas emissions, water consumption etc., it is difficult to prove losses for the franchisor.

Thus, contractual conditions are legally enforceable and legal consequences are expected in case of a breach of contract. In these terms, it could be said that private autonomy is a source of law.

4.2.2 Dealing the Agreement

Every contract is founded on an agreement having a specific object, form and reason that justifies the promise and the obligation. While the sources of law issued by institutions (laws, European Directives, treaties, etc.) find their effectiveness in compliance with the provisions that regulate their issuance, the contract, as a tool that regulates the relations between the contracting parties, finds its own

---

[3] Hawthorne (2008), p. 507.
[4] Pearce and Halson (2007), pp. 1–10.

effectiveness in the agreement between the parties in compliance with the framework that the system identifies for the validity and effectiveness of the contracts.

The existence of an agreement is determined objectively on the basis of the parties' words and actions. The objective evidence of an agreement is traditionally the existence of an offer and of corresponding acceptance. An offer is an expression of willingness to contract without further negotiation. An offer needs to be communicated to the other party. It is important to distinguish an offer from a mere invitation. An invitation is not an offer. It is just a way of simulating interest, to gain more information and to go on with negotiations. Generally speaking, advertisement, brochures etc. are just invitations. Acceptance is the answer to a specific offer, made with a binding intention. It must be communicated to the other party and conform to the offer. An acceptance must be unconditional and compliant with the exact terms proposed by the proponent. When the recipient alters the terms contained in the offer or adds a new term, that response is not an acceptance. It constitutes a counteroffer.

These general rules, which seem to be very clear in identifying the time and place of the constitution of the contractual legal bond, in practice can be open to doubts. Furthermore, the interpretation of the contract can create problems in determining the extent of the contractual obligation.[5]

It is for the parties to make their agreement and ensure that the terms are sufficiently concrete to be enforced. Courts, even in civil law system, will generally refuse to fill in any gaps. Therefore, courts, in practice, fill in the gaps if some evidence is available. Courts can particularly take commercial practice and previous performance into account.

As a general principle, when an essential term is missing, the agreement will not be complete enough to be enforced. When the law states that a contract is enforceable only if recorded in a particular way, the rule is described as a requirement of form. The general rule is that there is no requirement that contracts need to be made in writing and parties may decide whether written evidence is necessary. In commercial dealing, written evidence is almost inevitably available, taking into account the complexity and the value of obligations.

Thus, the legal concept of an agreement is different from the common definition of the convergence of interests between parties. It is important to consider the interpretation of a contract and the problems with evidence in case of judicial intervention in the execution of the contract (e.g., problems with providing proof of the exact content of a contract in a valid and enforceable oral agreement).[6]

---

[5] Perillo (2000), p. 427.
[6] Pearce and Halson (2007), pp. 1–10.

4.2.3 Limits to Freedom of Contract

Contracts need to be compliant with **imperative norms**, some countries extend the control of contracts to the conformity of general clauses like morality and public order. We can try to define the term "general clauses" as "flexible rules" that increase the role that judges play in the making of laws. Therefore, general clauses can play an important function in counterbalancing the abstract binding force of the law and the concrete social economic issues. General clauses are often applied when certain issues that arise are not lending themselves readily to clear or permanent definition. In these cases, it is not possible to solve the issue with an abstract norm, but it is important to solve the problem considering the concrete situation. Let us think about the meaning of public order. It comes from the French "ordre public" and evokes the fundamental principles of the legal system contained in the Constitution.

4.3 Judicial Intervention in Contract Matters

4.3.1 Illegal and Unfair Contract

As said contract will be considered illegal at its formation when it is contrary to the legal order. Contracts falling into this category cannot be enforced. The contract will be declared void by the judge and treated as if it was never entered into.

In some cases, there can also be a control of the substantial content of a contract, such as in the case of unfair terms specifically regarding consumers' contracts. According to EU Directive 93/13, in order to assess the fairness of the content of a contract the judge has to evaluate whether the rights and duties of the parties are balanced in accordance with the principle of good faith. In these terms, EU general clauses on fairness offer significant potential for improved consumer protection. The importance of the judicial assessment of fairness in consumer contract is well underlined by scholars. "Decisions to accept onerous or unbalanced contract terms are not necessarily a calculated risk assumed by consumers in return for a concession in price. Rather, the insights of behavioural economics suggest that there are significant limitations on the decision-making processes of consumers relating to 'rational, social, and cognitive factors', which are not necessarily improved by consumers being provided with more information about the incidental terms of their contracts. Such measures may not ensure that these terms become part of the decision by consumers to enter into a standard form contract in any meaningful sense".[7] The most common types of unfair terms are exclusion clauses that provide the right for one party to exclude his/her liability arising under the contract. The law restricts the use of such terms. In American law, the protection comes from the common law that can be defined as the collection of judicial precedents. In European

---

[7] Paterson (2009), p. 934. See also Carbonnier (2001); Willet (2012), pp. 412–440.

countries, national legislators have adopted specific rules regarding consumers' contracts according to the European Directive 93/13/CEE. Also, there are specific rules in Asian countries. For instance, art. 10 of the Japanese Consumer Contract Act enacted in 2000 and amended in 2006 provides that: "Clauses which restrict the rights of consumers or expand the duties of consumers beyond those under the provisions unrelated to the public order applicable pursuant to the Civil Code, the Commercial Code and such other laws and regulations and which, impair the interests of consumers unilaterally against the fundamental principle provided in the second paragraph of article 1 of the Civil Code, are void". The Australian Consumer Law's unfair contract provisions have found their way into Australian law, and the starting point can be found in an EU Directive.[8]

4.3.2 Damages in Case of Breach of Contract

Every breach of contract will give rise to a right to claim damages. A breach of contract will occur where, without lawful excuse, a party either fails or refuses to perform a contractual obligation.

A contract is discharged by the perfect performance of both parties. A contract can be also discharged by agreement between the parties.

The purpose of the contract is the performance of the parties; performance means the exact fulfilment of the promises made. Therefore, it is important to determine the content of promises. According to principles of subjective interpretation, interpreters might search the common will of parties even beyond the literal meaning of the contractual content.[9]

Moreover, agreements must be executed in good faith. Good faith in the execution of the contract is generally defined as the expressions of the duty of loyalty by each party of the contract so as not to offend the confidence that gave rise to the contract. According to the good faith rule, for instance, the debtor is also obliged to duties (such as duties of care or duties of information) not textually included in the contract but necessary to the fulfillment of the promises made.[10]

In some countries, like Italy and Germany, good faith takes a relevant role in integrating the contract with ancillary obligations according to the primary ones. The duty to perform a certain service and the duty to inform the counterparty about the possible negative effect of a certain performance serve as examples of this.[11]

The principle of good faith is of fundamental importance with regard to consumers' contracts in particular. For instance, Directive 93/13/CE, on unfair clauses in consumers' contracts (i.e., contracts between a consumer and a supplier),

---

[8] Svantesson and Holly (2010), pp. 3–14.

[9] Shavell (2006), pp. 290–291.

[10] Farnsworth (1963), p. 679; Summers (1968), pp. 232–233; Weigand (2004), p. 174.

[11] Dawkins (2014), pp. 283–295.

establishes that a contractual term which has not been individually negotiated shall be regarded as unfair if, contrary to the requirement of good faith, it causes a significant imbalance in the parties' rights and obligations arising under the contract, to the detriment of the consumer.

4.4 Tourism Contracts

4.4.1 B2B and B2C Contracts

In the following chapters we are going to consider the most common tourism contracts, divided in B2C (business to consumers) contracts and B2B (business to business) contracts. Among B2C contracts: hotel contract, tourist rental contract, travel package, multiproperty. Among B2B contracts: allottment, franchising, management.

"Consumer" generally means any natural person who is dealing for purposes that are outside his trade, business or profession.

A "Business" generally means any natural or legal person who is dealing for purposes relating to his trade, business or profession, whether publicly owned or privately owned.

The agreement is the central concept in the production of norms thanks to private autonomy, but we have to consider the importance of heteronomy in the production of contractual effects. The agreement, together with the interpretation, the integration of the contract with the law, conventional customs, and good faith create effects between the parties.[12]

The above considerations are of particular interest with regard to consumers contracts. The consumer is the weak part of the contract and need protection from unfair terms and unfair commercial practices.

4.4.2 Sustainable Contracts

The contract represents a tool to settle opposing interests between the parties, but it can represent a social lever when it produces effects that affect general interests in terms of environmental, social and market sustainability.[13] Regarding the latter, the contract may represent a balanced distribution of contractual rights and obligations, which allows it to be maintained in the interest of both parties over time for the benefit of the entire market sector and of the whole society.

---

[12] Falduto (2014).

[13] Pennasilico (2014a, b), p. 754; Lener (1974), p. 333; Patti (1979); Perlingieri (2005), p. 71 ss.

In terms of social and environmental sustainability, examples can be found in contracts of the tourism market like the so-called hotel green franchising contract.

Franchising is a contract where a franchisor provides a licensed privilege to the franchisee to do business, and offers assistance in organising, training, merchandising, marketing and managing in return for a monetary consideration. It is often used in the hospitality industry.

Eco-sustainable products and renewable energies represent one of the few successful businesses to date, which is why investing in a franchise in this sector could prove to be the right choice. The green approach can be applied to both products and services, which is why there are ecological franchises in very different areas, from clothing to food, from tourism to services for companies.

Each of the eco-sustainable franchising activities focuses on a particular behaviour that is essential for living a more eco-sustainable and eco-responsible life: reduction, reuse, and recycling.

The social goal is followed by the parties of the contract because there are advantages in the green choice:

- High loyalty business opportunities;
- They are aimed at sensitive consumers looking for reliable products;
- Accurate attention to cutting-edge marketing strategies;
- High rate of innovation and creativity;
- Good ease of access, economics, and logistics.

Three types of green franchising can be distinguished:

1. Ecological franchises dedicated to REDUCTION: choosing a franchise that deals with reduction means responding to the needs of companies and individuals regarding energy efficiency or the sale of products that reduce the production of waste, such as organic food sold in bulk or products ecologically obtained from recycling.

   For those who start a franchise business in this sector, the parent company normally guarantees all the necessary technical training, especially for renewable energy and plant services.

2. Ecological franchises focused on REUSE:

   Choosing a franchise that focuses on reuse means investing in a growing sector, such as the second-hand market, taking advantage of all the opportunities provided by e-commerce.

   Eco-responsible behaviours, such as the regeneration of cartridges or the reuse of children's clothing and accessories, are an established and consolidated trend in purchasing habits.

3. Ecological franchises specialized in RECYCLING:

   Choosing a franchise that enhances recycling and monetizes the separate collection of waste not only reduces the impact on the environment, but also offers tools of loyalty and additional income for those who already own a business.

In these terms, the contract forms the framework of the sources of law that design a sustainable economy: the franchisor provides a specific know-how in terms of reduction, reuse, and recycling, to the franchisee who is obliged to respect the eco-rules, as in the franchising contract.

References

Atiyah, P. S. (1979). *Rise and fall of freedom of contract*. Oxford University Press.

Buckley, F. H. (Ed.). (1999). *The fall and rise of freedom of contract*. Duke University Press.

Carbonnier, J. (2001). *Flexible droit*. LGDJ.

Cordero Moss, G. (2004). Lectures on comparative law of contracts. *Publications Series of the Institute of Private Law, University of Oslo, 166*, 35.

Dawkins, C. E. (2014). The principle of good faith: Toward substantive stakeholder engagement. *Journal of Business Ethics, 121*(2), 283.

Falduto, A. (2014). *The faculties of the human mind and the case of moral feeling in Kant's philosophy*. De Gruyter.

Farnsworth, A. (1963). Good faith performance and commercial reasonableness under the uniform commercial code. *University of Chicago Law Review, 30*, 67.

Hawthorne, L. T. (2008). Communication: Harmonisation of contract law characterized by formality and strong enforcement mechanisms imperative for economic development. *Uniform Law Review, 13*, 507.

Lener, A. (1974). *Ecologia, persona, solidarietà: un nuovo ruolo del diritto civile*. In N. Lipari (a cura di), *Tecniche giuridiche e sviluppo della persona* (p. 333). Laterza, Roma – Bari.

Paterson, J. (2009). The Australian unfair contract terms law: The rise of substantive unfairness as a ground for review of standard form consumer contracts. *Melbourne University Law Review, 33*, 934.

Patti, S. (1979). *La tutela civile dell'ambiente*. Cedam Padova.

Pearce, D., & Halson, R. (2007). Damages for breach of contract: compensation, restitution, and vindication. *Oxford Journal of Legal Studies*, 1.

Pennasilico, M. (2014a). Contratto e uso responsabile delle risorse naturali. *Rass. Dir. Civ.*, p. 754.

Pennasilico, M. (2014b). *Manuale di diritto civile dell'ambiente*. Esi, Napoli.

Perillo, J. M. (2000). The origins of the objective theory of contract formation and interpretation. *Fordham Law Review, 69*, 427.

Perlingieri, P. (2005). I diritti umani come base dello sviluppo sostenibile. Aspetti giuridici e sociologici. In P. Perlingieri (Ed.), *La persona e i suoi diritti. Problemi del diritto civile* (p. 71). Esi.

Shavell, S. (2006). On the writing and the interpretation of contracts. *Journal of Law, Economics, & Organization, 22*(2), 290.

Summers, R. S. (1968). "Good Faith" in general contract law and the sales provisions of the uniform commercial code. *Virginia Law Review, 54*, 232.

Svantesson, D. J. B., & Holly, L. (2010). An overview and analysis of the national unfair contract terms provisions. *Commerce Law Quarterly, 24*(3), 3.

Weigand, T. A. (2004). *The duty of good faith and fair dealing in commercial contracts in Massachusetts* (Vol. 88, p. 174). Massachusetts Law Review.

Willet, C. (2012). General clauses and the competing ethics of European consumer law in the UK. *The Cambridge Law Journal, 71*(2), 412.

Chapter 5
The Worldwide Concept of Sustainability and Tourism

Contents

5.1 Sustainability and Tourism	39
5.1.1 The Environmental and Social Impact of Tourism	39
5.1.2 Concepts of Sustainability	40
5.1.3 The Concept of Sustainability in UN Actions	41
5.2 Defining Sustainability in Tourism Sector	42
5.2.1 The Environmental and Social Impact of Tourism	42
5.2.2 Is Sustainability an Unfocused Concept?	44
5.2.3 Measuring Sustainability	45
5.2.4 Some Examples of Sustainable Tourism	48
5.3 The Role of Courts and Scholars	51
5.3.1 Courts, Scholars and Sources of Law	51
5.3.2 Scholars, Courts and Sustainability	52
References	53

5.1 Sustainability and Tourism

5.1.1 The Environmental and Social Impact of Tourism

Sustainability is becoming a keyword within tourism as well. This term is more frequently used in the sense of human sustainability on Earth, and eco-sustainability is the most common definition of sustainability. This definition is just a part of the wider concept of sustainable development, which means the development of human activity, including industrial and economic activity that meets the needs of both the present and future generations.

As previously said, tourism can affect environmental sustainability. Natural and historical attractions and tourism sites may be damaged by the multitude of tourists visiting them.

Governments are aware of this and recognize how important special economic incentives may be to the growth of the tourism industry according to eco-sustainability principles.

© The Author(s), under exclusive license to Springer Nature Switzerland AG 2021
S. Landini, *Sustainable Tourism Contracts*,
https://doi.org/10.1007/978-3-030-83140-0_5

As we have already seen, sustainable tourism and ecotourism are two possible ways of addressing the many environmental and social problems associated with tourism.

People are generally aware of their impact on the environment regarding tourism. Tourists tend to choose tourism offers that are marketed as ecological or sustainable.

5.1.2 Concepts of Sustainability

As it has been noted,[1] the terms "sustainable" and "nature" are used more and more in marketing material produced by the tourism industry. The degree to which the use of such terms can affect, in the present time, consumer purchasing decisions and corporate environmental performance is largely unknown.

Eco-tourism, as well as sustainable tourism, can be considered to be commonplace. Such concepts need to be determined through some basic standards that are globally recognized. Established by individual companies, industry associations, voluntary organisations, and government agencies, eco labels range in scale from single villages to worldwide sites, from single activities to entire destinations. They include voluntary codes, awards, and accreditation and certification schemes. Such eco-standards should be well defined and transparent. An effective framework of environmental regulation, independent audits and penalties for non-compliance should also be provided. The use of terms like eco-tourism and sustainable tourism in brochures, advertising materials etc. without respecting the ecological criteria should be considered as cases of unfair commercial practice.

We intend to consider some of the basic concepts used in definitions of sustainability that are recognized at international levels.

Many projects concerning sustainable forms of tourism have been proposed, but we would like to highlight the role of private autonomy and contracts in designing forms of sustainable tourism development.

In ecology, sustainability is commonly defined as the capacity of biological systems to remain diverse and productive over time. Eco-sustainability for humans is more complex. It can be defined as the long-term maintenance of well-being while also considering economic, political, social, and cultural dimensions.

The word sustainability in economic terms involves ecological economics where social, cultural, health aspects on one side, and monetary/financial aspects, on the other side, are integrated.

---

[1] Buckley (2002), pp. 183–208.

5.1.3 The Concept of Sustainability in UN Actions

The concept of sustainable development is commonly referred to in a statement of the report elaborated by the Brundtland Commission of the United Nations on March 20th, 1987 that reads: "sustainable development is development that meets the needs of the present without compromising the ability of future generations to meet their own needs".[2]

The Commission, recalling its resolution 38/161 of December 19th, 1983 on the preparation process for the Environmental Perspective to the Year 2000, welcomed the establishment of a special commission, which later came to be called the World Commission on Environment and Development, to make a report available on the environment and the global issues up to the year 2000 and beyond, including proposed strategies for sustainable development.

Moreover, the Commission recognized its instrumental role in revitalizing and reorienting discussions and deliberations on the environment and development. It emphasized the necessity of a new approach to economic growth, as an essential prerequisite for the eradication of poverty and for enhancing the resource base on which present and future generations depend.

At the 2005 World Summit on Social Development, it was noted that sustainability requires the reconciliation of environmental, social, and economic demands. These are the "three pillars" of sustainability. Such pillars have served as a common ground for numerous sustainability standards and certification systems in recent years.[3]

During the world summit, our common fundamental values were strongly reaffirmed, including freedom, equality, solidarity, tolerance, respect for all human rights, respect for nature and shared responsibility: these are all essential to international relations.

Current developments and circumstances require a consensus on major threats and challenges. Peace, security, development, and human rights are the pillars of the United Nations system and the foundations for collective security and well-being. These values are interlinked and mutually reinforcing. Of course, development is a central goal in itself and sustainable development, in its economic, social, and environmental aspects, constitutes a key element of the framework of United Nations activities.

The Earth Charter is another central document to help us in understanding a sustainable economy.

It speaks of "a sustainable global society founded on respect for nature, universal human rights, economic justice, and a culture of peace".[4] This Charter is a declaration of the fundamental ethical principles for building a just, sustainable, and peaceful global society. The Earth Charter Secretariat, Earth Charter Commission

---

[2] Adams (2006).

[3] United Nations General Assembly (2005).

[4] The Earth Charter Initiative (2000).

members, National Committees, partner organisations, and many other groups organised consultations focused on the ideas and principles to be included in the Earth Charter. These meetings took place over a five-year period from 1995 to 2000. The recommendations and comments generated by these consultations were forwarded to a drafting committee created by the Earth Charter Commission in December 1996. Professor Steven C. Rockefeller was appointed by the Commission to chair this committee.

This Chart is a document written with the purpose of creating new opportunities to build a democratic and human world.

To realize these aspirations, the Chart highlights the necessity to live with a sense of universal responsibility, by identifying ourselves with the whole Earth community as well as our local communities. Everyone shares a responsibility for the present and future well-being of the human race and the larger living world.

Such standards are particularly developed in the food industry, but there is a change in other sectors as well, such as the tourism sector.

The UNEP (United Nations Environment Programme) and the UNWTO list 12 principles of sustainable tourism: economic viability, local prosperity, employment quality, social equity, visitor fulfilment, local control, community well-being, cultural richness, physical integrity, biological diversity, resource efficiency, and environmental purity.[5]

According to such principles, sustainable tourism can be defined as: "tourism that takes full account of its current and future economic, social and environmental impacts, addressing the needs of visitors, the industry, and the environment and host communities".

5.2 Defining Sustainability in Tourism Sector

5.2.1 The Environmental and Social Impact of Tourism

Sustainable tourism development guidelines and management practices are applicable to all forms of tourism in all types of destinations. Sustainability principles refer to the environmental, economic, and socio-cultural aspects of tourism development, and a suitable balance must be established between these three dimensions to guarantee sustainability.

As a result of the above considerations, sustainable tourism should:

(1) Make optimal use of environmental resources, maintaining essential ecological processes and helping in the conservation of natural heritage and biodiversity.

---

[5]Making Tourism More Sustainable—A Guide for Policy Makers, UNEP and UWTO (2005), pp. 11–12.

5.2 Defining Sustainability in Tourism Sector

(2) Respect the socio-cultural authenticity of host communities; the tourism industry must conserve their man-made and natural cultural heritage and traditional values and contribute to inter-cultural understanding and tolerance.
(3) It is important to provide fairly distributed socio-economic benefits to all stakeholders, including stable employment, income-earning opportunities, social services to host communities, and a contribution to poverty alleviation.
(4) Sustainable tourism development requires the informed participation of all relevant stakeholders.
(5) Sustainable tourism should also maintain a high level of tourist satisfaction and ensure the tourists have a meaningful experience, raising their awareness about sustainability issues and promoting sustainable tourism practices amongst them.

Moreover, achieving sustainable tourism is a long-term process. It is also a continuous process and constant monitoring on the impact of tourism activities on the environment is required, introducing the necessary preventive and/or corrective measures whenever necessary.

The Covid 19 pandemic has highlighted the need to talk about sustainability in terms of health as well, by offering tourism that, in the long term, also allows workers and customers to act in a way that protects their own health and that of others. For this to happen, there will inevitably be great changes in tourism activities, as well as in everyone's habits.

These would be changes that concern the respect for interpersonal distances, the use of protective devices and systems, complying to safety protocols that will be prepared by both sector operators and health authorities to protect workers and customers, interpersonal relationships, and changes on work and travel.

Workers in the tourism industry, especially hotels and carriers, are providing health services and special conduct codes for employees and clients. Below are some of the actions they are taking:

- Deep cleaning and disinfection of all hotel rooms, restaurant areas and conference rooms, etc.;
- Equipping all public spaces with hand sanitizers;
- Staff training in the proper conduct of sanitary procedures and caring for the safety of guests as well as their own;
- Help and information in case of safety procedure.

We cannot understate that sustainable development, as defined by the UN, is not accepted worldwide without criticism.

5.2.2 Is Sustainability an Unfocused Concept?

Some economists are sceptical about the possibility of sustainable development and consider this term an oxymoron.[6]

Other authors think that the definition of sustainability is improving the quality of human life; sustainability is a task in progress and therefore a mere political process, so some definitions of the concept of sustainability set out common goals and values.[7] It implies responsible and proactive decisions that minimize negative impacts while balancing social, environmental, and economic growth to ensure desirable needs in the future. For these reasons, "sustainability" is also considered to be an "unfocused concept" like "liberty" or "justice" that merely describes a "dialogue of values that defies consensual definition".[8] It may be possible to propose an alternative definition of sustainability considering the UN's "three pillars". Some authors, in contrast to the three common criticisms on the concept of sustainability (it is vague, attracts hypocrites and fosters delusions), argue for an approach to sustainability that is integrative, action-oriented, goes beyond technical fixes, incorporates a recognition of the social construction of sustainable development and engages local communities in new ways. As Robinson highlighted in 2004: "if sustainability is to mean anything, it must act as an integrating concept. In particular, it is clear that the social dimensions of sustainability must be integrated with the biophysical dimensions... Clearly, the very concept of sustainability is predicated on a need to think across temporal scales. In addition, both the social and ecological dimensions of the term bring to the fore the need for spatial integration. The disciplinary division of knowledge in the university system means that many cross-scalar issues get lost in the 'white spaces' between disciplines. The concept of sustainability may have a role in helping to bridge some of those gaps".[9] In this perspective, it is necessary to move beyond concepts and towards action.

Another definition arises from the measurement of sustainability (including the sustainability of environmental, social, and economic domains, both individually and in various combinations). This term is based on indicators, benchmarks, audits, standards, and certification systems like Fairtrade.

The World Sustainability Society estimates the quality of sustainability governance for individual countries using the Environmental Sustainability Index and the Environmental Performance Index.

---

[6]Redclift (2009), pp. 33–50.

[7]Markus et al. (2006), pp. 801–839.

[8]Ratner (2004), pp. 50–69. Marshall and Toffel (2005), pp. 673–682; Blewitt (2008), pp. 21–24.

[9]Robinson (2004), p. 378.

5.2 Defining Sustainability in Tourism Sector

5.2.3 *Measuring Sustainability*

We think that the last two concepts (Robinson's theory of converting concepts into actions and the sustainability measurement theory) are similar and they could interplay in defining sustainability.

Below, we will consider examples of sustainable economies, taking into account some of the possible actions, the results of which can be measured through benchmarks, standards, etc.

We can, for example, consider the impacts of human consumption on the environment. This impact is reduced not only by consuming less, but also by making the full cycle of production more sustainable by taking into account the effects of individual lifestyle choices and spending patterns, the resource demands of specific goods and services, and the impact on the global economy.

The average consumption per capita in the developing world could be considered sustainable but population numbers are increasing and individuals are aspiring to high-consumption Western lifestyles. Consumerism in developing countries should raise the standard of living without increasing its environmental impact. This objective can be achieved by using strategies and technology that permit economic growth while avoiding environmental damage and resource depletion. For instance, we can look at promoting the so-called "short distribution chain". It emphasises the proximity between the producer and the consumer.

This reduces the negative impact of human consumption on the environment and, in particular, it enables a consistent reduction of carbon footprints. A carbon footprint commonly indicates the total greenhouse gas emissions caused by an organisation, event, product, or person.

These results can be measured with the creation of a sustainable consumerism standard. It is important to keep in mind that calculating the total carbon footprint is impossible because of the excessive amount of data required and the fact that carbon dioxide can also be produced by natural events. In any case, scientists have found a conventional way to quantify carbon footprints.[10]

Sustainable actions and their measurement criteria should be determined according to principles that are shared at an international level. We cannot understate the importance of UN policy on sustainable consumerism in determining the main goal of sustainable development and the interaction between sustainability, human rights, and other fundamental international principles specifically regarding tourism, such as the principle of hospitality. In 2010, the International Resource Panel launched by the United Nations Environment Programme (UNEP) published a report on the global scientific assessment of the impacts of consumption and production.[11]

---

[10]Wright et al. (2011), pp. 61–72.

[11]*Decoupling: natural resource use and environmental impacts of economic growth. International Resource Panel report*, 2011 http://www.unep.org/resourcepanel/.

The International Resource Panel was established in 2007 in order to offer an authoritative scientific assessment on the sustainability and the environmental impacts of use of natural resources. The information contained in the International Resource Panel's reports is intended to be policy relevant.

Sustainability issues are also expressed in ethical terms and consist in implementing social change: urban planning and transport, local and individual lifestyle, and ethical consumerism. "The relationship between human rights and human development, corporate power and environmental justice, global poverty and citizen action, suggest that responsible global citizenship is an inescapable element of what may at first glance seem to be simply matters of personal consumer and moral choice".[12]

A recent UNEP report proposes a green economy that "improves human well-being and social equity, while significantly reducing environmental risks and ecological scarcities": it "does not favour one political perspective over another but works to minimise excessive depletion of natural capital". The report makes three key findings: "that greening not only generates increases in wealth, in particular a gain in ecological commons or natural capital, but also (over a period of six years) produces a higher rate of GDP growth"; that there is "an inextricable link between poverty eradication and better maintenance and conservation of the ecological commons, arising from the benefit flows from natural capital that are received directly by the poor"; "in the transition to a green economy, new jobs are created, which in time exceed the losses in "brown economy" jobs. However, there is a period of job losses in transition, which requires investment in re-skilling and re-educating the workforce".[13]

Strategies to improve the sustainability of our social systems include: improved education and the political empowerment of women, especially in developing countries; greater regard for social justice, notably equity between the rich and the poor both within and between countries; and intergenerational equity.

These purposes can be considered in terms of the measurable actions designed to achieve them. As we have seen, regarding the reduction of carbon footprints, we can find conventional systems of measurement even if the actions are complex and composed of a plurality of factors.

The UNWTO is also trying to coordinate principles and indicators of sustainability deriving from the three dimensions of sustainable development.

The use of indicators is an effective tool in addressing sustainability principles, programmes, and projects at an international level.

For these reasons, the World Tourism Organisation has been promoting sustainable tourism indicators since 1990s as essential tools for policymaking, planning and management of destinations processes. The WTO has developed, together with the Rainforest Alliance and the United Nations Environment Programme (UNEP), "The

---

[12] Blewitt (2014).

[13] United Nations Environmental Program (2011). Towards a Green Economy: Pathways to Sustainable Development and Poverty Eradication—A Synthesis for Policy Makers.

5.2 Defining Sustainability in Tourism Sector

Global Sustainable Tourism Criteria" (GSTC), that are a set of 37 voluntary standards representing the minimum that any tourism business should aspire to reach in order to protect and sustain the world's natural and cultural resources while ensuring tourism meets its potential as a tool for poverty alleviation.

The Guidebook on Indicators of Sustainable Development for Tourist Destination, published in 2004, is the most comprehensive resource on this topic, the result of an extensive study on indicator initiatives worldwide, involving 62 experts from more than 20 countries. The publication describes over 40 major sustainability issues, ranging from the management of natural resources (waste, water, energy, etc.), to development control, satisfaction of tourists and host communities, preservation of cultural heritage, seasonality, economic leakages, or climate change, to mention just a few.

For each issue, indicators and measurement techniques are suggested with practical information sources and examples. The publication also contains a procedure to develop destination-specific indicators, their use in tourism policy and planning processes, as well as applications in different destination types (e.g. coastal, urban, ecotourism, small communities). Numerous examples and 25 comprehensive case studies provide a wide range of experiences at the company, destination, national and regional levels from all continents.

UNWTO organised a series of regional and national workshops on sustainable tourism indicators to train tourism officials and professionals on their application, using a demonstration technique and participatory approach at pilot destinations.

UNWTO is working on setting up Sustainable Tourism Observatories to promote the use of indicators in policy-making and planning processes at the national and local destination levels, following examples of similar UN initiatives.

The process of the creation of the GSTC has joined together more than 40 leading public, private, non-profit, and academic institutions to analyse thousands of worldwide standards and engage the global community in a broad-based stakeholder consultation process.

The Global Sustainable Tourism Criteria have come to a common understanding of sustainable tourism and represent the minimum that any tourism organisation should aspire to reach. Criteria are organised around four main themes:

1. Effective sustainability planning;
2. Maximising social and economic benefits for the local community;
3. Enhancing cultural heritage;
4. Reducing negative impacts on the environment.

The European Commission has also been developing and testing a list of key indicators for measuring the sustainability of tourism policies beginning with the work conducted by the UNWTO. In particular, we must mention two specific schemes implemented by the European Commission: QUALITEST and ECOLABEL.

The QUALITEST tool has been designed to evaluate the quality of the performance of tourist destinations and their related services.

The ECOLABEL is a voluntary certification for environmentally friendly tourist accommodations indicating that the Tourist Accommodation Service:

- Limits energy consumption;
- Limits water consumption;
- Reduces waste production;
- Favours the use of renewable resources and of substances which are less hazardous to the environment;
- Promotes environmental education and communication.

We must not forget the 2030 Agenda for Sustainable Development and the SDGs (Sustainable Development Goals).

The agenda is a commitment to eradicate poverty and achieve sustainable development by 2030 worldwide. It includes 17 goals and 169 targets.

Researchers have achieved various results regarding the implementation of the purposes expressed in the concept of sustainable tourism: environmental compatibility, promotion of nature conservation and benefits for the local population.[14]

5.2.4 Some Examples of Sustainable Tourism

Many projects have been proposed. It is worth looking at a tourism project in Mexico. It consisted of territorial planning that boosted sustainable development in the city of Toluca and the surrounding valley region.

The project derives from an analysis of the urban planning problem in Mexico and Latin America. This has been caused by a demographic explosion and continuous migration from the countryside to the city.

It is essential to modify such movements through sustainable practices, which can be summarized in some basic principles of sustainable urbanism, such as: the pedestrianization of cities, better urban connectivity and sustainable transport, diversity in housing and trade, higher quality in architecture and urban design, renovation, and maintenance of the traditional structure of human settlements, increased urban density, better quality of life for the inhabitants.

In the Toluca Valley, ethnic groups, such as the Matlazinca, Otomí and Mazahua peoples, dating back to pre-Columbian eras, take advantage of the richness of natural resources.

Promoted in the 1940s in the countryside and in the 1950-1960s within Mexico and in the Toluca Valley, the process of industrialization in Toluca is the main factor for transformations that have deteriorated the valley's resources.

As a result, ecosystems have disappeared, altering the population's lifestyle.

Urban growth has been chaotic; there is a lack of organisation in the road and public transport systems, resulting in traffic and pollution problems.

---

[14]Steck (1999).

5.2 Defining Sustainability in Tourism Sector

The concept of sustainable development is very general and is quite difficult to define. At the same time, it gives us the opportunity to identify different goals of sustainability.

In the case of Toluca, these goals are: to reduce the negative impact of the productive activities on the environment; to restore degraded ecosystems; to gradually substitute the activities that are most harmful to the environment; to modify the extravagant and consumerist lifestyle; to improve the quality of life of the population, especially the marginalized groups; and to conserve biodiversity.

"Harmonic Tourism" is tourism that is integrated in the local environment and that proposes actions that boost local and urban development. It strives to improve the quality of life through a rational use of environmental and cultural resources, favouring the conservation of ecosystems and their basic biological processes to generate social and economic benefits for the population.

"The cites do not have to be condemned to be an immense concentration with no identity, full of contradictions and parasites of their surroundings, they may and must be transformed into a space composed by a mosaic of integrated communities, with better conditions of habitability, communication and cultural identity, where the tourist activity can be developed focused on the benefit of the tourist, however, fundamentally on the benefit of the very inhabitants of said communities, where harmony between visitors and hosts is promoted, and between new technologies and traditional technologies, between natural and socio-cultural environments as well.

To achieve sustainable urban development the city must be environmentally planned, to do so their regional surrounding and other regions it has relations with must be taken into account. This is why integrative participative planning is proposed, which emphasizes the necessity to integrate the different sectors of the economic activity into a plan of sustainable development, where diverse (federal, state, municipal and local) dependencies and spheres of the government partake; that from a model of environmental ordering of the territory the sectorial programs which complement each other, not opposed to the principles of sustainability or other sectors, are proposed, in a parallel manner it is based upon the participation of the multiple actors of the community under study and the neighbouring communities, all this considered within the regional context. Among the main characteristics presented by participant integrative participation as a flexible and efficient instrument to make decisions, in addition to the aforementioned ones as principles of Sustainable Urbanism, one finds: the new environmental management that proposes an efficient and sustainable management of the available resources for regional development".[15]

In this context, harmonic tourism becomes the fostering element of economic activities under a scheme of restoration, rehabilitation, conservation, protection, and advantageous use of natural resources, as well as the rescuing and valuing of the local culture for the benefit of the visitor and resident.

---

[15] Serrano Barquin and Hernandez Moreno (2009).

In this example, we can see how sustainable tourism can be a purpose and a means to achieve social, cultural, and urban sustainability at the same time.

As of now, we have considered sustainable actions created by designing a particular system of distribution, production, urbanization etc.

Other examples of sustainable tourism can be found in contracts.

As said, contracts can also play a relevant role in designing sustainable tourism.

As we have previously seen, tourism operator organisations contribute to sustainability through strategy and policy development. For instance, the IHRA (International Hotel and Restaurant Association) is an association with various purposes. It aims at developing eco-tourism by promoting sustainability among their members, fighting the various issues of climate change and by promoting measures in place to reduce CO_2 emissions.

It is possible to introduce clauses in the statutes of these associations by ensuring that all members, or all of those members who want to cover a particular position, are compliant with predetermined targets of sustainable development.

For example, the IHRA has created the Emeraude Hotelier Certification.

The IHRA estimates that almost 80% of all hotels are small and medium enterprises (SMEs) at different stages of organisational development, and only 20% consist of large enterprises. There are only few international standards for the hospitality industry, and national regulations differ greatly from one nation to another. It seems to be necessary to find universally recognized standards that meet the different needs of hotels worldwide.

The creation of the Emeraude Hotelier Certification addresses this issue. Hotels will be awarded with the Emeraude Hotelier recognition if they successfully implement the guidelines stipulated to enhance sustainable tourism.

This certification should serve to motivate hotel management as well as staff to continuously develop sustainable practices.

The Emeraude Hotelier certification is based on a three-level scale. Depending on the number of criteria the hotel fulfils, it will be awarded with one, two or three Emeraudes.

Another way contracts are used as an instrument to achieve a high standard of sustainability involves the business partners of tourism companies.

As previously mentioned, in franchising contracts, special conditions usually contain obligations for franchisors to achieve the same standards, including sustainability standards, of the Francisee. Special penalties, or the resolution of the franchising contract, will be provided in the case of a violation of these conduct rules.

More generally, special "sustainability clauses" can be included in other B2B contracts of the tourism industry.

Let us look at supply contracts, tender contracts, and service contracts. Special clauses imposing the suppliers to guarantee particular standards of sustainability in supply contracts can be introduced, as well as in other B2B contracts.

In addition, in this case, special penalties or contract resolutions will operate in the case of a violation of these conduct rules.

To this point, we have given examples regarding B2B contracts. Something similar can be said about B2C contracts where special conditions can be reserved

5.3 The Role of Courts and Scholars

5.3.1 Courts, Scholars and Sources of Law

During the last century, the approach towards solving legal problems has been widely dogmatic and positivistic, particularly in civil law systems that are traditionally based on written normative acts in contrast to common law systems that are mainly based on the judicial precedents. Civil codes and written legislation have had a central task and it has been presumed that the law is a coherent system of rules by which it is possible to find the solution to any specific question.

If we consider the function of courts in law sources, concerning civil law systems as well, we wonder whether judges draw their decisions from legal rules and principles, or if they decide cases in the light of what is fair by examining the facts at hand.

It is worth noting Brocard law, which states "in claris non fit interpretatio", which means "what is clear doesn't need to be interpreted". The legal language is ambiguous because legal terms can generally have two or more distinct meanings. The clarity of the text is the result of an interpretation, not the premise to elude interpretation. In this perspective, all norms need to be interpreted and revisited by judges. Needless to say, civil codes usually recognize the possibility for interpreters to create law through the analogy rule. According to this principle, in situations of two similar cases, judges can decide the case that does not have its own rules, by applying the rules provided for in the other, similar case.

Nevertheless, it is correct to say that even in civil law systems, judges do not create laws solely by applying the interpretation rule of analogy.

The main referent of Law is Society. Judges decide cases not only by reading the abstract provisions contained in legal statutes; but they also determine fairness through the examination of the facts at hand and through the creation of law.

Therefore, it is now widely accepted that court decisions should be considered de facto as a source of law in civil law systems as well.

Something similar can be said about the role of legal scholars.

The object of study for most legal scholars is still positive national law, but scientific products are also notes under court decisions, papers, and monographs, that offer an interpretation of law. Generally speaking, regarding the crisis of formalism in the new European legal culture, Hesselink concludes that "in a code system the courts and the scholars together master the gap between the abstract rules and the specific cases (concretisation) that legislator has left. Legislator (necessarily) provides abstract rules, the scholars are the expert on what their specific implication are, and the courts (inspired by these scholars) decide what they mean in specific case".[16]

5.3.2 Scholars, Courts and Sustainability

With regard to the principle of sustainability, we must say that the intervention not only of judges, but also of scholars (not only jurists), has been fundamental in its construction.

On 25th September 1997 the International Court of Justice (principal judicial organ of the United Nations) used the concept of "sustainable development" in a decision for the first time.[17]

The judgement was delivered on a protracted dispute between Hungary and Slovakia over the construction and operation of dams on the river Danube which found both States in breach of their legal obligations. It called on both countries to carry out the relevant treaty between them while taking account of the factual situation that has developed since 1989.

Hungary and Czechoslovakia, in 1977, concluded a treaty for the building of structures at Gabcikovo in Slovakia and at Nagymaros in Hungary for the production of electric power, flood control and improvement of navigation on the Danube. In 1989, Hungary suspended and subsequently abandoned completion of the project alleging that it entailed grave risks to the Hungarian environment and the water supply of Budapest. Slovakia (part of the past Czechoslovakia) insisted that Hungary carry out its treaty obligations.

In its judgement, the Court found:

- that Hungary was not entitled to suspend and subsequently abandon, in 1989, its part of the works in the dam project, as laid down in the treaty signed in 1977 by Hungary and Czechoslovakia and related instruments;
- that Czechoslovakia was entitled to start, in November 1991, preparation of an alternative provisional solution (called "Variant C"), but not to put that solution into operation in October 1992 as a unilateral measure;
- that Hungary's notification of termination of the 1977 Treaty and related instruments on 19 May 1992 did not legally terminate them (and that they are consequently still in force and govern the relationship between the Parties);
- that Hungary and Slovakia must negotiate in good faith in the light of the prevailing situation, and must take all necessary measures to ensure the achievement of the objectives of the 1977 Treaty;
- that, unless the Parties agree otherwise, a joint operational regime for the dam on Slovak territory must be established in accordance with the Treaty of 1977;

---

[16]Hesselink (2002).

[17]Trevisan (2009–2010).

References 53

- that each Party must compensate the other Party for the damage caused by its conduct;
- and that the accounts for the construction and operation of the works must be settled in accordance with the relevant provisions of the 1977 Treaty and its related instruments.

The Court held that environmental law is relevant for the implementation of the Treaty and that the Parties could, by agreement, incorporate them through the application of several of its articles. It found that the Parties, in order to reconcile economic development with protection of the environment, "should look afresh at the effects on the environment of the operation of the Gabcikovo power plant. In particular, they must find a satisfactory solution for the volume of water to be released into the old bed of the Danube and into the side-arms of the river".

The 1992 Rio Declaration is generally considered to be the first international treaty to regulate both sustainable development and the so-called precautionary principle to avoid environmental harm in the present risky society. The United Nations High Level Political Forum on Sustainable Development (HLPF) was established in June 2013 through a Resolution made by the UN General Assembly as the main forum for sustainable development issues within the UN framework. Its establishment is one of the main outcomes of the United Nation conference on sustainable development (or Rio+20) that took place in Rio on 20–22 June 2012. The HLPF replaces the above-mentioned Commission for Sustainable Development, which was a functional Commission under the UN Economic and Social Council, established in 1992 at the World Summit on Sustainable Development.

We must remember, at the same time, that the concepts of sustainability and of sustainable development can be traced back to Hans Carl von Carlowitz (1645–1714), who used the concept of "Nachhaltigkeit" in German (translatable in English as "sustainability"). The impact of timber shortages on Saxony's silver mining and metallurgy industries was devastating. In his work Sylvicultura Oeconomica oder Anweisung zur wilden Baum-Zucht (Sylvicultura Oeconomica or the Instructions for Wild Tree Cultivation), Carlowitz formulated ideas for the "sustainable use" of the forest. Following his view, the amount of wood that is cut down should equate to the amount that can be regrown through planned reforestation projects. The concept evolved by taking into account the new challenges offered by economic development, and more recently by technology.[18]

References

Adams, W. M. (2006). *The Future of Sustainability: Re-thinking Environment and Development in the Twenty-first Century*. Report of the IUCN Renowned Thinkers Meeting.
Blewitt, J. (2008). *Understanding sustainable development* (p. 21). Routledge.

---

[18]Grober (2010). He recalls von Carlowitz (1713).

Blewitt, J. (2014). *Understanding sustainable development* (2nd ed.). Routledge.

Buckley, F. H. (2002). Tourism ecolabels. *Annals of Tourism Research, 29*(1), 183.

Grober, U. (2010). *Die Entdeckung der Nachhaltigkeit: Kulturgeschichte eines Begriffs.* Verlag Antje Kunstmann.

Hesselink, M. W. (2002). *The new European private law.* Kluwer Law International.

Markus, J., Milne, M. K., Kearins, K., & Walton, S. (2006). Creating adventures in wonderland: The journey metaphor and environmental sustainability. *Organization, 13*(6), 801.

Marshall, J. D., & Toffel, M. W. (2005). Framing the elusive concept of sustainability: A sustainability hierarchy. *Environmental and Scientific Technology, 39*(3), 673.

Ratner, B. D. (2004). Sustainability as a dialogue of values: Challenges to the sociology of development. *Sociological Inquiry, 74*(1), 50.

Redclift, M. (2009). Sustainable development (1987–2005): An Oxymoron comes of age. *Problems of Sustainable Development, 4*(1), 33.

Robinson, J. (2004). Squaring the circle? Some thoughts on the idea of sustainable development. *Ecological Economics, 48*, 369.

Serrano Barquin, R., & Hernandez Moreno, S. (2009). Harmonic Tourism, Factor of Sustainable Development In the City of Toluca, Mexico. *Theoretical and Empirical Researches in Urban Management, 4*(13), 5–24.

Steck, B. (1999). *Sustainable tourism as a development option practical guide for local planners, developers and decision makers.* TZ Verlagsgesellschaft.

The Earth Charter Initiative. (2000). *Annual report.* www.earthcharter.org

Trevisan, L. (2009–2010). The International Court of Justice's treatment of sustainable development and implications for Argentina v. Uruguay. *Sustainable Development Law and Policy, 10*, 40.

UNEP and UWTO. (2005). *Making Tourism More Sustainable - A Guide for Policy Makers*

United Nations Environmental Program. (2011). *Towards a Green Economy: Pathways to Sustainable Development and Poverty Eradication – A Synthesis for Policy Makers.*

United Nations General Assembly. (2005). *World summit outcome.* www.un.org

Von Carlowitz, H. C. (1713). *Sylvicultura Oeconomica, oder Haußwirthliche Nachricht und Naturmäßige Anweisung zur Wilden Baum Zucht* [Leipzig, 1713].

Wright, L. A., Kemp, S., & Williams, I. (2011). Carbon foot printing': towards a universally accepted definition. *Carbon Management, 2*(1), 61.

Part II
Consumer Contracts and Tourism

Chapter 6
Consumer Contracts and Sustainability

Contents

6.1	Consumer Contracts and Sustainability	57
	6.1.1 Sustainable Consumer	57
	6.1.2 Consumer and Tourism	58
	6.1.3 Why Do Consumers Need Protection?	60
6.2	Standard Contracts and Consumer Autonomy	61
	6.2.1 Consumers' Choice	61
	6.2.2 Consumers' Protection Against Unfair Terms	62
	6.2.3 Many of the Consumers' Rights Remain Unfulfilled	64
6.3	Consumers' Protection Private Law Remedies	66
	6.3.1 Different Remedies	66
	6.3.2 Consumers' Protection and Punitive Damages	66
References		68

6.1 Consumer Contracts and Sustainability

6.1.1 Sustainable Consumer

In terms of contracts with a consumer, defined as contracts between a company and a natural person who acts for consumer purposes, we can discuss sustainability through different perspectives.

Consumer choices can have significant economic, social, and environmental implications. Autonomy in consumer choices must therefore be preserved in order to allow consumers to be an active part of the contract. Consumer rights are central to achieving sustainable development, because, as said by Consumers International (Consumers International, known as the International Organisation of Consumers Unions (IOCU), is the membership organisation for consumer groups around the world), these rights contribute towards a fairer, safer, and healthier society, and a more equitable and efficient economy.

The term sustainability is also connected to contracts with consumers because, as is well-known, environmental and sustainability claims in product advertisement,

---

© The Author(s), under exclusive license to Springer Nature Switzerland AG 2021
S. Landini, *Sustainable Tourism Contracts*,
https://doi.org/10.1007/978-3-030-83140-0_6

including tourism products, have a strong impact. It is therefore necessary to distinguish the fair environmental claims from the unfair ones, considering the impact they can have on the economic behaviour of the consumer. Some authors compare the effects of four types of ads (advertisings): a functional green adv. promoting the environmental advantages of a product, an emotional green adv. using a visual representation of pleasant natural scenery, a mixed type green adv. using functional and emotional strategies, and a control group. Findings of an experimental study using a representative sample of U.S. consumers suggest that both the emotional and the mixed-type advs. significantly affect brand attitude, mediated by attitude toward the adv. These effects do not depend on consumers' green involvement. Functional advs, in contrast, only impact brand attitudes when involvement, measured as green purchase behaviour or green product attitudes, is high.[1]

For all these reasons, it is important to preserve consumers' autonomy in contracts.

The term B2C commonly indicates a transaction that occurs between a company and a consumer, as opposed to a transaction between companies (called B2B).

In the language of economics, a consumer is generally a person or a group of people who are the final users of products and or services generated within a social system.

There are also different aspects to it when taking into account the legal meanings of the word "consumer". Legal definitions merely stipulate as they depend on political choices of legislators. One of the most common legal definitions of "consumer" is provided in the European Directive 93/13/CE.

6.1.2 Consumer and Tourism

According to these directives, the term "consumer" means any natural person who is dealing for purposes that are outside his trade, business, or profession.

With regard to the tourism market, we must keep in mind that customers sometimes deal for purposes that are both outside and inside their trade, business, or profession. Business travellers are a good example of this. The tourism industry can be divided into leisure tourism and business tourism, which can be defined as the provision of facilities and services to delegates who attend meetings, congresses, exhibitions, and business events. The fact is that business and leisure travel worlds often collide. Moreover, business travellers like to, during some brief moments of their trip, break routines, do something new, try out new activities.

It is therefore difficult to make a clear distinction between leisure travellers and business travellers.

---

[1] Matthes et al. (2014), pp. 1885–1893.

6.1 Consumer Contracts and Sustainability

From the legal point of view, this conclusion could cause problems in the application of consumer contract law.

For example, Italian Law on consumer contracts, according to European Directive 93/13/CE on unfair terms (art. 33 of consumers' code—legislative decree (D. Lgs 206/2005), is applicable only in the case of a contract between a supplier and a natural person who is dealing for purposes that are outside his trade, business, or profession. Is it also applicable in the case of a contract between a company (a hotel company, for example) and a business traveller? We believe that, in this case, consumer interest should prevail according to the principle laid down under the heading of the 93/13/Directive: 'Protection of the economic interests of the consumers'. As stated in those European programmes: "acquirers of goods and services should be protected against the abuse of power by the seller or supplier, in particular against one-sided standard contracts and the unfair exclusion of essential rights in contracts". Regarding that point, we have to remember that the proposal of the Directive on travel packages issued on July 9th, 2013 offers a different level of protection to business travellers: "as it is not appropriate to grant the same level of protection to business travellers whose travel arrangements are made on the basis of a framework contract concluded between their employers and specialised operators often offering, on a business-to-business basis, a level of protection similar to the one stemming from this Directive (so-called managed business travel), such travel arrangements are excluded from the scope".[2]

On 8 October 2008 the European Commission published a proposal for a consumer rights directive. The proposed directive was the provisional outcome of the review of the consumer acquis that the Commission launched with its Action Plan in 2004.2 The aim was to revise the four directives that according to the Commission regulate 'the contractual rights of consumers,' namely the directives on doorstep selling, unfair contract terms, distance contracts, and the sale of consumer goods and guarantees. As someone underlined "The mail purpose of this review, according to the Commission, is to achieve 'a true internal market for "business-to-consumer" trade (b2c).' The proposal contains nothing about business-to business (b2b) agreements and refers to 'a new beginning in the area of the contractual rights of consumers.

The proposed directive fits very well with a sharp distinction between b2c and b2b contracts and comprises several features that—especially as a combination—provide an optimal basis for a future European consumer (contract) code".[3]

The Consumers right Directive 2011/83/EU has been amended by Directive (EU) 2019/2161 of 27 November 2019 on better enforcement and modernisation of Union consumer protection rules. As announced in the New Consumer Agenda of November 2020, the Commission is going to update the guidance documents on the Unfair Commercial Practices Directive and the Consumer Rights Directive by 2022.

---

[2] Hesselink (2010), pp. 57–102.

[3] Ibidem.

National laws usually provide special dispositions aimed at consumer protection that has a specific impact on tourism contracts (i.e., travel package contracts, time share contracts, unfair terms, unfair commercial practices).

6.1.3 Why Do Consumers Need Protection?

A study conducted by the Office of Fair Trading (OFT), dealing with UK consumers, published in February 2011, found that consumers rarely read contracts in full before entering them. Thus, they are usually unaware of some of the terms to which they are agreeing. Consumers can also make mistakes in interpreting terms and conditions that they are unaware of.

Moreover, we have to consider some other factors that are related to the contract:

- Lengthy boilerplate terms are often in fine print and written in technical and complicated legal language;
- Access to the full terms may be difficult or impossible before acceptance. Often the document being signed is not the full contract;
- There may be social pressure to sign. For instance, the salesperson may imply that the customer is being unreasonable if he reads the terms. If the purchaser is at the front of a queue there could be additional pressure to sign quickly. Sometimes suppliers give customers a gift (also small), which socially obliges the customer to be co-operative and to conclude the transaction;
- Information asymmetry can be another disadvantage for consumers. Firms usually know the distribution of tastes and prices across consumers. At the same time, individual consumers are unaware of this distribution. In a market with such information asymmetry, a firm is able to maximize its profits by setting the price to attract consumers who would give the product a high rating. As someone noted "Consumer policy increasingly places emphasis on the role of information in allowing consumers to protect themselves and promoting a competitive economy. Increasing the information available to consumers is undoubtedly beneficial, but this article cautions that the limitations of consumer protection though information also have to be recognized. In particular, emphasis is placed on the insights provided by behavioral economics which suggests that consumers may not always respond to information provided as rationally as traditional economic models sometimes assume. One implication of this is that the way information rules are framed needs to be revisited. Other consumer policy approaches (altering the default rules, using bans and regulations, and risk sharing) need to be considered alongside a strategy of information provision. To analyze which approach should be adopted or to find the appropriate balance between different

approaches requires policy makers to engage more fully with the legal and consumer policy research community".[4]

Many consumer purchases are problematic when conditions are involved, whether they are in writing or in complex oral terms. Personal and social conditions also play a relevant role. Younger people are more likely to have problems with their contracts, while older consumers use prior experience and knowledge as a source of understanding. At the same time, the increased use of technology has, in some cases, inverted the conditions mentioned above: young people, in fact, are usually more informed on e-commerce and possible unfair commercial practice on the web.

Consumers with higher incomes, in higher social classes, and consumers who have received a higher level of education reported more problems. This may be because they are accustomed to driving a hard bargain.

Moreover, the purchase method is significant as a transaction can be conducted face-to-face, over the phone, or via Internet. The purchase method can influence consumers' understanding of the terms and conditions. This may depend on the different nature and degree of interaction between the parties of the contract, the accessibility and presentation of the terms and conditions, the timing of when information is presented, or the time available to assess information and make a decision.[5]

According to the results obtained by the OFT, the most common problems were related to goods and services not meeting expectations. In some cases, there could be a problem with the contract: 78% of consumers stated that terms were in dispute between the consumer and the trader, and in over half of these cases consumers felt that the trader had interpreted the terms to their own advantage. Other contract-specific problems included unexpected terms and conditions (34%), cancellation problems (28%) and unreasonable charges and penalties (27%), others.

6.2 Standard Contracts and Consumer Autonomy

6.2.1 Consumers' Choice

Consumer contracts are usually standard contracts (sometimes known as adhesion or boilerplate contracts): these are contracts between two parties where the terms and conditions of the contract are set by one of the parties, and the other party has little or no ability to negotiate terms. It is commonly said that the other party is placed in a "take it or leave it" position.[6]

---

[4] Howells (2005), p. 349 ff. See also Grundmann et al. (2001); Weatherill (1994), p. 49; Schwartz and Wilde (1979), pp. 630–638; Whitford (1973), p. 400; Sunstein and Thaler (2003), p. (1159); Becher (2008), p. 45.

[5] Viscusi (1996), pp. 661–665; Bainbridge (2000), p. 102; Hanson and Kysar (1999), p. 630.

[6] Rackoff (1988), p. 1174 ff.

There is a debate on whether, and to what extent, courts should enforce standard form contracts. On the one hand, they undoubtedly have an important role in promoting economic efficiency since they reduce transaction costs. On the other hand, signatories can accept unjust terms in these contracts. For instance, terms might be considered unfair if they allow the seller to avoid all liability, unilaterally modify terms, or terminate the contract. These terms are not only unfair from a legal point of view, but they may also be economically inefficient if they place the risk of a negative outcome on a consumer who is not in the best position to take precautions. Moreover, standard form contracts are usually drafted by lawyers who are instructed to minimize the firm's liability, and not necessarily drafted to implement managers' competitive decisions.

There are a number of reasons why such terms may be accepted by consumers: standard form contracts are rarely read; standard form contracts may exploit unequal power relations and they may not present enough information about the purchased product.

Some would argue that, in a competitive market,[7] consumers have the ability to shop around for the supplier who offers them the most favourable terms. However, where there are oligopolies, consumers may still only have access to contracts with similar predetermined terms, without any opportunity for negotiation. Moreover, in a competitive market, there could not be any real opportunity for negotiation. Many people do not read or understand the terms so there may be very little incentive for a company to offer favourable conditions.

6.2.2 Consumers' Protection Against Unfair Terms

As we have previously mentioned, in many countries, there are laws protecting consumers from unfair terms. In American law, protection mainly comes from the common law. In European Union countries, specific rules have been adopted by national legislators according to European Directive 93/13/CEE on unfair clauses in consumer contracts. Asian countries also have specific rules for B2C contracts. It is worth looking at the Japanese Consumer Contract Act enacted in 2000 and amended in 2006.[8]

According to Directive 93/13, a contractual term which has not been individually negotiated shall be regarded as unfair if, contrary to the requirement of good faith, it causes a significant imbalance in the parties' rights and obligations arising under the contract, to the detriment of the consumer. A term shall always be regarded as not individually negotiated where it has been drafted in advance and the consumer has therefore not been able to influence the substance of the term, particularly in the

---

[7] Waterson (2003), p. 129.

[8] Weatherill (2013); Ramsay (2012); Howells et al. (2010); Howells and Weatherill (2005); Reich et al. (2014).

6.2 Standard Contracts and Consumer Autonomy

context of a pre-formulated standard contract. Unfair terms are considered to be void and without effects.

Article 3 of Directive 93/13 contains an indicative and non-exhaustive list of the terms that may be regarded as unfair.

Below are some of the clauses relating to the hospitality industry:

(a) excluding or limiting the legal liability of a seller or supplier in the event of the death or personal injury of a consumer resulting from an act or omission of that seller or supplier;

(b) inappropriately excluding or limiting the legal rights of the consumer vis-à-vis the seller, or supplier, or another party in the event of total or partial non-performance or inadequate performance by the seller or supplier of any of the contractual obligations, including the option of offsetting a debt owed to the seller or supplier against any claim which the consumer may have against him;

(c) making an agreement binding on the consumer, whereas the provision of services by the seller or supplier is subject to a condition whose realization depends on his own will alone;

(d) permitting the seller or supplier to retain sums paid by the consumer where the latter decides not to conclude or perform the contract, without providing for the consumer to receive compensation of an equivalent amount from the seller or supplier where the latter is the party cancelling the contract;

(e) requiring any consumer who fails to fulfil his obligation to pay a disproportionately high sum in compensation;

(f) authorizing the seller or supplier to dissolve the contract on a discretionary basis where the same facility is not granted to the consumer, or permitting the seller or supplier to retain the sums paid for services not yet supplied by him where it is the seller or supplier himself who dissolves the contract;

(g) enabling the seller or supplier to terminate a contract of indeterminate duration without reasonable notice except where there are serious grounds for doing so;

(h) automatically extending a contract of fixed duration where the consumer does not indicate otherwise, or when the deadline fixed for the consumer to express this desire not to extend the contract is unreasonably early;

(i) irrevocably binding the consumer to terms with which he had no real opportunity of becoming acquainted before the conclusion of the contract;

(j) enabling the seller or supplier to alter the terms of the contract unilaterally without a valid reason which is specified in the contract;

(k) enabling the seller or supplier to alter unilaterally without a valid reason any characteristics of the product or service to be provided;

(l) providing for the price of goods to be determined at the time of delivery or allowing a seller of goods or supplier of services to increase their price without, in both cases, giving the consumer the corresponding right to cancel the contract if the final price is too high in relation to the price agreed when the contract was concluded;

(m) giving the seller or supplier the right to determine whether the goods or services supplied are in conformity with the contract, or giving him the exclusive right to interpret any term of the contract;

(n) limiting the seller's or supplier's obligation to respect commitments undertaken by his agents or making his commitments subject to compliance with a particular formality;

(o) obliging the consumer to fulfil all his obligations where the seller or supplier does not perform his;

(p) giving the seller or supplier the possibility of transferring his rights and obligations under the contract, where this may serve to reduce the guarantees for the consumer, without the latter's agreement;

(q) excluding or hindering the consumer's right to take legal action or exercise any other legal remedy, particularly by requiring the consumer to take disputes exclusively to arbitration not covered by legal provisions, unduly restricting the evidence available to him, or imposing on him a burden of proof which, according to the applicable law, should lie with another party of the contract.

In the field of tourism contracts, the following should be noted as clauses at risk of unfairness: clauses of derogation from jurisdiction by territory; jurisdiction waiver clauses and arbitration clauses; price revision clauses; complaint and denunciation clauses; clauses that give the organiser the right to modify or cancel the contract; clauses governing the onerous withdrawal of the tourist; liability limitation clauses.

Consumer protection takes place not only through the nullity of unfair clauses but also through a regulation of the consumer's right to information in order to reduce the information asymmetry of B2C contracts and also through the introduction of consumer withdrawal rights.

In this regard, the provisions on timeshare contracts can be considered as we are going to see in the next paragraphs.

Given the role that the economic behaviour of consumers can play in the way businesses make green choices, it becomes important to promote the active participation of consumers in building the market. It is important that the consumer knows his rights and has the possibility to exercise them to protect his freedom of choice of products and services.

6.2.3 Many of the Consumers' Rights Remain Unfulfilled

However, many of the rights enshrined in law remain mostly unfulfilled, as three major problems persist:

(1) consumers' lack of knowledge of the rights and of the methods for the correct use of the same rights, as well as their lack of aptitude to act consciously and to carefully evaluate consumption choices. This lack of education / information is also common in the entrepreneurial world, so the professional often does not know that he has certain obligations towards the consumer;

6.2 Standard Contracts and Consumer Autonomy

(2) the deficiencies in the law enforcement system, or in the implementation of the law, which favour less correct operators, both due to control bodies lacking the means and resources, and the continuous evolution of contractual forms, marketing techniques and sales channels, also linked to technological advancements;

(3) a judicial system that is unable to effectively perform its function of guaranteeing justice to consumers and deterring incorrect behaviour. Furthermore, the globalization of markets and electronic commerce have made the cross-border consumer relationship easy and frequent, which consequently creates problems in applying the law internationally, and imaginable difficulties with fighting fraud and violations perpetrated by remote countries, even outside of the European Union.

This situation produces damage on both an individual level, as there is a high number of consumers who suffer violations of their rights every year, and a collective level, and more generally on a macroeconomic level as well, because the market needs trust to develop and production needs competitiveness. These elements are closely linked to the fairness of relations between businesses and consumers.

In fact, unfair commercial practices and other violations of the Consumer Code are often implemented in the context of unfair competition, which allows the seller to maintain low prices, saving, for example, on after-sales services or by resorting to additional costs that are charged to the consumer after the contract is signed.

Therefore, it is paramount that every consumer knows, on a case-by-case basis, the forms of caution that need to be taken before committing to a purchase and that he/she is able to resort, when needed, to the qualified and impartial assistance of institutions (where provided) and consumer associations that are taking action to promote consumer education.

New dimensions of consumer education are also beginning to emerge as people become more aware of the need for ethical consumerism and sustainable consumer behaviour in our increasingly globalized society.

It is important to remember that consumer education focuses not only on consumers' rights but also on function skills, such as skills that are related to processing information relating to consumer behaviour. Two aspects that influence this process are: cognitive abilities and environmental influences, particularly interpersonal events.[9]

---

[9]Weeks et al. (2016), pp. 198–209.

6.3 Consumers' Protection Private Law Remedies

6.3.1 Different Remedies

In terms of consumer protection remedies, it is worth remembering a famous distinction: preventive measures, restitution, and punishment.[10]

The promulgation of codes of conduct inspired by customer satisfaction principles can be considered to be a preventative measure. Moreover, many existing consumer legislations are based on the presumption that consumers have the necessary information needed to compare products in the marketplace. This kind of measure can be considered to be a preventative measure.

Restitution is usually defined as reparations made by providing an equivalent product or compensation for loss damages or injury caused, or the restoration of property rights previously taken away.

We can consider, in terms of restitution, the invalidity of contracts in the violation of imperative norms (like in case of unfair terms) or the rescission of contracts in case of misrepresentation (a false statement of fact made by one party to another party), the invalidity or violability of contracts in case of a mistake (it is an erroneous belief, at contracting, that certain facts are) and consequently the refunding of payments.

6.3.2 Consumers' Protection and Punitive Damages

Consumers can also claim damages in case of a violation of their rights.

Actual damages are monetary compensation awarded to an injured party in order to compensate the individual for losses. When monetary compensation goes beyond that which is necessary to compensate the individual for losses, a sanction is issued to punish the wrongdoer (so-called punitive damage).

Consumers were limited to seeking actual damages. The most significant change brought by consumer protection legislation is that in some countries punitive damages are available to an injured consumer.

Punitive damages (also known as exemplary damages) may be awarded by a judge (or a jury) in addition to actual damages, which compensate a plaintiff for the losses suffered due to the harm caused by the defendant. Punitive damages are a measure of punishing the defendant in a civil lawsuit recognized in some American States.

Punitive damages are a settled principle of common law in US. They are generally a matter of state law although we have some important judgments of the U.S. Supreme Court. In particular, the U.S. Supreme Court, in BMW of North America v. Gore, 517 U.S. 519, 116 S. Ct. 1589, 134 L. Ed. 2d 809 (1996), also

---

[10]Cohen (1975), p. 24 ff.

6.3 Consumers' Protection Private Law Remedies

developed guidelines for assessing punitive damages. The Court held that the "degree of reprehensibility of defendant's conduct" is the most important indication of reasonableness in measuring punitive damages. In 1993 the U.S. Supreme Court in the case TXO Productions Corp. v. Alliance Resources Corp., 509 U.S. 443, 113 S. Ct. 2711, 125 L. Ed. 2d 366 (1993), stated that the Due Process Clause of the fourteenth Amendment to the U.S. Constitution prohibits a state from imposing a "grossly excessive" punishment on a person held liable in tort. Whether a verdict is grossly excessive must be based on an identification of the state interests that a punitive award is designed to serve. If the award is disproportionate to the interests served, it violates due process.[11]

In other countries, such as Italy and Germany, punitive damages are not foreseen by the law. In general, legal systems are increasingly recognizing relevance of non-pecuniary damage, they are determined on an equitable basis and have no function that is not strictly compensatory.[12]

Concerning this issue, it is worth remembering some cases where damages were awarded for delayed baggage and delayed flights.

In a Scottish case (O'Carroll v Ryanair, Sheriff Court, 2008), the Sheriff Court awarded damages against an airline for "stress, inconvenience, frustration and disruption" to the holiday as a result of the delayed baggage of the claimant. The appeal was to the Sheriff Principal of Grampian, Highland and Islands at Aberdeen. The airline argued in the appeal that the court did not have jurisdiction and that the basis of the award for damages were not permissible under Articles 19 and 29 of the Montreal Convention. In particular, according to art. 29, "in the carriage of passengers, baggage and cargo, any action for damages, however founded, whether under this Convention or in contract or in tort or otherwise, can only be brought subject to the conditions and such limits of liability as are set out in this Convention without prejudice to the question as to who are the persons who have the right to bring suit and what are their respective rights. In any such action, punitive, exemplary or any other non-compensatory damages shall not be recoverable." The Sheriff Principal rejected the airline's appeal stating that the awarding of damages for stress and inconvenience was available under Scots Law and was not excluded by Article 29 of the Montreal Convention as it did not amount to punitive, exemplary, or non-compensatory damages.

In the Brunton v Cosmosair case (Keighley County Court, November 25th. 2002), the claimant had booked a holiday for himself and his family in Mallorca. On arrival, he discovered that two of his bags were still in the UK. In addition to replacement costs, he claimed compensation for loss of amenity of the holiday, discomfort, and loss of enjoyment. The district judge rejected the latter on grounds that this was not recoverable under the Warsaw Convention, which is an international treaty governing certain incidents that occur on board an aircraft during flights

---

[11] Owen (1994), p. 39.

[12] Tolani (2011), p. 1 ff.

between signatory nations. This convention was modified by the above Montreal convention.

In the Lucas v Avro case (Sheffield County Court, March 15th, 1994), Lucas booked a flight-only holiday from Avro, but a mistake was made on the tickets issued: the return flight was in fact 24 hours later than indicated. The district judge rejected a claim for damages for mental distress on grounds that a flight-only contract did not include an obligation to provide peace of mind or freedom from distress.

In the Parker v TUI UK Travel case (Central London County Court, October 30th, 2006) Mr. Parker claimed damages for a delayed flight to Heathrow. The court held that the contract was just a contract of carriage, not a contract for a holiday. It was therefore not a contract for enjoyment and, for this reason, the claim for loss of enjoyment failed. In terms of punitive remedies, it is particularly worth remembering penalties awarded by Administrative Authorities in cases of Unfair Commercial Practice according to Directive 2005/29/EC.

References

Bainbridge, S. M. (2000). Mandatory disclosure: A behavioral analysis. *University of Cincinnati Law Review, 68*, 1023.

Becher, S. (2008). Asymetric information in consumer contracts: The challenge that is yet to be met. *American Business Law Journal, 45*, 723–774.

Cohen, D. (1975). Remedies for consumers protection: Prevention, restitution or punishment. *Journal of Marketing, 39*, 24 ff.

Grundmann, S., Kerber, G., & Weatherill, S. (Eds.). (2001). *Party autonomy and the role of information in the internal market*. De Gruyter.

Hanson, J., & Kysar, D. (1999). Taking behaviouralism seriously: The problem of market manipulation. *New York University Law Rev, 74*, 630.

Hesselink, M. W. (2010). Towards a sharp distinction between B2B and B2C? On consumer, commercial and general contract law after the consumer rights directive. *European Review of Private Law, 18*, 57.

Howells, G. (2005). The potential and limits of consumers empowerment of information. *Journal of Law and Society, 32*, 349.

Howells, G., Ramsay, I. M., & Wilhelmsson, T. (2010). *Handbook of research on international consumer law. Research handbooks in international law*. Edward Elgar.

Howells, G., & Weatherill, S. (2005). *Consumer protection law*. Ashgate.

Matthes, J., Wonneberger, A., & Schmuck, D. (2014). Consumers' green involvement and the persuasive effects of emotional versus functional ads. *Journal of Business Research, 67*(9), 1885.

Owen, D. G. (1994). Punitive damages overview: Functions, problems and reform. *Villanova Law Review, 39*, 363.

Rackoff, T. D. (1988). Contract of adhesion. An essay in reconstruction. *Harvard Law Review, 96*, 1174.

Ramsay, J. (2012). *Consumer law and policy: Text and materials on regulating consumer markets*. Hart.

Reich, N., Micklitz, H. W., Rott, P., & Tonner, K. (2014). *European consumer law. vol. Ius communitatis series*. Intersentia.

References

Schwartz, A., & Wilde, L. (1979). Intervening in markets on the basis of imperfect information: A legal and economic analysis. *University of Pennsylvania Law Review, 127*, 630.

Sunstein, C., & Thaler, R. (2003). Libertarian paternalism is not an Oxymoron. *University of Chicago Law Rev, 70*, 1159.

Tolani, M. (2011). U.S. Punitive damages before German Courts: A comparative analysis with respect to the Ordre public. *Annual Survey of International and Comparative Law, 17*, 1.

Viscusi, K. (1996). Individual rationality, Hazard warnings and the foundations of Tort law. *Rutgers Law Review, 48*, 661.

Waterson, M. (2003). The role of consumers in competition and competition policy. *International Journal of Industrial Organisation, 21*, 129.

Weatherill, S. (1994). The role of the informed consumer in European community law. *Consumer Law Journal, 2*, 49.

Weatherill, S. (2013). *EU consumer law and policy*. Edward Elgar.

Weeks, C. S., Mortimer, G., & Page, L. (2016). Understanding how consumer education impacts shoppers over time: A longitudinal field study of unit price usage. *Journal of Retailing and Consumer Services, 32*, 198.

Whitford, W. (1973). *The functions of disclosure regulation in consumer transaction* (Vol. 1973, p. 400). Wisconsin Law Rev.

Chapter 7
Hospitality Industry and Contracts

Contents

7.1 Hospitality Industry Market	71
7.1.1 Tradition and Innovation in Hospitality Industry	71
7.1.2 Food&Beverage	74
7.1.3 Sustainable Hospitality	75
7.2 The Hotel Accommodation Contract	77
7.2.1 Content of Hotel Contract	77
7.2.2 Green Hotel	78
7.2.3 Breach of Hotel Contract	80
7.2.4 Hotelkeepers' Liability	81
7.2.5 Hotel Contract vs Tourist Lease Contract	83
7.3 Tourism in Sharing Economy	84
7.3.1 Timeshare and Tourism	84
7.3.2 Timeshare in EU Directive	85
7.3.3 Home Exchange and Tourism	86
References	88

7.1 Hospitality Industry Market

7.1.1 Tradition and Innovation in Hospitality Industry

The hospitality industry is part of the service industry and it includes hotels, resorts, bed and breakfasts, campsites, restaurants, cruise lines, airlines, other forms of travel, event planning etc.[1]

Hotels represent the main source of income and hotel accommodation contracts can be considered as the standard form of hospitality industry contracts. Norms regulating hotel-keepers' liability, which we will discuss in the next paragraph, are generally applicable to other forms of the hospitality industry as well.

---

[1] Victorino et al. (2005), p. 555 ff.

© The Author(s), under exclusive license to Springer Nature Switzerland AG 2021
S. Landini, *Sustainable Tourism Contracts*,
https://doi.org/10.1007/978-3-030-83140-0_7

Agritourism enterprises represent another increasingly important source of income. They are defined differently in different parts of the world. They are generally defined as any agricultural-based operation or activity that brings visitors to a farm or ranch, sometimes referring specifically to farm stay. Agritourism usually includes a variety of activities: buying products directly from a farm stand, navigating a corn maze, picking fruit, feeding animals, or staying at a B&B on a farm.[2]

Agritourism helps preserve rural lifestyles and landscapes, including strengthening local networks, culture and traditions.

About the Eu Regulations on Rural development, see EU regulation 1303/2013—presents common rules applicable to the European structural and investment funds (ESIF); EU regulation 1305/2013—support for rural development by the European agricultural fund for rural development (EAFRD); EU regulation 1306/2013—on the financing, management and monitoring of the common agricultural policy; EU regulation 1310/2013—support for rural development by the European agricultural fund for rural development (EAFRD); EU regulation 807/2014—support for rural development by the European agricultural fund for rural development (EAFRD) and introducing transitional provisions; EU regulation 640/2014—the administration, withdrawal of support or conditions of penalties applicable to direct payments, rural development support and cross compliance; EU regulation 809/2014—how EU regulation 1306/2013 on the administration and control system, rural development measures and cross compliance should be applied.

The Commission in the recent communication on the Multiannual Financial Framework (MFF) mentioned a more common agricultural policy. CAP (Community Agricultural Policy) will have to support the transition to a fully sustainable agricultural sector development of dynamic rural areas, ensuring healthy, safe and high quality food for over 500 million consumers [COM (2018) 322 final—Regulation QFP]. On 1 June 2018, the European Commission presented the legislative proposals on the future of the CAP for the period after 2020.

The development of agritourism enterprises can be considered to be part of European policy on sustainable rural development as detailed in European regulation 1257/1999, which establishes the framework for Community support for sustainable rural development. In fact, this regulation establishes that support for rural development, relating to farming activities and their conversion, may include: the improvement of structures in agricultural holdings and structures for the processing and marketing of agricultural products, the conversion and reorientation of agricultural production potential, the diversification of activities with the aim of providing complementary or alternative activities, the maintenance and reinforcement of viable social fabric in rural areas, the development of economic activities and the maintenance and creation of employment with the aim of ensuring better exploitation of existing inherent potential, the preservation and promotion of a high nature value and a sustainable agriculture respecting environmental requirements.

---

[2]Privitera (2010); Busby and Rendle (2000), pp. 635–642; Maetzold (2002).

7.1 Hospitality Industry Market

The common agricultural policy (CAP) supports the vibrancy and economic viability of rural communities through rural development measures. The rural development measures reinforce the CAP's market measures and income supports with strategies and funding to strengthen the EU's agri-food and forestry sectors, environmental sustainability, and the wellbeing of rural areas in general. Agritourism is part of sustainable development since it allows farmers to promote their estates and geographical locations and, when associated with the sale of home-made products, adds value to their agricultural production.

Bed and Breakfasts (well known as B&Bs) are considered to be part of Agritourism, but this hospitality industry phenomenon is no longer limited to only rural areas. B&Bs are small lodging establishments that offer overnight accommodation and breakfast. Bed and breakfasts are usually private homes with fewer than 10 bedrooms available for commercial use.

The hospitality industry has been greatly innovated by new forms of tourism such as medical tourism and sport tourism.

Medical tourism typically consists of a movement from a more developed nation to another area of the world for medical care to find treatment at a lower cost. Medical tourism is different from the traditional model of international medical travel where patients generally travel from less developed nations to major medical centers in more developed countries for treatments that are unavailable in their own communities. Services that are typically sought by travelers are joint replacements, dental surgery and cosmetic surgery. However, every type of health care, including psychiatry, alternative treatments, convalescent care and even burial services are available.

Typical lodging for medical tourism includes clinics and spas. The term spa comes from the name of the Belgian town of Spa, whose name can be traced back to Roman times, when the settlement was called Aquae Spadanae. Spa towns or spa resorts are lodgings associated with water treatment (like balneotherapy), typically offering various health treatments. The belief in the curative powers of mineral waters goes back to prehistoric times and it is popular worldwide.

Sport tourism is also a phenomenon that has become globally popular due to famous international events such as the Olympic Games or Super Championships. It is clear that there is an important connection between sports and tourism: contributing to the execution of development plans, promoting national and international friendships and promoting an understanding between people and communities.[3]

Sport tourism refers to travel involving athletes and observers of a sporting event. Therefore, sport tourism requires special lodgings near sporting event locations and functional to the sporting event organization.

---

[3] Kurtzman and Saubar (1993), p. 30; Penot (2003), pp. 100–101.

7.1.2 Food&Beverage

Moreover, food service is considered to be part of the hospitality industry. Increasingly important aspects of this sector are catering and banqueting contracts.

A catering contract is an agreement between a hiring party and a company offering catering services. This contract typically includes prices, terms and conditions of payment, information on food and beverage served, as well as the time of the event and how long food and beverage will be made available for. It will also specify whether the meal will be served seated or in buffet style and indicate whether or not the caterer will provide trays of food circulating among guests.

We need to distinguish catering from banqueting. The term banqueting consists of the activity of food and drink preparation in the organization of a banquet. Thus, banqueting provides food and drink that is cooked and prepared on site by a chef. Banqueting also includes the preparation of tables, waiter services, and the supply of tables, chairs, napkins, tablecloths, tableware, dishware etc.

Another sector of the hospitality industry is event planning. It is important to draw a careful event planning contract, which is an agreement between an event planner and a client for the planning, organization, and management of an event.

The agreement will contain information about the party and the event (location, time, a detailed description of all services to be performed by the event planner). The event planner will provide the services indicated in the detailed description contained in the contract. Usually, this description is found in a separate document attached to the contract.

The event planner will be responsible for the planning, organization and management of all the details that are necessary for the performance of the services outlined in the description, including, but not limited to, the event site, negotiating any leases or obtaining any permits or licenses, parking, insurance, the rental of any equipment, and the negotiating of fees and services to be provided by any contractor, vendor or other service provider.

In the case of events organized for the promotion of a company, the event planner agrees to use the company's name, logo or trademark in any material used by the event planner in promotion of the event, including, but not limited to, any public announcements in newspapers, magazines, billboards, tickets, or television and radio announcements. The event planner further agrees to only use the company's name, logo or trademark for purposes relating to the event and for no other purposes without the prior written consent of the company. For these promotional events, special clauses concerning the preparation of any promotional documents or promotional material will be inserted.

The event planner agrees that all works conducted at the event site shall be performed in accordance with all the applicable laws of the governing jurisdiction to provide a safe working environment for the event workers and the general public.

The parties acknowledge that the event planner is an independent contractor with respect to the client and has no authority or power to incur debts, obligations or commitments of any kind whatsoever for, or on behalf of, the client, or to bind the client to any contract, agreement or employment agreement, unless specifically requested in writing by the company.

Special conditions provide payment terms and conditions. Event planners shall be paid in full usually no later than 2 weeks before the event. Payments may be via cash, check, or money order. The event planner usually asks for a deposit when the agreement is concluded. If the client should cancel this agreement a certain number of days (usually 90) before the event date, any payments made to the event planner shall be refunded in full. A predetermined cancellation fee shall be applied if the client cancels within a certain number of days (usually 30) before the event date. After that period of time the client usually has to pay the entire amount.

7.1.3 Sustainable Hospitality

The hospitality industry becomes important when it comes to sustainability from at least three points of view.

Some authors focused on possible sustainable interventions of hotels operators including sustainable food systems, hotel energy solutions, impacts of technology, water and food waste management, green hotel design, certification and ecolabelling systems and the evolving nature of corporate social responsibility strategies.[4]

They examine the concept of sustainability in hospitality industry and conclude that industry may need to examine how it defines sustainability, to extend its sustainability reporting to embrace materiality and external assurance and to address the issues of sustainable consumption and continuing economic growth if it is to demonstrate a worthwhile and enduring commitment to sustainability.[5]

The first concerns the possibility of building guidelines for tour operators aimed at reducing polluting emissions. Hotelier associations have been active in this regard for a long time. One of this sector's most important organizations is the IHAR. It is a very old professional union. In January 1869, 45 hoteliers gathered in Koblenz, Germany to create an alliance under the name of ALL HOTELIER ALLIANCE (AHA) to defend their interests, to grow and to organize.

In April 1921, various local European, African, and Latin American hotel associations decided to merge into a new international Association: INTERNATIONAL HOTELS ALLIANCE (IHA). In November 1947, after the end of the Second World War and the creation of the United Nations, Hoteliers from the International Hotels Alliance met together with The European Aubergistes Association and the Asian Innkeepers Association and decided to merge into a large International Association to globally defend the private sector from governments, public sectors, the military etc.. . . thereby creating the INTERNATIONAL HOTELS ASSOCIATION (IHA), established in London. In October 1960, The New York Hotels Association asked to

---

[4]Legrand et al. (2017).

[5]Peter et al. (2016).

join the IHA. On November 1st, 1997, the IHA merged with the International Organisation of Hotels and Restaurants and together, they became a single legal entity named the INTERNATIONAL HOTELS AND RESTAURANTS ASSOCIATION (IHRA), which is still active today.

This association has various purposes. It aims to provide a full and complete platform for the formation of industry positions, international representation, information dissemination, and international connections in the hospitality industry worldwide. The IHRA promotes the hospitality industry's various points of view and updates standards and various technical issues for hospitality worldwide. It also aims to develop eco-tourism by promoting sustainability among their members, fighting various issues relating to climate change and promoting measures put in place to reduce CO_2 emissions.

Secondly, sustainability is also linked to new forms of hospitality that aim to enhance the local cultural heritage and favor the repopulation of abandoned rural areas. Let us think, for example, about dispersed hotels. It is an Italian model that aims to enhance ancient villages using existing buildings and therefore not impacting the environment with new ones.

They are characterized by bedrooms that are located in several buildings close to each other, generally within the ancient country, but managed centrally, and therefore generally equipped with a main structure that is capable of providing the reception, a breakfast room and all the typical services of a classic hotel. There are certain cases where the concept of a dispersed hotel does not stop at hospitality, intended for sleeping and having breakfast, but that involve the entire village, which offers a whole set of services related to the territory and local food and wine. The term 'albergo diffuso' was coined for the first time in 1982 in Friuli, an Italian Region, more precisely in Carnia, which, at the time was struggling with reconstruction after an earthquake and with the urgent need to find initiatives aimed at revitalizing the villages to avoid depopulation. With different variations and regional regulations, several dispersed hotels have been created, through renovations where the enhancement of the existing buildings is combined with the use of more eco-friendly modern materials that allow thermal and acoustic insulation and a reduction of waste. Even for interiors and furnishings, they tend to favor traditional objects and furnishings by re-adapting them or reusing them in a modern style, through eco-design principles that aim to extend the life cycle of an object, giving it new life. Recalling the previous idea on the importance of the tourism association in the development of the environmentally friendly, the ADI (national association of dispersed hotels) was born in 2006 in order to give guidelines for current and future dispersed hotels, with the aim of enhancing and promoting this form of horizontal tourism, where guests, instead of being hosted in classic structures, find accommodation in the village and in contact with the locals, often custodians of the most authentic and lively popular traditions.

Thirdly, hospitality industry policies also become important when it comes to counteracting over-tourism. We are referring to the influx of tourism in places that everyone wants to see because they are "famous" and attract many "hit and run" tourists who just stop for a few photos and then leave for the next famous stop. This type of mass tourism causes pollution, the devastation of nature and the discomfort of local populations.

Many identify one of the causes of over-tourism as the proliferation of non-hotel locations. The reference is to short-term tourist lease and home exchanges. On this front, however, as we will see better later, it is necessary to make distinctions, and sometimes non-hotel locations represent an opportunity for sustainable tourism in terms of more experiential tourism that brings tourists closer to the everyday life of the environment visited. In this way, short-term leases in the suburbs of cities that are famous for their art, or in places that do not allow the development of hotel structures, if not very costly in terms of environmental impact, represent a way of developing sustainable tourism and avoiding over-tourism.

7.2 The Hotel Accommodation Contract

7.2.1 Content of Hotel Contract

The rights and obligations of customers of hotels and other tourist lodgings are provided in special regulations published by professional unions: in general, legislative provisions and, in particular, in contracts. Accommodation contracts are generally atypical contracts. In international law there is no unified legal source that regulates the hotel contract. There are different solutions of individual countries regarding the contract, these solutions can be summarized in the two legal systems: Anglo- American, where the institute is covered by numerous precedents and special laws, and European Continental, where the hotel contract is based mainly on the business practices and very few legal solutions of individual countries.

The idea of creating an international convention on the unification of decisions on hotel- contract began by UNIDROIT (International Institute for the Unification of Private Law) in 1977 at the meeting in Rome, and in 1979 the first text of the draft convention on the hotel contract was created. The draft was discussed until 1986, when the idea of making a convention on the hotel contract ceased to exist due to the impossibility of formulating clauses that would satisfy all the countries in the same way. The draft of convention on the hotel contract regulated all relevant issues: (1) the field of contract application (articles 1 and 2), (2) the terms of the contract (article 3), (3) the duration of the contract (article 4.), (4) the hotel-keeper's liability (article 5 and articles 11–15) and (5) the liability of the guest (article 6) and his obligation of payment the services (articles 9 and 10).[6]

The rights and obligations of customers and hotelkeepers are normally ruled conventionally by standard contracts that usually contain the above regulations, published by professional unions.

---

[6]Radolović (2010), p. 1093 ff.

We can make a list of rules that commonly regulate accommodation contracts. The hotelkeeper is compelled to rent the empty rooms of his hotel to any customer, and to allocate and to provide all comforts advertised by the hotel (e.g., swimming pool, sports, night club, etc). The services that the hotel offers are very varied. For example, with the evolution of the world of work and the development of smart working, or work done outside the workplace without a strict schedule and without workplace restrictions, the hospitality industry, and in particular hotels, has adapted to the demands of what has been defined as a "workcation", formed by the words work and vacation, overlapping work times and rest times. The hotels offer spaces to work in peace and safety in a location of leisure. The rooms offer a dedicated high-speed Wi-Fi connection, coffee corner and press service, which are all services that hotels were already accustomed to offering to congress or business tourism.

The hotelkeeper can deny the rental, if the customer: (a) is sick; (b) is intoxicated (c) is dirty (d) could be dangerous to other guests of the hotel.

On the other hand, the customer is bound: (a) to accept the room that was booked by him or with his command via a third person, unless it is not in accordance with his order; (b) to maintain the room up to the end of the period that was agreed, otherwise he is compelled to provide compensation to the hotelkeeper; (c) to pay the price.

Moreover, the customer is compelled: (a) to sign all corresponding documents on entry to the hotel; (b) to deliver the key of his room to the reception when exiting the hotel; (c) to meet his visitors at the public premises of the hotel. Visitors can enter the rooms only with the approval of hotelkeeper.

The following is usually prohibited: (a) customers cooking meals in the hotel rooms, as well as dining in them, except for customers who have ordered room service; (b) washing of clothing in the rooms; (c) placement of all kinds of baggage in the corridors of the hotel; (d) movement of furniture in the rooms and making holes in the walls in order to hang photographs or other objects; (e) keeping of all kinds of domestic animals without the permission of hotelkeeper; (h) gambling; (i) music and all kinds of gatherings that cause noise or nuisance to other customers; (j) use of towels, etc. outside of the rooms.

The customer is compelled to behave politely towards hotel personnel and to report any complaint against them to the manager; in turn, they are bound to satisfy the customer to the greatest possible extent.

7.2.2 Green Hotel

The offer of green hotel rooms which are highly attractive to customers is of particular interest in hotel contracts.[7] The reference is to hotel rooms built according to an eco-sustainable philosophy: glass and wood, minimalist style, an immense park, tree houses, etc. The green advantages include: the energy saving techniques

---

[7]Millar and Baloglu (2011), pp. 302–331; Butler (2008), pp. 234–244.

7.2 The Hotel Accommodation Contract

obtained through solar and photovoltaic panels; the materials used for the construction, wood and stone, combined with the floor heating and cooling systems. The interior furnishings can be made by craftsmen who have recycled the wood found in abandoned mountain huts. These are interventions made through an eco-compatible choice, without neglecting comfort, design and cutting-edge equipment. We also speak of green building with structures surrounded by nature, built with specific techniques of green building, based on natural materials. The structures are also designed to fit perfectly into the surrounding environment. Other aspects of green hotels are: use of untreated natural wood, eco-compatible and Klimahouse Nature certified architecture, intelligent use of light and bio-air conditioning. In this case, the accurate description of the "green services" is part of the offer, precisely because it influences the customer's choice. So much so that the customer could act for a breach of contract when, in reality, the structure is not respectful of the promised green standards.

There are usually booking procedures regarding the formation of accommodation contracts. The consumer makes a specific and unconditional offer (providing dates in/out, rates, hotel, type of bedroom) to stay and to pay. The hotelkeeper is compelled to provide a written answer by electronic methods quickly (usually within 3 days), that he accepts or declines the room request that has been communicated to him in written form, by phone or by fax, and in an affirmative case, is entitled to ask for a percentage of the price (usually 25%) of an overnight stay for all the days of stay that have been requested.

The reservation request is considered valid with the receipt of a deposit that was determined as above or with the written acceptance of the reservation by the hotelkeeper.

Sometimes customers prefer to make online reservations through a website knowing the hotel standard, dates, and type of room, but not knowing the exact identity of the hotel, in order to obtain a cheaper rate.

From the point at which customers make a reservation, the website acts solely as an intermediary between them and the accommodation provider, transmitting the details of the reservation to the relevant accommodation provider and sending the customer a confirmation email for, and on behalf of, the accommodation provider.

By making a reservation with an accommodation provider, customers accept and agree to the relevant cancellation and no-show policies of that accommodation provider, and to any additional (delivery) terms and conditions of the accommodation provider that may apply to the reservation or the stay, including for services rendered and/or products offered by the accommodation provider.

By completing a booking, customers usually agree to receiving an email, which the website may send closer to the arrival date, giving information on the destination and providing certain information and offers relevant to the booking and the destination.

Booking a hotel online is very easy and cheap but customers may find some surprises at the end of their stay if they do not read all of the information on the website carefully.

In the Frainier v. Priceline.com case (Frainier v. Priceline.com, No. B225920, Calif. App. 2nd Dist. Div. 3, 2012), Frainier and other online users of Priceline. com's online hotel booking services filed a suit against Priceline.com, claiming that the online company quoted them with a "total charges" price that did not include an additional per-night "resort fee" charged by the hotel. Plaintiffs alleged breach of contract, fraudulent inducement, negligent misrepresentation and violation of the unfair competition law, and other causes of actions under state law. The district court granted summary judgment for Priceline.com and the plaintiffs appealed. The court of appeals held that although Priceline.com omitted the "resort fee" charges from the "total charges" page, it had disclosed those fees elsewhere in its website. The court noted that Priceline.com placed a bold-faced, large-type notice including "important information," just below the "total charges" line. When users clicked on that important information notice, users were taken to a new page containing a disclosure that was short and contained a message stating that additional hotel fees or charges could apply. Thus, the court affirmed "this disclosure clearly stated that the offer price did not include mandatory resort fees charged by the hotel to the customer at checkout. Priceline did not represent to customers that they would pay nothing in addition to the 'total charges.' Instead, it expressly stated that hotels might make additional charges, some which might be mandatory (such as resort fees) and some of which might be optional (parking, phone calls, or minibar charges)."

7.2.3 Breach of Hotel Contract

Special norms rule no-show and hotel overbooking. A no-show is when a passenger/guest neither cancels his or her reservation nor shows up. Overbooking is a practice that airlines, hotels, and concert and other public show arrangers use to sell more tickets than the actual number of people they can accommodate. It aims to avoid empty seats or rooms due to no-shows and is legally sanctioned so long as it is not abused.

The hotelkeeper must offer the rooms that have been accepted in a written or fax request or by contract with the customers. In the opposite case, he is compelled to ensure their stay in another hotel of at least the same quality and in the same city, and that would offer the same comforts and conditions of stay (sea, sports, etc), as those that are advertised for his own hotel.

In this case, the hotelkeeper must cover the cost of transport and the difference of price that may exist between his hotel and the other one from his own expenses. Where the above is not possible, the hotelkeeper is compelled to compensate the customer with the total cost of the stay.

A person who books a room for a predetermined time period but does not use it for all or part of that time period, owes the hotelkeeper a percentage of the price (usually half the price) that was agreed for the period that he did not use the room. If, however, the customer warned the hotelkeeper in advance (usually 48 hours before

7.2 The Hotel Accommodation Contract 81

the arrival date), then he is exempt from the compensation and the hotelkeeper is compelled to directly return the advance that was collected.

The customer is eligible to make use of: (a) the room or apartment that is rented; (b) the communal areas of the hotel that are intended for the customers.

Room rentals last for one day, unless it is otherwise explicitly agreed between the hotelkeeper and the customer. The rental is then considered to be renewed reciprocally for each following day, provided that the hotelkeeper informs the customer when the hire expires or the customer informs the hotelkeeper that he will not continue the hire. This notice should be made on the previous day, otherwise it is not in effect for the same day, but for the next one.

When the room hire is terminated the customer is compelled to vacate the room usually before the 12th hour. Staying beyond this hour results in the customer being charged with a partial payment of the price for the running day.

If the room is let for a certain amount of time, the hotelkeeper is not entitled to interrupt the hire before the time that was agreed passes, unless the customer: (a) violates contractual obligations; (b) becomes sick from a contagious illness or another illness that causes nuisance to the remaining customers of the hotel (c) violates the common morals.

7.2.4 Hotelkeepers' Liability

Special provisions are contained in the convention on the liability of hotelkeepers concerning the property of their guests signed in Paris, on December 17th, 1962.

A hotelkeeper shall be liable for any damage to, destruction, or loss of property brought to the hotel by any guest who stays at the hotel and has sleeping accommodation put at his disposal.

Property is defined as: everything which is at the hotel during the time when the guest has the accommodation at his disposal; everything which the hotelkeeper, or a person for whom he is responsible, takes responsibility for outside the hotel during the period for which the guest has the accommodation at his disposal; or everything which the hotelkeeper, or a person for whom he is responsible, takes responsibility for, whether in the hotel or outside it, during a reasonable period preceding or following the time when the guest has the accommodation at his disposal; shall be deemed as property brought to the hotel.

Generally, liability is limited. The liability of a hotelkeeper shall be unlimited: where the property has been deposited with him; where he has refused to receive property which he is bound to receive for safe custody. A hotelkeeper shall be bound to receive securities, money and valuable articles; he may only refuse to receive such property if it is dangerous or if it is of excessive value or cumbersome in relation to the size or standing of the hotel.

The hotelkeeper shall be liable and shall not have the benefit of the limitation on his liability where the damage, destruction or loss is caused by a wilful act, omission, or negligence on his part or the part of any person for whose actions he is responsible.

Any notice or agreement purporting to exclude or diminish the hotelkeeper's liability given or made before the damage, destruction or loss has occurred shall be null and void.

The provisions shall not apply to vehicles, any property left within a vehicle, or live animals.

A hotelkeeper shall not be liable when the damage, destruction or loss is due: to the guest or any person accompanying him or in his employment, or any person visiting him; to an unforeseeable and unstoppable act of nature or an act of war; to the nature of the article.

This Convention shall apply to the metropolitan territories of the contracting parties. Many countries have ratified this convention. Among them are Belgium, France, Germany, Ireland, Italy, Lithuania, Luxembourg, Malta, Poland, Serbia, Slovenia, and the United Kingdom.

Accommodation contracts can be concluded by the tourist, by a travel agency or by a tour operator on behalf of the tourist. Travel agencies and tour operators are able to offer rooms at cheap prices through allotments. Some authors focused on the impact of smart contracts in hospitality industry. Hotels can be instantly updated right from the time that a guest leaves her home for the airport to when she checks in for her flight and even upon arrival at the hotel. Smart contracts can be adopted to facilitate both minor and major transactions in the hospitality industry. Hotels and travel agencies, for example, could streamline their business relationships with smart contracts on block chain platforms.[8]

Allotments are used to designate a certain block of pre-negotiated hotel rooms (but also carrier seats) that have been bought out and held by a travel agency, travel organizer, or tour operator. Allotments can be purchased for a specific period of time, part of a season or for any single dates and then resold to travel partners and final customers.

National law rarely regulates allotment contracts. Their content is usually regulated by business practices (see the code of practice on relations between hoteliers and travel agents drawn up by the IHRA and UFTAA United Federation of Travel Agents Associations) or by private autonomy. Allotment contracts are related to the bookings of a specific capacity (certain number of beds, hotel rooms or carrier seats).

According to the allotment contract, and in the case of hotel allotments, the hotelkeeper undertakes the duty to provide the availability of a certain number of beds or rooms established in the contract to the travel agency, to provide services to the travel agency's guests, and to pay a certain commission to the travel agency. In exchange, the travel agency undertakes the obligation to make the bookings or notify the hotelkeeper about the impossibility to comply with the contractual terms and pay the cost of services, if the travel agency used the contracted accommodation.

---

[8]Buhalis (2001), p. 21 ff.; Willie (2019), pp. 112–120; Dogru et al. (2018).

The Hotel Accommodation Contract portion begins:

There are two distinct kinds of allotment contracts: (i) allotment contracts with the right of unilateral withdrawal from the contract (the real allotment contract), and (ii) allotment contracts with the guarantee charge (the "full for empty" allotment contract).

The hotelkeeper is liable for any damages due to a breach of the allotment contract. His liability is normally divided into two types: (i) general liability—that derives from the contract between the agency and the hotelkeeper and (ii) special liability—characteristic only of the allotment contract. In the case of liability for a breach of the allotment contract, the hotelkeeper will reimburse the total pecuniary and non-pecuniary damage to the travel agency or its guest.

The hotelkeeper's compensation of pecuniary damages to guests and travel agencies includes loss of profits. The most significant non-pecuniary damages which the agency may suffer include first of all a violation of reputation. The most common cases of non-pecuniary damages that the guest may suffer from the allotment contract's breach include: (i) failed vacation; (ii) missing the goals of the guest's sojourn; (iii) various types of discomfort, discontent and distress.

7.2.5 Hotel Contract vs Tourist Lease Contract

With regard to tourist lease contracts (or lease contracts), it is important to remember that lease contracts are strongly regulated by national law in the interest of the lessee.

The term 'lease' indicates a transfer of the right to possession and use of good for a term in return for consideration.

A lease contract is an agreement concerning the lease, between two parties: the lessor, who is a person transferring the right to possession and use of good under a lease, and the lessee, who is a person acquiring the right to possession and use of good under a lease.

Tourist lease contracts allow the lessee the availability of the structure, with the agreement of the lessor, for a certain period of time. Arrival and departure dates are provided in the contract.

The contract contains all the lease conditions, which usually include the following: a description of the structure, the cost per week, the total to be paid including utilities, bed linens and bath towels, and extra costs (i.e., extra bed for an adult; extra bed for an infant, heating, etc.).

Also, the formation of this contract is usually composed of a booking and a definitive contract.

To confirm the reservation, clients should deposit a percentage of the total amount due (usually 25%). The receipt should be sent along with the reservation. Payment of the balance due should be paid in cash upon arrival.

A deposit for the house is usually given to the owner at the beginning of the stay. This sum will be given back on departure, providing no damage was made to the house, furniture or property.

The lessees are responsible for the house, the furniture and all the accessories. All problems, damage or missing objects and/or accessories should be communicated immediately to the owner so that these problems can be resolved during the lessees' stay. The lessees must abide by the rules that should be displayed in the house.

In the case of cancellation, the advance for the confirmation (deposit) will be fully retained.

In the case of early departure, the clients are required to pay the entire price of the booking period agreed with the owner. The lessor and lessee can also meet on a dedicated platform that could be described as a business model that creates value by facilitating exchanges between two or more interdependent groups, usually consumers and producers, owners and lessees, etc. Phenomena like Airbnb changed the market structure in the accommodation industry in less than a decade.[9]

7.3 Tourism in Sharing Economy

7.3.1 Timeshare and Tourism

The idea of sharing a travel and an accommodation is one of the recent frontiers of Tourism. The idea is part of the so called sharing economy and collaborative consumption. The term "collaborative consumption" was coined by Marcus Felson and Joe L. Spaeth in their paper "Community Structure and Collaborative Consumption: A routine activity approach" published in 1978 in the journal American Behavioral Scientist.[10] According to their opinion, sharing. economy is based on the human will to help each other and share their time and properties, which can be returned in either material on non-material form.

Timeshare and long term lease can represent a form of share economy. Timeshare is an arrangement whereby several joint owners have the right to use a property as a holiday home under a time-sharing scheme.

The timeshare concept was born in Europe in the late 1960s. The timeshare industry grew in the 70s and 80s around the world and it was very prominent in the U.S., particularly in places such as Florida and Hawaii.

Initially, timeshare properties were marketed as investments. Timeshares are not, in fact, investments and one should not buy a timeshare with the expectation of reselling it for a profit. However, beginning in the 1990s, the timeshare industry experienced a renaissance because people were realizing that the concept of timeshare is a real vacation option. Timeshares have become a very popular option for many tourists who love going back to the same destination and enjoy the place as well as the apartment they visited in the previous years. However, in many cases,

---

[9] Srnicek (2017), pp. 254–257.
   Aznar et al. (2019) (21), pp. 119–123.
[10] Botsman and Rogers (2010) 2nd ed.

consumers' organisations find problems with the misleading or deceptive conduct of sellers.

For instance, the clients simply sign a contract with the purpose of buying the right to stay in a specific apartment during a certain period of time, but the contract includes another agreement concerning a time-sharing exchange that mediates the stays in other facilities. This, however, incurs additional costs.

7.3.2 Timeshare in EU Directive

In European countries, timeshares are regulated according to the latest Directive, Directive 2008/122/EC, of the European parliament and of the council of January 14th, 2009 on the protection of consumers regarding certain aspects of timeshares, long-term holiday products, resale and exchange contracts.

This Directive aims particularly at regulating new holiday products and certain transactions related to timeshares, such as resale contracts and exchange contracts, that are not covered by the first Directive on Timeshares, Directive 94/47/CE.

In fact, since the adoption of Directive 94/47/EC of the European Parliament and of the Council of October 26th, 1994 regarding the protection of purchasers from certain aspects of contracts relating to the purchase of rights to use immovable properties on a timeshare basis, timeshares have evolved and new holiday products similar to them have appeared on the market.

According to Directive 2008/122, a 'timeshare contract' means a contract lasting more than 1 year under which a consumer, for consideration, acquires the right to use one or more overnight accommodations for more than one period of occupation. A 'long-term holiday product contract' is an agreement lasting more than 1 year under which a consumer, for consideration, acquires primarily the right to obtain discounts or other benefits in terms of accommodation, either on its own, or together with travel or other services. A 'resale contract' is a contract under which a trader, for consideration, assists a consumer to sell or buy a timeshare or a long-term holiday product. An 'exchange contract' is a contract under which a consumer, for consideration, joins an exchange system which allows that consumer access to overnight accommodation or other services in exchange for granting other people temporary access to the benefits of the rights deriving from that consumer's timeshare contract.

In order to provide consumers with the opportunity to fully understand their rights and obligations under the contract, they should be allowed a period during which they may withdraw from the contract without having to justify the withdrawal and without bearing any cost. A right of withdrawal was provided in Directive 94/47CE.

The length of this period varies between Member States, and experience shows that the length prescribed in Directive 94/47/EC was not long enough. The period should therefore be extended in order to achieve a high level of consumer protection and more clarity for consumers and traders. The length of the period, the modalities for and the effects of exercising the right of withdrawal should be harmonized.

According to art. 6 of Directive 2008/122, Member States shall ensure that the consumer is given a period of 14 calendar days to withdraw from the timeshare, long-term holiday product, resale or exchange contract, without giving any reason. The withdrawal period shall be calculated: (a) from the day of the conclusion of the contract or of any binding preliminary contract; or (b) from the day when the consumer receives the contract or any binding preliminary contract if it is later than the date referred in point (a).

Member States shall ensure that, where the consumer exercises the right to withdraw from the timeshare or long-term holiday product contract, any exchange contract ancillary to it or any other ancillary contract is automatically terminated, at no cost to the consumer. An 'ancillary contract' is a contract under which the consumer acquires services which are related to a timeshare contract or long-term holiday product contract and which are provided by the trader or a third party on the basis of an arrangement between that third party and the trader, like loan contracts.

Consumers should have effective remedies in the event that traders do not comply with the provisions regarding pre-contractual information or the contract. In addition to the remedies existing under national law, consumers should benefit from an extended withdrawal period where traders have not provided information. The exercise of the right of withdrawal should remain free of charge during that extended period regardless of what services consumers may have enjoyed. It is obvious that the expiration of the withdrawal period does not preclude consumers from seeking remedies in accordance with national law for breaches of the information requirements.[11]

The timeshare therefore offers accommodation together with other services and, in this way, it is similar to the hotel contract insofar as the owner acquires a property right, although limited in time in use. In this field, green offers are also available in relation to construction materials and energy saving, such as in Green Multi-properties. These aspects will be particularly relevant in this field because they are an integral part of the economic evaluation of the deal: the fact that the building is built according to energy saving criteria will affect costs and it must therefore be well described in the contract as part of the information for the buyer who represents, as shown by the EU Directive, the weak part of the contract primarily due to information asymmetry.

7.3.3 Home Exchange and Tourism

We can also include the practice of house swapping, commonly known as home exchange, in the hospitality industry. This has become an alternative kind of vacation as part of the collaborative consumption movement.

---

[11] Hart (1980), pp. 49–57; Id., (1982), pp. 19–31; Hovey (2002), pp. 141–160.

7.3 Tourism in Sharing Economy

The term home exchange refers to the swapping of homes on either a temporary, or more permanent basis.

We can consider some international associations whose purpose is home swapping. Home exchange communities are non-profit organisations that have pioneered the global experience of home exchange holidays since the early 1950s.

To use the service offered by such associations, membership is required. These organisations currently provide their services to their members via the Internet. To become a member of a home exchange community (hereinafter The Community), one must subscribe to a contract providing that "the Community" will allocate a username and password to the member in order to access the "Members only" area of the site. The members will be required to use their username and password each time they log on to the site, giving them access to information available about accommodations. The contract of membership is an agreement between a physical person and a legal person (the Community) for leisure purposes.

The use of the site and the information on the site is at the risk of the members themselves. The information that is provided on the site is for general information only and is subject to change. "The Community" does not warrant that information contained on the site is complete, accurate, or up-to-date. Any aspect of the site may be changed, supplemented, deleted or updated without notice at the sole discretion of "the Community".

Copyright in the site (including, without limitation, text, graphics, logos, icons, sound recordings and software) is owned or licensed by "the Community". Members must not reproduce, transmit, distribute, adapt, modify, sell, publish or otherwise use any of the material on the site except as permitted by statute or with "the Community's" prior written consent.

Members acknowledge that all information they provide on the Community's web site, including personal information is complete, accurate and current.

It is a condition of the agreement that information uploaded by members does not contain any viruses, worms, Trojans or other programs or materials that have the ability to alter, delay, damage or interfere with the operation of the site, are not false or misleading, and do not contravene any law, statute or regulation.

It is a condition of the agreement that member's information does not contain text, images or website URLs that promote, either implicitly or explicitly, any product or service that is provided by individuals, companies or organisations other than the "the Community".

Special conditions concern the Privacy Policy and membership termination.

"The Community" reserves the right to suspend or terminate membership and access to or use of the site, the information and/or the services, at any time, if members breach any of their obligations under the agreement.

Home swapping is part of the sharing economy that is a sustainable alternative to the currently unsustainable economy. It is framed by its proponents as a "transformative force that drives the shift from the ownership-based economy to the economy that celebrates the ideas of shared access, higher levels of utilisation of already produced but underutilised goods and exchange of services that otherwise are hard to find on the formal market".[12]

References

Aznar, J., Maspera, J., & Quer, X. (2019). A game theory approach to Airbnb and hotels competition. *European Journal of Tourism Research, 21*, 119.

Botsman, R., & Rogers, R. (2010). *What's mine is yours. How collaborative consumption is changing the way we live* (2nd ed.). Harperbusiness.

Buhalis, T. (2001). *Tourism distribution channels: Practices, issues and transformations* (p. 21). Thomson.

Busby, G., & Rendle, S. (2000). The transition from tourism on farms to farm tourism. *Tourism Management, 21*, 635.

Butler, J. (2008). The compelling "Hard Case" for "Green" hotel development. *Cornell Hospitality Quarterly, 49*(3), 234.

Dogru, T., Mody, M., & Leonardi, C. (2018). Blockchain technology & its implications for the hospitality industry. *Boston Hospitality Review*, 6.

Hart, C. W. (1980). Timesharing: Part of the hotel equation. *The Cornel Hotel and Restaurant Administration Quarterly, 21*(3), 49.

Hart, C. W. (1982). The timeshare feasibility study: Forecasting sales Performance. *The Cornell Hotel and Restaurant Administration Quarterly, 23*(1), 19.

Heinrichs, H. (2013). Sharing economy a potential new pathway to sustainability. *Gaia, 22*, 228.

Hovey, M. (2002). Is timeshare ownership an investment product? *Journal of Financial Services Marketing, 7*(2), 141.

Kurtzman, J., & Saubar, J. (1993). Sport as a tourist endeavour. *Journal of Tourism and Sport, 1*.

Legrand, W., Sloan, P., & Chen, J. S. (2017). *Sustainability in the hospitality industry: Principles of sustainable operations*. Routledge.

Maetzold, J. (2002). *Nature-Based Tourism & Agritourism Trends: Unlimited Opportunities*. kerrcenter.com.

Martin, C. J. (2016). The sharing economy: A pathway to sustainability or a nightmarish form of neoliberal capitalism? *Ecological Economics, 121*, 149.

Millar, M., & Baloglu, S. (2011). Hotel guests' preferences for green guest room attributes. *Cornell Hospitality Quarterly, 52*(3), 302.

Penot, J. (2003). Sport tourism and tourism generated by sporting events. *Journal of Sport Tourism, 8*(2), 100.

Peter, J., Hillier, D., & Comfort, D. (2016). Sustainability in the hospitality industry. *International Journal of Contemporary Hospitality Management, 28*, 36.

Privitera, D. (2010). *The importance of organic agriculture in tourism rural*, anubis.kee.hu

Radolović, O. (2010). Hotel guest's liability for non-payment of hotel services in comparative law. *World Academy of Science, Engineering and Technology, 2010*, 1093.

---

[12] Voytenko Palgan et al. (2017), pp. 70–83. On Sharing Economy Heinrichs (2013), pp. 228–231; Martin (2016), pp. 149–159.

References

Srnicek, N. (2017). The challenges of platform capitalism: Understanding the logic of a new business model. *Junction, 23*(4), 254.

Victorino, L., Verna, R., Plaschka, G., & Dev, C. (2005). Service innovation and customer choice in the hospitality industry. *Managing Service Quality*, 555.

Voytenko Palgan, Y., Zvolska, L., & Mont, O. (2017). Sustainability framings of accommodation sharing. *Environmental Innovation and Societal Transitions, 23*, 70.

Willie, P. (2019). Can all sectors of the hospitality and tourism industry be influenced by the innovation of Block chain technology? *Worldwide Hospitality and Tourism Themes, 11*, 112.

Chapter 8
Travel Contracts and Sustainable Mobility

Contents

8.1 Transport Law 91
    8.1.1 Transport Law and Consumers' Protection 91
    8.1.2 Transportation Contract 92
8.2 European and International Transportation Laws 93
    8.2.1 Maritime Transportation Law 93
    8.2.2 Air Transport 97
    8.2.3 Rail Transport 99
8.3 Sustainable Mobility and Tourism 100
    8.3.1 Sustainable Mobility 100
    8.3.2 Sustainable Transport and Travel 101
References 102

8.1 Transport Law

8.1.1 Transport Law and Consumers' Protection

As we have highlighted in the first part, transport is the necessary pre-condition to tourism and the different eras of tourism can be identified with particular modes of transport. Tourism is a matter of being elsewhere and that implies the use of transport. Therefore, it is a matter of fact that the evolution of tourism is strictly connected to the development of modern transport and other aspects of tourism have followed the evolution of modes of transport.

The connection between transport and tourism also transformed transport law. Transport law can be complemented by a series of norms that give rights to passengers. Therefore, it is correct to say that these regulations are giving transport law a consumer dimension. As someone notes "EC transport law is set to be complemented by a series of Regulations giving rights to passengers for almost

---

© The Author(s), under exclusive license to Springer Nature Switzerland AG 2021
S. Landini, *Sustainable Tourism Contracts*,
https://doi.org/10.1007/978-3-030-83140-0_8

every mode of transport. These Regulations not only give transport law a distinct consumer dimension but also add new elements to European private law".[1]

8.1.2 Transportation Contract

A transportation contract is an agreement between a Carrier and a Passenger, which is any person that is transported based on a voyage ticket issued by the carrier and/or agencies authorized thereto. The object of the agreement is the provision of transport. The carrier undertakes to transport the passenger and/or luggage, vehicles etc. under the general conditions, which the Passenger undertakes to examine and observe in their entirety prior to the purchase and/or booking of the voyage ticket. Also, the formation of this contract is usually composed by booking and definitive contract.

The transport service refers to the route indicated on the ticket, which sometimes includes accommodation on board.

Transportation will be regulated by transport law, which includes all national and international laws governing the conveyance of passengers or goods, especially as a commercial enterprise, pertaining to both the method and the means. It includes highways, mass transit, aviation, rail, and maritime and motor carriers.

Transportation contracts are usually regulated by the following general conditions: the voyage ticket is personal; it may not be transferred and it is valid solely for the voyage indicated on the ticket. The passenger is required to retain the ticket carefully in order to justify his entitlement to travel and exhibit it to any Officer or personnel of the Company that may request it.

The price indicated on the voyage ticket is the current tariff of the carrier in force on the date of issue. The tariff is not fixed and may be subject to increases or decreases.

In case of accommodation on board, the passenger shall occupy the cabin or seat indicated on the ticket and where the ticket does not indicate any cabin or seat, it will be indicated by the captain or the on-board purser.

Special dispositions regulate the check-in time. Passengers who do not attend the check-in at the established time, or who do not board as indicated on the boarding card, will generally not be entitled to a refund and must instead complete the payment of the price of the voyage if they have not yet paid it in full.

There will also be no refunds in the following cases: (i) embarkation refused for safety reasons, even if the passenger attends within the above indicated times; (ii) if the passenger holds documentation which is unsuitable for disembarking at the final destination; (iii) if the Passenger, after having checked in, does not attend for embarkation at a suitable time; (iv) if the passenger is not indicated as the ticket holder.

---

[1] Karsten (2007), pp. 17–136.

Refunds are usually provided in case of cancellations. Cancellations must be notified by the passenger to the company directly or via the travel agent within the terms reported in the general conditions and with the application of the penalties indicated in the general conditions.

In some cases, passengers accept, prior to departure, that changes can be made to the timetable provided on the voyage ticket. The Company, in case of situations of its own need and/or force majeure, has the option to cancel the indicated departure time, to add or omit stopovers, and to begin the voyage from a different place than expected.

In the event of the cancellation of a voyage, or an extended delay, passengers shall be entitled to refreshments and meals, depending on their waiting time. These provisions shall be applied in relation to the anticipated length of the delay and the distance of the destination. In addition, the carrier shall provide accommodation, if necessary, and transport to the place of accommodation. Passengers will be informed by the carrier on preparations relating to acquiring refreshments, transport and hotel accommodation.

The carrier is not liable for the damages caused to passengers by the delay or the failure to perform the transport should such circumstance derive from chance, force majeure, adverse weather conditions, strikes or any technical breakdowns arising from force majeure or other causes not attributable to it and, in any event, in compliance with the provisions.

Since the passenger is the weaker party in the transport contract, passengers' rights in this respect should be safeguarded. Thus, national and international law regulate delayed departures, cancellations and overbookings. Transport is regulated at a European level, with particular regard to the protection of the passenger.

8.2 European and International Transportation Laws

8.2.1 Maritime Transportation Law

With regard to maritime transportation, international conventions, EU directives and regulations have greatly improved safety standards in sea transport. The improvements were particularly brought about by the three legislative packages adopted in the wake of disasters. We can recall some well known cases. On 8th December 1999, the Maltese-flagged tanker Erika, departed Dunkerque bound for Livorno, carrying around 31,000 tons of heavy fuel oil. In the early afternoon of the 11th December 1999, Erika experienced a structural failure as she was crossing the Bay of Biscay in heavy weather. The vessel first began to list heavily and then, after the list was corrected, broke in two on 12 December, some 40 nautical miles off the southern tip of Brittany. As a result, the vessel foundered some 30 nautical miles south of the Pointe de Penmarch, causing major oil spill in French waters. The damage caused to the environment and the exceptionally high cost of the damage caused to fisheries and tourism make the Erika oil spill an environmental tragedy. The Prestige oil spill occurred off the coast of Galicia, Spain, caused by the sinking of the 26 year old structurally deficient oil tanker MV Prestige in November 2002, carrying 77,000 tonnes of heavy fuel oil. During a storm, it burst a tank on 13th November and French, Spanish, and Portuguese governments refused to allow the ship to dock. The spill polluted thousands of kilometers of coastline and more than one thousand beaches on the Spanish, French and Portuguese coast, as well as causing great harm to the local fishing industry.

Another famous accident was "Costa Crociere" Disaster. On the evening of January 13, 2012, the Costa Concordia, which was to make a Mediterranean cruise from Civitavecchia via Savona, Marseille, Barcelona, Palma de Mallorca, Cagliari to Palermo, is shipwrecked off the port of Giglio Island. At 21:45, it collided with a small offshore rock formation called "Scogli delle Scole" about 500 m from the port of the island, Giglio Porto. The hull was slashed over almost 70 m, it hit licked and went down with a slope of 65 degrees a few hours later.

At the time of the accident 3216 passengers and 1013 crew members were on board. The accident causes the death of 32 people as well as 193 injured. In addition, a Spanish diver died during the salvage work in February 2014. The Costa Concordia is the largest passenger ship which has ever sunk.

With regard to Erika I package, Directive 2001/105/EC of 19 December 2001 strengthened and standardised the legal provisions laid down in Directive 94/57/EC on ship inspection and survey organisations. In particular, it introduced a system of liability in the event of proven negligence. Directive 2001/106/EC of 19 December 2001 made port State control mandatory for potentially hazardous vessels and introduced a 'blacklist' of ships which can be refused access to EU ports.

Regulation (EC) No 417/2002 of 18 February 2002 set a fixed timetable for withdrawing single-hull oil tankers from service and replacing them with safer double-hull vessels. Following the Prestige oil tanker disaster, a more rigorous timetable was adopted in Regulation (EC) No 1726/2003 of 22 July 2003. Regulation (EU) No 530/2012 of 13 June 2012 on the accelerated phasing-in of double-hull or equivalent design requirements for single-hull oil tankers subsequently repealed Regulation (EC) No 417/2002 and countered certain potential exemptions under IMO rules. It specified that, for the transport of heavy grade oil, only double-hull oil tankers would be allowed to fly the flag of a Member State, and it banned all single-hull oil tankers, irrespective of the flag, from ports or offshore terminals or from anchoring in areas under the jurisdiction of Member States.

With regard to Erika II package, Directive 2002/59/EC of 27 June 2002 established a Community vessel traffic monitoring and information system (SafeSeaNet). Before a ship is allowed to enter a port in a Member State, its owners are responsible for providing certain information to the relevant port authorities, particularly in the case of dangerous or polluting cargoes. The directive made it mandatory for ships to be equipped with automatic identification systems (AIS) and voyage data recorders (VDRs) or 'black boxes'. The authorities of the relevant Member States have the right to prohibit ships from leaving a port in unfavourable weather conditions. Regulation (EC) No 1406/2002 of 27 June 2002 established a European Maritime Safety Agency (EMSA). EMSA's role is to provide Member

States and the Commission with scientific and technical support, and to ensure that safety rules in maritime transport are enforced. Its remit has considerably expanded over time to incorporate pollution control (operational assistance at the request of Member States) and satellite-based monitoring systems. Regulation (EU) No 100/2013 of 15 January 2013 amended the EMSA Regulation, clarifying EMSA's core and ancillary tasks, as well as detailing the role it should play in facilitating cooperation between Member States and the Commission, by:developing and operating the EU Long-Range Identification and Tracking of Ships (LRIT) European Data Centre and SafeSeaNet; providing relevant vessel positioning and Earth observation data to the competent national authorities and relevant EU bodies; and providing operational support to Member States concerning investigations related to serious casualties.

The third maritime safety package and port State control have been adopted on 2008. Following intense negotiations, Parliament and the Council reached agreement in December 2008 on a third legislative package comprising two regulations and six directives. A recast of the Directive on port State control (Directive 2009/16/ EC of 23 April 2009) to ensure more frequent and more effective inspections under new monitoring mechanisms linked to potential risk, thereby bringing the procedures, instruments and work done in accordance with the Paris Memorandum of Understanding within the field of application of EU law; Directive 2009/21/EC of 23 April 2009 on flag State requirements, which enabled compliance on the part of ships flying a Member State flag to be monitored more effectively; Directive 2009/ 17/EC of 23 April 2009 amending the Directive establishing a Community vessel traffic monitoring and information system (SafeSeaNet), aimed to improve the framework legal conditions concerning places of refuge for ships in distress and to further develop SafeSeaNet.Regulation (EC) No 391/2009 and Directive 2009/15/ EC of 23 April 2009 established common rules and standards for ship inspection and survey organisations, and were aimed at creating an independent quality-monitoring system to eliminate the remaining flaws in inspection and certification procedures for the world fleet. Directive 2009/18/EC of 23 April 2009 establishing the fundamental principles governing the investigation of accidents in maritime transport set out the standard principles for investigations at sea of marine casualties and incidents involving vessels flying the flag of an EU Member State and occurring in the territorial sea or internal waters of a Member State. The directive also established a system for pooling findings, known as the 'permanent cooperation framework', between EMSA, the Commission and the Member States. Regulation (EC) No 392/2009 of 23 April 2009 on the liability of carriers of passengers by sea in the event of accidents (based on the 1974 Athens Convention relating to the Carriage of Passengers and their Luggage by Sea as amended by its protocol of 2002). Directive 2009/20/EC of 23 April 2009 set out the requirements for port State control in respect of ship owners' certificates of insurance against maritime claims.

Safety at sea is a key element of maritime transport policy with a view to protecting passengers, crew members, the marine environment and coastal regions. Given the global nature of maritime transport, the International Maritime Organisation (IMO) develops uniform international standards. The primary international agreements include the International Convention for the Prevention of Pollution from Ships (MARPOL) adopted on 2nd November 1973 at IMO, the International Convention for the Safety of Life at Sea (SOLAS) adopted on 1st November 1974 and the International Convention on Standards of Training, Certification and Watchkeeping for Seafarers (STCW) adopted on 7th July 1978. While prompt amendment of EU law to incorporate these international law-based agreements is a major objective of the EU's maritime transport policy, additional measures are also adopted at EU level.

MARPOL Convention includes regulations aimed at preventing and minimizing pollution from ships—both accidental pollution and that from routine operations—and currently includes six technical Annexes. Special Areas with strict controls on operational discharges are included in most Annexes.

The main objective of the SOLAS Convention is to specify minimum standards for the construction, equipment and operation of ships, compatible with their safety.

At European law level, with regard to passengers ship safety and ship inspection, the common rules and standards for ship inspection and survey organisations and for the relevant activities of maritime administrations (classification societies) were laid down in Directive 94/57/EC of 22 November 1994. Safety on ships providing scheduled services between two EU ports is regulated by Directive 2009/45/EC of 6 May 2009, which consolidated and recast the safety rules and standards for passenger ships established by Directive 98/18/EC. Directive 98/41/EC of 18 June 1998 on the registration of persons sailing on board passenger ships made it possible for passenger numbers to be monitored and for rescue operations to be mounted more efficiently in the event of an accident. The rules on minimum qualifications for seafarers were updated in 2019 on the basis of a Commission proposal. Following adoption by Parliament and the Council, Directive (EU) 2019/1159 was published in the Official Journal on 12 July 2019.

In 2016, the Commission put forward three legislative proposals, which were voted on in plenary on 4 October 2017 and published on 30 November 2017. The first of the resulting directives, Directive (EU) 2017/2108 of 15 November 2017 amending Directive 2009/45/EC on safety rules and standards for passenger ships, sought to clarify and simplify the safety rules and standards for passenger ships. The idea behind the directive was to make the rules easier to update, monitor and enforce. Amendments to the previous directive included removing inconsistent and incorrect references, providing new definitions of different types of ships, clarifying the definition of equivalent material, excluding ships under 24 m and simplifying the definitions of sea areas. A database has also been established by the Commission to increase transparency and facilitate the notification of exemptions, equivalences and additional safety measures. The second, Directive (EU) 2017/2109 of 15 November 2017 amending Council Directive 98/41/EC on the registration of persons sailing on board passenger ships operating to or from ports of the Member States of the Community and Directive 2010/65/EU on reporting formalities for ships arriving in and/or departing from ports of the Member States, updated and clarified the existing requirements for the counting and registration of passengers and crew on board passenger ships. Amendments included updating the definition of 'port areas'

8.2 European and International Transportation Laws

in order to incorporate information on the nationality of the persons on board, and obliging companies to store lists of passengers and crew in a National Single Window. The third proposal led to the adoption of Directive (EU) 2017/2110 of 15 November 2017 on a system of inspections for the safe operation of ro-ro passenger ships and high-speed passenger craft in regular service, which amended Directive 2009/16/EC and repealed Council Directive 1999/35/EC. This updated and clarified the existing survey requirements for ro-ro ferries and high-speed craft and provided for a system of ship-based inspections prior to the commencement of a regular service, which can be combined with a flag state survey on a yearly basis.

The passenger of a ship is, in any event, guaranteed by articles 16, 17 and 18 of EU Regulation n. 1177/2010 concerning the rights of passengers when travelling by sea and inland waterway and amending Regulation (EC) No 2006/2004.

The protection of passengers should cover not only passenger services between ports situated in the territory of the Member States, but also passenger services between such ports and ports situated outside the territory of the Member States, taking into account the risk of distortion of competition on the passenger transport market.

Carriers should provide for the payment of compensation for passengers in the event of the cancellation or delay of a passenger service based on a percentage of the ticket price, except when the cancellation or delay occurs due to weather conditions endangering the safe operation of the ship or to extraordinary circumstances which could not have been avoided even if all reasonable measures had been taken.

Passengers should be fully informed of their rights under this Regulation in formats that are accessible to everybody, so that they can effectively exercise those rights. They should be able to exercise their rights by means of appropriate and accessible complaint procedures implemented by carriers and terminal operators within their respective areas of competence or, as the case may be, by the submission of complaints to the body or bodies designated to that end by the Member State concerned.

8.2.2 Air Transport

At the international level, with regard to air transportation, a Convention for the Unification of Certain Rules Relating to International Carriage by Air was agreed in Montreal on May 28th, 1999, setting new global rules on liability in the event of accidents for international air transport, replacing those in the Warsaw Convention of 1929 and its subsequent amendments. The Montreal Convention provides for a regime of unlimited liability in the case of death or injury of air passengers.

At the level of European Union law the main rules on air transportation are contained in regulation 889/2002, amending Council Regulation (EC) No 2027/97, on air carrier liability in the event of accidents.

The regulation 889/2002 was issued because it was necessary to amend Council Regulation (EC) No 2027/97 of October 9th, 1997 on air carrier liability in the event of accidents in order to align it with the provisions of the Montreal Convention, thereby creating a uniform system of liability for international air transport. All provisions of the Montreal Convention relevant to such liability shall govern the liability of a Community air carrier in relation to passengers and their baggage.

Eu Regulation 889/2002 and the Montreal Convention reinforce the protection of passengers and their dependants. In the internal aviation market, the distinction between national and international transport has been eliminated and it is therefore appropriate to have the same level and nature of liability in both international and national transport within the Community.

All air carriers shall in respect of carriage by air provided or purchased in the Community, provide each passenger with a written indication of:

- the applicable limit for that flight on the carrier's liability in respect of death or injury, if such a limit exists;
- the applicable limit for that flight on the carrier's liability in respect of destruction, loss of or damage to baggage and a warning that baggage greater in value than this figure should be brought to the airline's attention at check-in or fully insured by the passenger prior to travel;
- the applicable limit for that flight on the carrier's liability for damage occasioned by delay.

Regulation (Ec) No 261/2004 of the European Parliament and of the Council of February 11th, 2004 establishes common rules on compensation and assistance to passengers in the event of denied boarding and of cancellation or long delay of flights, repealing Regulation (EEC) No 295/91.

This Regulation governs denied boarding (in case of overbooking, for example) and cancellation or long delays, without restricting the rights of the operating air carrier to seek compensation from any person, including third parties, in accordance with the applicable law.

Where boarding is denied, the air carriers call for volunteers to give up their reservations, in exchange for benefits, instead of denying passengers boarding, and by fully compensating those that are denied boarding in the end.

Passengers that are denied boarding against their will should be able to either cancel their flights, with the reimbursement of their tickets, or to continue them under satisfactory conditions, and should be adequately cared for while awaiting a later flight. Volunteers should also be able to cancel their flights, with the reimbursement of their tickets, or continue them under satisfactory conditions.

In case of a cancellation, preventive measures should be adopted. In order to avoid trouble and inconvenience to passengers caused by the cancellation of flights, carriers must inform passengers of cancellations before the scheduled time of departure, in addition to offering them reasonable rerouting, so that the passengers can make other arrangements.

If they fail to do this, air carriers should compensate passengers, except for when the cancellation occurs in extraordinary circumstances that could not have been avoided even if all reasonable measures had been taken.

8.2 European and International Transportation Laws

Passengers whose flights have been cancelled should be able to either obtain the reimbursement of their tickets or to obtain re-routing under satisfactory conditions and should be adequately cared for while awaiting a later flight.

Passengers should be fully informed of their rights in the event of denied boarding, cancellation or long delay of flights, so that they can effectively exercise their rights.

At an international level, passengers' rights are recognized by a code of conduct recently adopted by the IATA (International Air Transport Association), which is the trade association for the world's airlines, representing some 240 airlines that cover 84% of total air traffic.

At the 69th IATA AGM in June 2013, the industry unanimously adopted a set of core principles for consumer protection legislation. Air Transport Contracts are usually compliant with the rules contained in the IATA code of conduct.

According to these principles, passengers should have clear, transparent access to the following information:

– fare information, including taxes and charges, prior to purchasing a ticket;
– the airline actually operating the flight in case of a codeshare service.

A basic principle is that there should be no compromise between safety and passenger rights protection.

Passenger entitlements enshrined in regulations should reflect the principle of proportionality and the impact of extraordinary circumstances.

Therefore, safety-related delays or cancellations, such as those resulting from technical issues with an aircraft, should always be considered as extraordinary circumstances in order to exonerate air carriers from liability for such delays and cancellations.

The company recognizes the right to re-routing, refunds or compensation in cases of denied boarding and cancellations, where circumstances are within the carrier's control. In case of a delay, the company recognizes the right to re-routing, refunds or care and assistance to passengers affected by delays where circumstances are within the carrier's control.

8.2.3 Rail Transport

Regarding rail transportation at a European level, we have regulation (EC) no 1371/2007 of the European parliament and of the council of October 23rd, 2007 on rail passengers' rights and obligations.

According to such regulation, users' rights to rail services include the receipt of information regarding the service both before and during the journey.

Whenever possible, railway undertakings and ticket vendors should provide this information in advance and as soon as possible.

Railway undertakings should cooperate to facilitate the transfer of rail passengers from one operator to another by providing through tickets whenever possible.

The provision of information and tickets to rail passengers should be facilitated by adapting computerized systems to a common specification.

Railway undertakings should be obliged to be insured, or to make equivalent arrangements, for their liability to rail passengers in the event of an accident.

At the international level, there is the Convention concerning International Carriage by Rail (COTIF) signed in Bern on May 9th, 1980 and amended by the Protocol for the modification of the Convention concerning International Carriage by Rail of June 3rd, 1999 (the so-called Vilnius Protocol). When the 1980 Convention concerning International Carriage by Rail (COTIF) came into effect in 1985, this marked the birth of the Intergovernmental Organisation for International Carriage by Rail, known today as the OTIF.

8.3 Sustainable Mobility and Tourism

8.3.1 Sustainable Mobility

Climate change is at the top of UN priorities. There is also common understanding and strategy for the need to increase the capacity of countries in dealing with this challenge.

UNECE (United Nation Economic Commission for Europe) collected some mainstreams for CO_2 abatement and improved fuel efficiency in the transport sector:

- Innovative vehicle technologies, advanced engine management systems and efficient vehicle powertrains;
- The use of sustainable biofuels, not only of the first generation (vegetable oil, biodiesel, bio-alcohols and biogas from sugar plants, crops or animal fats etc.), but also of the second (biofuels from biomass, non-food crops including wood) and third generations (biodegradable fuels from algae);
- Consumer information (campaigns for eco-driving, use of public transport and modal transport etc.);
- Legal instruments (such as tax incentives for low carbon products and processes, taxation of CO_2 intensive products and processes, etc.);
- An improved transport infrastructure together with Intelligent Transport;
- Systems (ITS) to avoid traffic congestion and to foster the use of intermodal transport (road, rail and waterways).
- We can remember other international agendas:
- The Millennium Development Goals (MDG), in particular MDG 7 to ensure environmental sustainability;
- The Kyoto Protocol, adopted on 11 December 1997. Owing to a complex ratification process, it entered into force on 16 February 2005. Currently, there are 192 Parties to the Kyoto Protocol;

- UN General Assembly Resolution A/RES/63/32, titled "Protection of global climate for present and future generations" (PDF);
- UN Framework Convention on Climate Change (UNFCCC).

At the end of 2020 European Commission presented landmark Sustainable and Smart Mobility Strategy.

According to the EU strategy all large and medium-sized cities should have a sustainable urban mobility plan by 2030. This should include integrated electronic ticketing facilities for multimodal transportation and automated mobility should be deployed on a large scale.

8.3.2   Sustainable Transport and Travel

Sustainable transport and travel (also referred to as "sustainable mobility") play an important role in the development of sustainable tourism as tourism-related transport, especially road and air traffic, is on the rise, and it contributes considerably to reducing greenhouse gas emissions, pollution and climate change. Developing and encouraging the use of different modes of transport that have a low impact on the environment, e.g., cycling, walking, car sharing, fuel-efficient transport systems and the use of electric vehicles, is key in reducing travelers' ecological footprint. To achieve this, consistent and innovative sustainable mobility strategies and measures need to be formulated and introduced at the destination and at the business level. It is also possible to introduce tourism transport networks to promote sustainable mobility. Recent research indicates that if bicycle facilities are integrated into public transport networks (bike parking, bike racks on buses and tramways, bike lanes), both the use of bicycles and the use of public transport are boosted. With regard to bicycles in tourism, we have to remember that it is part of sustainable mobility and can improve the form of sustainability in terms of regional development. In fact, it could be useful in assisting with the revitalization and diversification of rural and regional areas. In this way, the planning and provision of infrastructure and information are key considerations in maximizing the economic development benefits of this form of tourism for regional areas.[2] Sustainable mobility would imply not only a change in the means of transport but also a reduced level of mobility. As this would entail new forms of tourism, other than those solely based on auto- and aero mobility, it represents a major challenge for the future development of tourism.[3]

In this way, travel packages become an instrument of sustainable tourism since they bring together travelers who use the same means of transport and they can offer sustainable mobility packages together with accommodation.

---

[2] Gronau (2007), pp. 265–275.

[3] Høyer (2020), pp. 147–160; Hopkins (2020), pp. 129–143; Hardy and Jagannath (2020), pp. 263–283; Tomej and Janne Liburd (2020), pp. 222–239. See also Lumsdon and Owen (2004), pp. 157–169.

Moreover, tour operators can help by introducing indications of what the tour-operating sector considers to be 'good practice', which can be drawn from voluntary initiatives such as existing eco-labels and codes of conduct. The problem is that the practical implementation of such guidance varies greatly from one tour operator to another, depending on different types of factors, such as size, financial capacity, corporate structure, operational location, organisational culture, etc.

Some scholars investigate the dimensions of what is currently referred to as 'good practice' in the tour operating industry, with the aim of exploring their comprehensiveness and sufficiency as tools for making mass tourism a more sustainable business.[4] In particular the achievement of sustainability in tourism is dependent upon a number of prerequisites, in particular the adoption of a new 'social paradigm' regarding the consumption of tourism or, more simply stated, the need for all tourists to become 'fair' and 'responsible' tourists.

References

Gronau, W. (2007). Encouraging behavioral change towards sustainable tourism: A German approach to free public transport for tourists. *Journal of Sustainable Tourism, 25*(2), 265–275.

Hardy, A., & Jagannath, A. (2020). Using innovations to understand tourist mobility in national parks. *Journal of Sustainable Tourism, 28*(2), 263–283.

Hopkins, D. (2020). Sustainable mobility at the interface of transport and tourism. *Journal of Sustainable Tourism, 28*(2), 129–143.

Høyer, K. G. (2020). Sustainable tourism or sustainable mobility? The norwegian case. *Journal of Sustainable Tourism, 28*(2), 147–160.

Karsten, J. (2007). Passengers, consumers, and travelers: The rise of passenger rights in EC transport law and its repercussions for community consumer law and policy. *Journal of Consumer Policy, 30*, 17–136.

Lumsdon, L., & Owen, E. (2004). Tourism transport: The green key initiative. In L. Lumsdon & S. J. Page (Eds.), *Tourism and transport: Issues and agenda for the new millennium* (pp. 157–169). Elsevier.

Monica Tepelus, C. (2005). Aiming for sustainability in the tour operating business. *Journal of Cleaner Production, 13*, 99–107.

Srinivasan, G. (2014). Environmental sustainability: The tour operator's perceptions. *Tourisms, 9*, 127–143.

Tomej, K., & Janne Liburd, J. (2020). Sustainable accessibility in rural destinations: A public transport network approach. *Journal of Sustainable Tourism, 28*(2), 222–239.

---

[4] Srinivasan (2014), pp. 127–143; Monica Tepelus (2005), pp. 99–107.

Chapter 9
Mass Travel Contracts

Contents

9.1   Inclusive Tour 103
    9.1.1 From Thomas Cook's Idea to Mass Tourism 103
    9.1.2 Regulation of Mass Tourism 104
9.2   International Law 104
    9.2.1 International Convention on Travel Contracts 104
    9.2.2 General Obligation on the Tour Organizer and on the Traveller 105
    9.2.3 General Obligation on the Intermediary 107
9.3   Travel Packages and European Union Law 107
    9.3.1 The First Directive on Travel Package 107
    9.3.2 The New Directive 108
9.4   Ruined Holiday 112
    9.4.1 Non-Material Damage in Case of Travel Contracts 112
    9.4.2 Ruined Holiday Damage According to the Directive 2302/2015 113
    9.4.3 One of the Leading Case on Ruined Holiday Damage 115
    9.4.4 Non Material Damage and Green Tourism Services 116
References 116

9.1 Inclusive Tour

9.1.1 From Thomas Cook's Idea to Mass Tourism

Inclusive tours as budget-friendly package tours permitted the development of mass tourism defined as the act of visiting a leisure destination with large amounts of people at one time.

The acronym IT stands for "inclusive tour", i.e., a tourism product that consists of transport from the place of departure to the destination, accommodation at the destination and other possible recreational or business tourist services. All these products are purchased by a firm called a "tour operator", which combine them and sell them at a single price to tourists.

© The Author(s), under exclusive license to Springer Nature Switzerland AG 2021   103
S. Landini, *Sustainable Tourism Contracts*,
https://doi.org/10.1007/978-3-030-83140-0_9

It is commonly believed that Thomas Cook's operations in the 1850s and 1860s were inclusive tours. In fact, Cook put together all the elements of his excursion and sold them as a single package.

The IT industry flourished after World War II for several reasons:

- there was a new mass tourism generation thanks to economic and social conditions founded on principles of equality;
- many military aircrafts were converted to civilian use;
- the desire of the consumer to move away from a period of austerity;
- new legal and economic policy with the aim of developing tourism. In this perspective.

9.1.2 Regulation of Mass Tourism

The Diplomatic Conference on the Travel Contract (CCV) meeting in Brussels in 1970, assessing the development of tourism and its economic and social role and recognizing the need to establish uniform provisions relating to travel contracts, signed an international convention on travel contracts. The convention established general duties on the tour organizer and on the intermediary in order to protect travellers considering the information asymmetry in mass travel contracts.[1]

It is usually said that mass tourism contracts have led to over-tourism and they are considered to be the opposite of sustainable tourism. As already mentioned, in reality, they can represent a positive influence towards sustainable tourism by collecting more travellers who intend to reach the same destination in order to reduce emissions in transport, thus favouring the combination of sustainable transport (train and bicycle for example) and encouraging travellers to reach destinations that they had not previously considered because they were not as famous.

9.2 International Law

9.2.1 International Convention on Travel Contracts

According to the international convention on the contract of travel signed in Brussels on April 23rd, 1970, a travel contract can either be an organised travel contract or an intermediary travel contract: an "Organised Travel Contract" is any contract whereby a person undertakes in his own name to provide for a client at an inclusive price, a combination of services comprising transportation, accommodation separate from the transportation, or any other service relating thereto; an "Intermediary Travel

---

[1] Sanchez Lima (2018), pp. 149–197; Twigg-Flesner and Micklitz (2010), pp. 201–207.

Contract" is any contract whereby a person undertakes to provide for a client, for a price, either an organised travel contract or one or more separate services that make a journey or sojourn possible. "Interline" or other similar operations between carriers shall not be considered as intermediary travel contracts.[2]

According to international rules as well, a "Travel Organiser" used to be distinguished as any person that habitually or regularly performs organised travel contracts, whether or not such activity is his main business and whether or not he exercises such activity on a professional basis; and a "Travel Intermediary" (or the "seller") as any person that habitually or regularly performs intermediary travel contracts, whether such activity is his main business or not and whether he exercises such activity on a professional basis or not.

Travel contracts are regulated by norms prevailing in the respective country where travel services are affected. Special rules are contained in the International Convention relating to the contract of travel.

This Convention shall apply to any travel contract concluded by a travel organizer or intermediary, where his principal place of business or, failing to have any such place of business, his habitual residence, or the place of business through which the travel contract has been concluded, is located in a Contracting State.

This Convention shall apply without prejudice to any special law establishing preferential treatment for certain categories of travellers.

9.2.2 General Obligation on the Tour Organizer and on the Traveller

With regard to the general obligations of travel organizers, intermediaries and travellers, the Convention provides that the travel organizer and the intermediary shall safeguard the rights and interests of the traveller according to the general principles of law and good usages in this field.

On the other hand, the traveller shall, in particular, furnish all the necessary information that is specifically requested from him and comply with the regulations relating to the journey, sojourn or any other service.

The travel organizer shall issue a travel document bearing his signature, although a stamp may be affixed instead of the signature. The travel document shall include the following: (a) place and date of issue; (b) name and address of the travel organizer; (e) name of the traveller or travellers and if the contract was concluded by another person, the name of such person; (d) places and dates of the beginning and end of the journey and sojourns; (e) all necessary specifications concerning transportation, accommodation as well as all ancillary services included in the price; (f) where applicable, the minimum number of travellers required; (g) the inclusive price covering all the services provided for in the contract; (h) circumstances and

---

[2] Simons (1987), pp. 3–10.

conditions under which the traveller may cancel the contract; (i) any clause providing for arbitration; (j) a statement that, notwithstanding any clause to the contrary, the contract is subject to the provisions of this Convention; (k) any other terms the parties may agree upon.

The travel document shall be the evidence of the terms of the contract. A breach of contract by the travel organizer shall affect neither the existence nor the validity of the contract, which shall remain subject to this Convention. The travel organizer shall be liable for any loss or damage resulting from such breach.

Unless the parties agree otherwise, the traveller may substitute another person in for the purpose of carrying out the contract, provided that such person satisfies the specific requirements relating to the journey. A special right of cancellation is provided.

The traveller may cancel the contract in whole or in part at any time. In this case he has to compensate the organising travel agent in accordance with domestic law or the provisions of the contract.

The travel organizer may, without indemnity, cancel the contract, in whole or in part, if before the contract or during its performance, circumstances of an exceptional character manifest themselves, of which he could not have known at the time of the conclusion of the contract, and which, had they been known to him at that time, would have given him a valid reason not to conclude the contract.

The travel organizer may also, without indemnity, cancel the contract if the minimum number of travellers stipulated in the travel document has not been reached, provided that the traveller has been informed of that at least fifteen days before the date on which the journey or sojourn was due to begin.

In the case of a cancellation of the contract before its performance, the travel organizer shall refund in full any payments received from the traveller. In the event of a cancellation of the contract during its performance, the travel organizer shall take all necessary measures in the interest of the traveller; furthermore, the parties shall compensate each other in an equitable manner.

The price is determined by the contract but an increase in the price is possible as a consequence of changes in exchange rates or in the tariffs of carriers, and provided that this possibility has been anticipated in the travel document. If the increase in the inclusive price exceeds 10%, the traveller may cancel the contract without compensation or reimbursement. In that case, the traveller shall be entitled to a refund of all sums paid by him to the travel organizer.

Special norms regulate organizer's liability. The travel organizer shall be responsible for the acts and omissions of his employees and agents, when acting in the course of their employment or within the scope of their authority, as if such acts and omissions were his own. The travel organizer shall be liable for any loss or damage caused to the traveller as a result of non-performance, in whole or in part, of his obligations to organise as resulting from the contract or this Convention, unless he/she proves that he/she acted as a diligent travel organizer.

Also, where the travel organizer entrusts the provision of transportation, accommodation or other services connected with the performance of the journey or sojourn to a third party, he/she shall be liable for any loss or damage caused to the traveller as a result of total or partial failure to perform these services, in accordance with the rules governing such services. The travel organizer shall be liable according to the same rules for any loss or damage caused to the traveller during the performance of the services, unless the travel organizer proves that he/she has acted as a diligent travel organizer in the choice of the person or persons performing the service.

In this case, insofar as the travel organizer has paid compensation for any loss or damage caused to the traveller, he/she shall be subrogated in any rights and actions the traveller may have against a third party responsible for such loss or damage.

9.2.3 General Obligation on the Intermediary

With regard to the intermediary travel contract, CCV provides that any contract concluded by a travel intermediary with a travel organizer or with persons providing separate services, shall be deemed as concluded by the traveller.

The travel intermediary shall be liable for wrongful acts or defaults he/she commits in performing his obligations. Wrongful acts or defaults are assessed in terms of the duties of a diligent travel intermediary.

The travel intermediary shall not be liable for non-performance, in whole or in part, of journeys, sojourns or other services governed by the contract.

Private autonomy in a travel contract is limited by this convention. In fact, any stipulation that would directly or indirectly derogate from the provisions of this Convention shall be null and void, insofar as it would be detrimental to the traveller. In particular, any clause that assigns the travel organizer or intermediary the benefit of insurance taken out by the traveller, or that shifts the burden of proof shall be null and void. The nullity of such a stipulation shall not imply the nullity of the other provisions of the contract.

9.3 Travel Packages and European Union Law

9.3.1 The First Directive on Travel Package

Tourism plays an important role in the economy of the Union, and package travel, package holidays and package tours ('packages') represent a significant proportion of the travel market. For this reason, Council Directive 90/314/EEC lays down a number of important consumer rights in relation to package travel, with particular regard to information requirements, the liability of traders in relation to the performance of a package, and protection against the insolvency of an organizer or a retailer. However, it was necessary to adapt the legislative framework to market developments in order to make it more suitable for the internal market, to remove ambiguities and to close legislative gaps. On July 9th, 2013 the Commission proposed a reform of the Travel Packages Directive 90/314 to bring it up to date with the developments in the travel market. In December of 2015, Directive (EU) 2015/2302 of the European Parliament and of the Council of November 25th, 2015 on package travel and linked travel arrangements came into effect, amending the Regulation (EC) No 2006/2004 and Directive 2011/83/EU of the European Parliament and of the Council, and repealing Council Directive 90/314/EEC.

The adoption of Directive 90/314/EEC on package travel in 1990 created important rights for European travellers purchasing package holidays, typically consisting of passenger transport and accommodation. This particular Directive ensures that consumers receive essential information before and after signing a package travel contract. It provides that organizers and/or retailers are responsible for the proper performance of the package, even if the services are provided by subcontractors, and regulates what happens if there are changes to the package travel contract. It also provides that travellers receive a refund of pre-payments and are repatriated in the event of the organizer's and/or retailer's insolvency.

Directive 90/314 reflects an old reality of the travel market: the structure of the travel market was much simpler in 1990 than it is today and the Internet did not exist.

9.3.2 The New Directive

Of course, the Directive has been innovated by CJEU ruling. The judgment of the European Court of Justice "Club-Tour Case C-400/00 of 30 April 2002" clarified that the notion of "pre-arranged combination" also covers travel services combined by a travel agent at the customer's express request just before the conclusion of a contract between the two.

Despite the above-mentioned CJEU ruling, it remains unclear to what extent modern ways of combining travel services are covered by the Directive.

During the last decade, the Commission undertook a comprehensive review of the consumer acquisitions leading to the adoption of Directive 2008/122/EC on timeshares and Directive 2011/83/EU on consumer rights. The revision of Directive 90/314/EEC is part of this revision program.

The new Directive 2015/2302 entered in force from 1st July 2018. In particular, the Directive contains a new definition for travel packages in accordance with the case law of the Court of Justice.

According to the case law of the Court of Justice of the European Union, with regard to the interpretation of Directive 314/1990, since travel services may be combined in many different ways, the European Commission affirms that is necessary to consider as packages all combinations of travel services that contain features which travellers typically associate with packages, notably that separate travel services are put together into a single travel product for which the organizer assumes responsibility for exact performance. It should make no difference whether travel services are combined before any contact with the traveller or at the request of or according to the selection made by the traveller. The same principles should apply

9.3 Travel Packages and European Union Law

irrespective of whether the booking is made through a high street travel agent or online.

At the same time, travel packages should be distinguished from assisted travel arrangements, where online or high street agents assist travellers in combining travel services leading the traveller to conclude contracts with different providers of travel services, including booking processes, which do not contain those features and in relation to which it would not be appropriate to apply all obligations applying to packages.

According to Article 2 of Directive 314/1990, "package means the pre-arranged combination of not fewer than two of the following when sold or offered for sale at an inclusive price and when the service covers a period of more than twenty-four hours or includes overnight accommodation: (a) transport; (b) accommodation; (c) other tourist services not ancillary to transport or accommodation and accounting for a significant proportion of the package. The separate billing of various components of the same package shall not absolve the organizer or retailer from the obligations under this Directive".

Art. 3 of the new Directive states that "the term package means a combination of at least two different types of travel services for the purpose of the same trip or holiday, if: those services are put together by one trader, including when at the request or according to the selection of the traveller, before a contract on all services is concluded; or, irrespective of whether separate contracts are concluded with individual travel service providers, those services are:

  (i) purchased from a single point of sale within the same booking process,

  (ii) offered or charged at an inclusive or total price,

  (iii) advertised or sold under the term 'package' or under a similar term,

  (iv) combined after the conclusion of a contract by which a trader entitles the traveller to choose among a selection of different types of travel services, or

  (v) purchased from separate traders through linked online booking processes where the traveller's name or particulars needed to conclude a booking transaction are transferred between the traders at the latest when the booking of the first service is confirmed.

Art. 3 also contains a stricter definition of a 'travel service', which is: (a) the carriage of passengers, (b) accommodation other than for residential purposes, (c) car rental or (d) any other tourist service not ancillary to the carriage of passengers, accommodation or car rental.

According to art. 3, a travel package needs to be distinguished from an 'assisted travel arrangement', that is "a combination of at least two different types of travel services for the purpose of the same trip or holiday, not constituting a package, resulting in the conclusion of separate contracts with the individual travel service providers, if a retailer facilitates the combination: (a) on the basis of separate bookings on the occasion of a single visit or contact with the point of sale; or

(b) through the procurement of additional travel services from another trader in a targeted manner through linked online booking processes at the latest when the booking of the first service is confirmed."

In order to clarify the purpose of the new definition of a travel package contained in art. 3, it is worth recalling a leading case of the CJEC c-400/00 Club-Tour, Viagens e Turismo SA v. Alberto Carlos Lobo Gonçalves Garrido.

Mr. Lobo Gonçalves Garrido purchased, for an inclusive price, a holiday consisting of air tickets and accommodation for 2 weeks, full board, in the holiday village of Gregolimano (Greece) from Club-Tour.

For that purpose, Club-Tour bought a holiday from the travel agency Club Med Viagens Lda ('Club Med'). It was Club Med that undertook to make the necessary reservations at the holiday village of Gregolimano for accommodation, meals and transfers, to organise and publish the holiday program, and to fix the overall price.

On their arrival at the holiday village, Mr. Lobo Gonçalves Garrido and his family noticed that it was infested by thousands of wasps, which prevented them—throughout their stay—from fully enjoying their holiday. Moreover, the immediate request by Mr. Lobo Gonçalves Garrido for the transfer of himself and his family to another village could not be dealt with by Club-Tour, as the Club Med that it contacted stated that it was not possible to arrange appropriate alternative accommodation.

Thereby, on his return home, Mr. Lobo Gonçalves Garrido refused to pay the price of the holiday agreed with Club-Tour. Before the Tribunal Judicial da Comarca do Porto, Club-Tour denied that the Directive applied to the present proceedings, arguing that the holiday that was sold was outside its scope and asked for the payment of the holiday price.

The Tribunal Judicial da Comarca do Porto referred the following questions to the European Court of Justice for a preliminary ruling: "Does a package organised by the agency, at the request and on the initiative of the consumer or a strictly defined group of consumers in accordance with their wishes, including transport and accommodation through a tourism undertaking, at an inclusive price, for a period of more than 24 h or including overnight accommodation, fall within the scope of the concept of "package travel" as defined in Article 2(1)?

May the expression "pre-arranged" which appears in the Directive be interpreted as referring to the moment when the contract is entered into between the agency and the customer?".

With regard to the first question, the CJEC affirms that the word 'package' used in Article 2(1) of Directive 314/1990 must be interpreted as including holidays organised by a travel agency at the request of and according to the specifications of a consumer or a defined group of consumers.

According to CJCE's opinion: "the Directive, which is designed amongst other things to protect consumers who buy 'package' holidays, gives a definition of that term in Article 2(1) whereby it is enough, for a service to qualify as a 'package', if, first, the combination of tourist services sold by a travel agency at an inclusive price includes two of the three services referred to in that paragraph (namely transport, accommodation and other tourist services not ancillary to transport or accommodation and accounting for a significant proportion of the package), and, second, that service covers a period of more than 24 hours or includes overnight accommodation."

There is nothing in the definition of the travel package contained in art. 2 of Directive 314/1990 suggesting that holidays organised at the request and in accordance with the specifications of a consumer or a defined group of consumers cannot be considered as 'package' holidays within the meaning of the Directive.

9.3 Travel Packages and European Union Law

With regard to the second question, the Court affirms that, taking into account the purposes of Directive 314/1990, the term 'pre-arranged combination' used in Article 2(1) of the Directive must be interpreted as including combinations of tourist services which are put together at the time when the contract is concluded between the travel agency and the consumer.

As said, the new Directive tried to solve all these interpretation problems by adapting the law to the new form of inclusive tour.

In case of occurrences, duration contracts (contracts that you expect will remain in force for a lengthy period), generally speaking, may provide that the professional party may unilaterally make changes related to the price of the goods to be delivered or the service to be rendered provided that the consumer has been notified within a reasonable time to be able to, if necessary, to terminate the contract. With regard to travel packages, the Directive contains special norms on the alteration of the price or of other package travel contract terms. According to Art. 10 price increases shall be possible only as a direct consequence of changes in:

- the price of the carriage of passengers resulting from the cost of fuel or other power sources;
- the level of taxes or fees on the travel services included in the contract imposed by third parties not directly involved in the performance of the package, including tourist taxes, landing taxes or embarkation or disembarkation fees at ports and airports; or
- the exchange rates relevant to the package.

According to Art. 11 the organiser may not unilaterally change other package travel contract terms unless:

- the organiser has reserved that right in the contract;
- the change is insignificant; and
- the organiser informs the traveller of the change in a clear, comprehensible and prominent manner on a durable medium.

In this case, the traveller may, within a reasonable period specified by the organizer, accept the proposed change; or terminate the contract without paying a termination fee.

Art. 12 on the right for consumers to withdraw before the start of the package contains a norm that has had an important role in the present pandemic situation, where there is a necessity to withdraw from travel packages due to the lockdown and travel restrictions enacted in some countries.

According to Article 12:

Where the traveller terminates the package travel contract under this paragraph, the traveller may be required to pay an appropriate and justifiable termination fee to the organiser.

The traveller shall have the right to terminate the package travel contract before the start of the package without paying any termination fee in the event of unavoidable and extraordinary circumstances (like a pandemic) occurring at the place of destination or its immediate vicinity and significantly affecting the performance of the package, or which significantly affect the carriage of passengers to the destination.

In the event of a termination of the package travel contract under this paragraph, the traveller shall be entitled to a full refund of any payments made for the package but shall not be entitled to additional compensation.

Of course, mediation of conflicts between consumers and travel operators is welcome. The Commission recommendation of May 13th, 2020 aims to ensure that vouchers become a viable and more attractive alternative to reimbursements for cancelled trips in the context of the current pandemic, which has also heavily strained travel operators financially.

Moreover, tour operators have reinvented themselves in the current period with flexible offers and last-minute contracts that can be cancelled without penalties. Furthermore, tourist packages have become an excellent tool for implementing "workcation", allowing smart workers to move and work in safe and healthy environments, with the possibility of safe leisure and of effectively carrying out their work duties.

9.4 Ruined Holiday

9.4.1 Non-Material Damage in Case of Travel Contracts

Another important aspect of travel package law concerns non-material damages in the case of loss of enjoyment of a holiday.

In the field of package holidays, in some countries there is an obligation to provide compensation for non-material damage that causes significant distortions of competition.

In Italy, for instance, art. 47 of the Italian Tourism code (legislative decree May 23rd, 2011, n. 79) introduces the concept of "damage for a ruined holiday" (Danno da vacanza rovinata), which is comprehensive of non-material damage.

A solution has been found in the new travel packages Directive and, before that, in the case law of the CJEC regarding European Union Law.

According to point 34 of the premises of the new Directive, "Compensation should also cover non-material damage, such as compensation for loss of enjoyment of the trip or holiday because of substantial problems in the performance of the relevant travel services. The traveller should be required to inform the organizer without undue delay, taking into account the circumstances of the case, of any lack of conformity he perceives during the performance of a travel service included in the package travel contract. Failure to do so may be taken into account when determining the appropriate price reduction or compensation for damages where such notice would have avoided or reduced the damage".

The provision contained in Directive 314/1990 generated an interpretation problem regarding non-material damage compensation.

According to art. 5 of this Directive, "Member States shall take the necessary steps to ensure that the organizer and/or retailer party to the contract is liable to the consumer for the proper performance of the obligations arising from the contract, irrespective of whether such obligations are to be performed by that organizer and/or retailer or by other suppliers of services without prejudice to the right of the organizer and/or retailer to pursue those other suppliers of services. With regard to the damage resulting for the consumer from the failure to perform or the improper performance of the contract, Member States shall take the necessary steps to ensure that the organizer and/or retailer is/are liable unless such failure to perform or improper performance is attributable neither to any fault of theirs nor to that of another supplier of services, because:—the failures which occur in the performance of the contract are attributable to the consumer;—such failures are attributable to a third party unconnected with the provision of the services contracted for, and are unforeseeable or unavoidable;—such failures are due to a case of force majeure . . . ., or to an event which the organizer and/or retailer or the supplier of services, even with all due care, could not foresee or forestall. . . .In the matter of damages arising from the non-performance or improper performance of the services involved in the package, the Member States may allow compensation to be limited in accordance with the international conventions governing such services. In the matter of damage other than personal injury resulting from the non-performance or improper performance of the services involved in the package, the Member States may allow compensation to be limited under the contract. Such limitation shall not be unreasonable. . . . The consumer must communicate any failure in the performance of a contract which he/she perceives on the spot to the supplier of the services concerned and to the organizer and/or retailer in writing or any other appropriate form at the earliest opportunity. This obligation must be stated clearly and explicitly in the contract."

9.4.2 *Ruined Holiday Damage According to the Directive 2302/2015*

The new norm proposed by the European Commission takes into account the problems of interpretation related to the above disposition and the case law of CJEC C- 168/00 Simone Leitner v. TUI Deutschland GmbH & Co. KG.

Simone Leitner and her family booked a package holiday (all-inclusive stay) with TUI at the Pamfiliya Robinson club in Side, Turkey for the period from July 4th to 18th, 1997.

On July 4th, 1997 Simone Leitner, who was 10 years old, and her parents arrived at the club. There they spent the entire holiday and had all their meals. About a week after the start of the holiday, Simone Leitner showed symptoms of salmonella poisoning due to the food offered in the club. In fact, many other guests in the club also fell ill with the same illness and presented the same symptoms.

The illness, which lasted beyond the end of the holiday, manifested itself in a fever of up to 40 degrees over several days, circulatory difficulties, diarrhoea, vomiting and anxiety. Her parents had to look after her until the end of the holiday.

After the end of the holiday, a letter of complaint concerning Simone Leitner's illness was sent to TUI. Since no reply to that letter was received, Simone Leitner, through her parents, brought an action for damages in the sum of ATS 25,000.

The Austrian Court, at first, awarded the claimant only ATS 13,000 for the physical pain and suffering caused by the food poisoning and dismissed the remainder of the application, which concerned the compensation for the non-material damage caused by loss of enjoyment of the holiday.

The Court considered that, if the feelings of dissatisfaction and negative impressions caused by disappointment must be categorised, under Austrian law, as non-material damage, they could not give rise to compensation because there is no express provision in any Austrian law for compensation for non-material damage of that kind.

The claimant appealed to the Landesgericht Linz, which assesses that the text of Article 5 of Directive 314/1990 is not precise enough to draw any definite conclusion about non-material damage in case of loss of enjoyment of a holiday. Thus, the Landesgericht Linz decided to halt proceedings and to refer a question to the Court for a preliminary ruling.

With this question, the national Court seeks to ascertain whether Article 5 of the Directive must be interpreted as conferring, in principle, on consumers a right to compensation for non-material damage resulting from failure to perform or the improper performance of the obligations inherent in the provision of package travel.

The CJEU states that it is clear from the second and third recital in the preamble to Directive 314 that its purpose is to eliminate the disparities between the national laws and practices of the various Member States in the field of package holidays which are liable to give rise to distortions of competition between operators established in different Member States. It is a matter of fact that, in the field of package holidays, the existence in some Member States but not in others of an obligation to provide compensation for non-material damage would cause significant distortions of competition. In fact, as the Commission has pointed out, non-material damage is a frequent occurrence in that field.

Given that the Directive is designed to offer protection to consumers, and that compensation for non-material damages arising from the loss of enjoyment of a holiday is of particular importance to consumers, the CJEC concludes that Article 5 of the Directive implicitly recognizes the existence of a right to compensation for damage other than personal injury, including non-material damage.

The problem of non-material damage in the case of loss of enjoyment of a holiday is diffused worldwide. It is worth remembering a famous English case: Milner v. Carnival Plc (3).

9.4.3 One of the Leading Case on Ruined Holiday Damage

On June 19th, 2006, Mr. and Mrs. Milner booked a cruise with Carnival, which was the maiden around the world voyage of the Queen Victoria vessel. The vessel was to depart from Southampton on January 6th, 2008, to cruise around the world for 106 nights, and to return to Southampton on April 22nd, 2008. During the voyage, the couple were to be accommodated in cabin 7083, which is a Princess Grade cabin situated on deck 7. They chose that location, refusing a free upgrade to a superior cabin, because that area is least affected by the ship's movements in poor weather.

Unfortunately, the convex metal floor plate in the Milners' room flexed loudly, particularly as the vessel reached open seas, causing noise and vibration in the cabin. After two sleepless nights, Mr. and Mrs. Milner were provided with alternative accommodation in the form of suite 6083, which had no natural light. Moreover, their luggage remained in suite 7083, meaning that they needed to move between the two cabins: sleeping in suite 6083 and dressing in suite 7083.

After that, they had to change cabins multiple times to make way for the passengers who had originally booked it. Eventually they disembarked the Queen Victoria at Honolulu. They remained in Hawaii until the 25th March, when they boarded the Queen Elizabeth II.

The trial judge awarded the claimants £2500 each for the diminution in value of the holiday; £7500 each for the distress and disappointment and £2000 for the wasted expenditure on gowns which were unlikely to be worn.

The Court of Appeal assesses damages by comparing the expectations raised by the defendant tour operator against the reality of the experience actually provided. In the Milners' case, the expectations were 'sky high', as the Court said. The cruise was advertised to be '... a legendary experience exceeding expectations' and an '... unprecedented event in Cunard's long and illustrious history'. Using this approach, the Court concluded that the value of the cruise was diminished by about one third when evaluating what the overall experience was compared to that which was not provided balanced against that which was enjoyed. It therefore awarded Mr. and Mrs. Milner £3500(Milner v Carnival Plc [2010] 3 All ER 701).

This judgment focuses on some important issues of loss of enjoyment of a vacation: (i) different contracts for holidays vary greatly. It would be a grave mistake to look at the facts in a similar case and compare those facts with the facts in another case as a means of establishing the measure of damages; (ii) in assessing damages, judges have to take into account the type of holiday (a special occasion, such as a honeymoon, should attract more damages than an ordinary package holiday), the features of the holiday which were regarded as the primary features of a holiday will make a difference (for example, a traveller who is a sports fan will suffer more disappointment if he is not able to use the promised sports facilities); the difference between the expectations set by the tour operator and the reality of the experience actually provided. All of these considerations come from a basic feature of tourism product: "selling holidays is selling dreams".

9.4.4 Non Material Damage and Green Tourism Services

It is a question of seeing in which cases the failure to offer green tourism services promised in the contract represents an injury in terms of private interests worthy of compensation. We can propose three different cases. The first case is that of a tourist lease or a timeshare with energy costs higher than expected because the building does not respect the advertised energy saving fees. In this case, however, the pecuniary damage is not attributable to a loss of enjoyment of the holiday.

The second case is that of offering green services such as a greater contact with nature, relaxation areas on hay or salt coatings for heliotherapy. In this case, there is economic damage due to the absence of the promised services, but also non-pecuniary damage due to the non-enjoyment of the expected holiday.

The third case is that of environmental claims relating to the advertising of the green nature of the tourist offer (for example construction with environmentally friendly materials), when such claims don't correspond to the truth. In this case, unfair commercial practice could happen, which will see the intervention of public authorities and claims for compensation.[3]

The problem with this case is that the nature of the loss is not pecuniary, which makes the quantification of the damage unpredictable. Some authors gave an answer moving from Millners' case "It appears therefore, that following the Milner case, a measure can be placed upon the intangible emotion that is enjoyment, or more specifically, loss of that enjoyment, following breach of a holiday contract. Introducing guidelines creates a starting point for negotiations which ultimately could speed up settlements and reduce costs and the need for court time. Of course, the type of holiday experienced has to firstly be agreed in order to establish within which bracket the damages will fall and where negotiations should begin. This therefore invites arguments as to what type of holiday is deemed to be 'special' and what is simply ordinary".[4]

References

Prager, S. (2011) The assessment of damages in holiday cases: The impact of Milner V Carnival Plc. *Travel Law Quarterly*, p. 13.

---

[3] Prager (2011), p. 13 ff.
[4] Scargill (2010), p. 204 ff.

References

Sanchez Lima, M. G. (2018). *Traveler vulnerability in the context of travel and tourism contracts* (p. 149). Springer.

Scargill, C. (2010). Loss of enjoyment in holiday claims–lottery or science? *Travel Law Quarterly, 2*, 204.

Simons, M. S. (1987). An overview of international trends in hospitality and tourism law. *International Journal of Hospitality Management, 6*(1), 3.

Twigg-Flesner, C., & Micklitz, H. W. (2010). Think global - towards international consumer law. *Journal of Consumer Policy, 33*(3), 201.

Chapter 10
Unfair Commercial Practices

Contents

10.1	Martketing Strategies in Tourism Market	119
	10.1.1 Marketing in Brief	119
	10.1.2 DAGMAR Model	121
	10.1.3 Commercial Practices	122
10.2	Best Commercial Practices	123
	10.2.1 Illegal and Unfair Advertising	123
	10.2.2 Unfair Commercial Practices in EU Law	125
	10.2.3 Unfair Commercial Practices and Unfair Commercial Terms	128
	10.2.4 Some Cases	130
	10.2.5 Environmental Claims and Green Claims	136
References		140

10.1 Martketing Strategies in Tourism Market

10.1.1 Marketing in Brief

According to the Chartered Institute of Marketing, "Marketing is the management function which organises and directs all those business activities involved in assessing customer needs and converting customer purchasing power into effective demand for a specific product or service, and in moving that product or service to the final consumer or user so as to achieve the profit target or other objective set by the company or other organisation". In other words "marketing is about anticipating demand, recognizing it, stimulating it and finally satisfying it. It is understanding what can be sold, to whom, when, where and in what quantities".[1]

Marketing involves activities of:

– Market planning that is needed to meet short term and long-term objectives of tourism companies (achieving a certain level of sales, increasing the profitability,

---

[1] Holloway and Plant (1992), 2nd edition, p. 4.

© The Author(s), under exclusive license to Springer Nature Switzerland AG 2021   119
S. Landini, *Sustainable Tourism Contracts*,
https://doi.org/10.1007/978-3-030-83140-0_10

reducing business risk (by diversifying the product range, for instance), obtaining a measured increase in the return on capital invested by the company).

– Market research that is the planned and systematic collection and analysis of data designed to help the management organisation to take decisions and to monitor the results of the decisions taken. Market research aims at understanding the needs and wants of consumers, taking into account all variables that affect human needs. Variables affecting the demand for goods and services may be divided into two categories: demographic variables and psychographic variable (such as lifestyle and personality).

"Successful new strategic tourism planning initiatives will require that decision makers not only understand historical and contemporary trends and movements in the business environment but will require the ability to predict new key emerging developments and shifts—this will lead to the development of innovative and effective strategies...Tourism is essentially a social phenomenon and, although like all industries it is influenced by the society in which exist, tourism is unusual in that it involves a large-scale, if temporary, transfer of individuals between different societies...One of the most important demographically related changes is the democratization of tourism...Global urbanization is another significant demographic shift starting in the twentieth century and one that has a variety of effects for tourism providers. Resulting increases in congestion, pollution, poverty, unemployment and crime can all have a significant impact on the demand for tourism. (Having regard to lifestyle) research carried out in several countries, in particular a large-scale study by the Stanford Research Institute in California, USA, indicates that there is a clearly defined trend away from an outward-directed lifestyle towards inward-directed and integrated values. Several recent studies indicate that post-materialistic values, in other words, growing non materialistic needs, environmental care, diminishing concerns about career, prestige and status, etc. will gain importance....New luxuries will become time and simplicity, stillness and peace of mind—intangible like purpose, meaning, fulfilment and quality of life are gaining importance...This movement will need to be reflected in the type of tourism products offered".[2] Determining product policy, which means getting the right product. This process involves product differentiation, the creation of a particular image or "personality" for the company and its products, launching a new product etc.

– Pricing the product, which means determining the price of a product. It is well known that the price of a product says something about the product to consumers and that by manipulating price in combination with the qualities of the product, it is possible to orientate sales.

– Designing marketing communications. The marketing manager has, in particular, four ways of communicating its promotional messages to consumers:—by advertising the product through selected media such as television or the press; by using

---

[2]Moutinho (2011), pp. 2–5.

10.1.2 DAGMAR Model

Marketing communication is a significant part of the relationship between tourism companies (hotels, travel agencies, tour operators etc.) and consumers. Consumers can be reached at three different levels by communication processes.

At a cognitive level, clients must be made aware of the product. The company has to convince the consumers that its product serves their needs. Moreover, it is important to turn the consumer into a loyal user of the company's products.

The objects of this process can be summarized using the DAGMAR model: Defining Advertising Goals for Measured Advertising Results (DAGMAR), which is an advertising model proposed by Russel H. Colley in 1961.[3]

At an affective level, communication must make the client sympathetic to the product and/or the company. Social and cultural influences play very relevant roles here. Social influence causes new products and fashions to spread through society. Culture is the key element that unites the group. Cultural values can influence the way people choose tourism products.

The message must affect consumer behavior, by motivating them to buy the product. It is important to consider the five main components in a tourism product: destination attractions and the environment; destination facilities and services; the accessibility of the destination; the image of the destination; the price for the consumers. These tourism product components largely determine the consumer's choice and influence the buyer's motivation.

According to DAGMAR, each purchase prospect goes through four steps: 1. Awareness; 2. Comprehension; 3. Conviction; 4. Action.

These steps, also known as the ACCA advertising formula, derive from the AIDA advertising formula, which is an acronym used in marketing and advertising that describes a common list of events that may occur when a consumer engages with an advertisement:

- A—Attention (Awareness): attracts the attention of the customer.
- I—Interest: raises customer interest by focusing on and demonstrating advantages and benefits (instead of focusing on features, as in traditional advertising).
- D—Desire: convince customers that they want and desire the product or service and that it will satisfy their needs.
- A—Action: lead customers towards taking action and/or purchasing.

Colley identifies about 50 objectives; in terms of tourism marketing, the following are sufficient:

---

[3]Colley (1961).

- Those associated with informing customers about the product;
- Those ordered to persuade clients to buy;
- Those whose purpose is to remind the customers of the product and/or the company.

In designing the message to consumers, the Marketing Manager has to take into account the following factors: the source of the message; the message appeal; the channel to be used and the target audience. "ICT (information and communication technology) was first used to speed up the processing and communication of information within companies, then between the company and its trade partners, and more recently, through the Internet, between company and its end user customers. This has had a powerful effect in service industries, such as tourism, because information is fundamental to the creation and selling of intangible holiday and travel experience. Information is the life-blood of tourism".[4]

The major factor will be the source, since it establishes the credibility of the message and its effectiveness. A message gains credibility, for instance, if the person delivering the message is seen as an expert on the subject, as a friend or as someone closely associated with the product, etc.

While designing a marketing process, it is important to consider legal limits to commercial practices.

10.1.3 Commercial Practices

A commercial practice is a conduct, a commercial communication and all forms of advertising (direct marketing and product package included) that a company uses to promote, sell or provide goods or services to consumers.

The law generally considers a commercial practice as unfair when it is contrary to the requirements of professional diligence and it materially distorts, or is likely to materially distort, the economic behaviour of the average consumer whom it reaches or to whom it is addressed.

Advertising is also part of commercial practice and it refers to forms of communication that are distributed at the initiative of economic operators through media (such as television, radio, newspapers, banners, mail, Internet, etc.) as part of an intentional and systematic means to affect individual attitudes and choices in relation to the consumption of goods and services.

This advertising practice still includes forms of communication that promote a business image as perceived by consumers as well, even when there is no immediate form of selling specific goods or services involved.

---

[4]Middleton et al. (2009), 4th ed., pp. 242–243.

10.2 Best Commercial Practices

10.2.1 Illegal and Unfair Advertising

Advertising methods and means of distribution are continuously evolving thanks to the imagination of advertisers, technological developments and the development of new marketing techniques. New advertising channels, such as the Internet, continue to emerge alongside traditional distribution methods, like television, dailies and periodicals, banners, direct marketing (mailings, phone calls and door-to-door sales), radio, cinema and product packaging itself.

Moreover, advertising with technology can represent a means to persuade consumers into commercial transactions that they might otherwise avoid. For this reason, many governments worldwide regulate and control false, deceptive or misleading advertising, stemming from the basic principle that customers have the right to know what they are really buying.

Advertising can also be unfair in terms of the principle of fair competition between companies. Generally speaking, advertisements must not unfairly discredit, disparage or attack other products, services, advertisements or companies, or exaggerate the nature or importance of competitive differences.

With regard to Unfair Commercial Practices and B2B Relationships, some kinds of advertising models can represent unfair commercial practices regarding B2B relationships. Generally speaking, advertising can be defined as the making of a representation in any form in connection with a trade, business, craft or profession in order to promote the supply of goods or services, including immovable property, rights and obligations.

Given that advertising is a very important means of giving information to the market about goods and services, a competitive internal market needs to have some basic provisions governing the form and content of advertising, with particular regard to comparative advertising. If conditions of fairness are met, this form of advertising will help demonstrate objectively the merits of the various comparable products. Comparative advertising, when it compares material, relevant, verifiable and representative features and is not misleading, may be a legitimate means of informing consumers of their advantage.

It is therefore correct to say that comparative advertising can stimulate competition between suppliers of goods and services to the consumer's advantage.

On the other hand, misleading and unlawful comparative advertising can lead to distortion of competition within the internal market. Advertising is considered misleading when it deceives or is likely to deceive the persons to whom it is addressed or whom it reaches and, by reason of its deceptive nature, is likely to affect their economic behaviour and/or, for those reasons, injures or is likely to injure a competitor.[5]

---

[5] Micklitz (2009); Micklitz (2010), pp. 229–242.

Conditions of permitted comparative advertising, as far as the comparison is concerned, are established at the national law level in order to determine which practices relating to comparative advertising may distort competition, be detrimental to competitors and have an adverse effect on consumer choice. Such conditions of permitted advertising generally include criteria of objective comparison of the features of goods and services.

It is obvious that differences between the state laws on misleading advertising hinder the execution of advertising campaigns beyond national boundaries and affect the free circulation of goods and services.

For these reasons, directives exist at the European level in order to harmonize the national advertising laws in Member States. Regulating advertising is necessary for the proper functioning of the internal market. The adoption of a directive is the appropriate instrument because it lays down uniform general principles and at the same time allows the Member States to choose the form and appropriate method by which they can obtain these objectives in accordance with the principle of subsidiarity.

Council Directive 84/450/EEC of September 10th, 1984 concerning misleading and comparative advertising has been substantially amended several times [by Directive 97/55/EC of the European Parliament and of the Council and by Directive 2005/29/EC of the European Parliament and of the Council].

The most recent one is Directive 2006/114/EC of the European Parliament and of the Council of December 12th, 2006 concerning misleading and comparative advertising.

According to Article 3 of this Directive, when determining whether advertising is misleading, all of its features shall be taken into account, and in particular any information concerning:

(a) the characteristics of goods or services (e.g., their availability, nature, execution, composition, method and date of manufacture or provision, fitness for purpose, uses, quantity, specification, geographical or commercial origin, the results to be expected from their use, the results and material features of tests and the checks carried out on the goods or services);
(b) the price or the manner in which the price is calculated, and the conditions on which the goods are supplied or the services provided;
(c) the nature, attributes and rights of the advertiser, such as his identity and assets, his qualifications and ownership of industrial, commercial or intellectual property rights or his awards and distinctions.

Article 4 lists the hypothesis of permitted comparative advertising:

(a) when the comparison is not misleading within the meaning of Articles 2(b), 3 and 8(1) of this Directive or Articles 6 and 7 of Directive 2005/29/EC ("Unfair Commercial Practices Directive");
(b) when advertising compares goods or services meeting the same needs or intended for the same purpose;

10.2 Best Commercial Practices

(c) when advertising objectively compares one or more material, relevant, verifiable and representative features of those goods and services, which may include price;

(d) when advertising does not discredit or denigrate the trademarks, trade names, other distinguishing marks, goods, services, activities or circumstances of a competitor;

(e) for products with a designation of origin, in each case, advertising relates to products with the same designation;

(f) when advertising does not take unfair advantage of the reputation of a trademark, trade name or other distinguishing marks of a competitor or of the designation of origin of competing products;

(g) when advertising does not present goods or services as imitations or replicas of goods or services bearing a protected trademark or trade name;

(h) when advertising does not create confusion among traders, between the advertiser and a competitor or between the advertiser's trademarks, trade names, other distinguishing marks, goods or services and those of a competitor.

Member States shall ensure adequate and effective means to prevent misleading advertising and enforce compliance with the provisions on comparative advertising in the interests of traders and competitors.

Such means shall include legal provisions for individuals or organisations regarded under national law as having a legitimate interest in fighting misleading advertising or regulating comparative advertising. In particular, individuals or organisations may: (a) take legal action against such advertising; or (b) bring such advertising before an administrative authority competent either to decide on complaints or to initiate appropriate legal proceedings.

Also, the evolution of technology has had a deep impact on commercial practice.

Effective and high-speed ICT infrastructure and software applications in the travel and tourism industry are crucial for tourism development. Technology allows customer–management relations and supply chain management to be combined into a single source, facilitating operations such as product selection, ordering, fulfilment, tracking, payment and reporting. Technology also cuts costs by enabling the provider to be in direct contact with the consumer and it also impacts employment because of the need for maintenance for ICT equipment.

10.2.2 Unfair Commercial Practices in EU Law

Developments in technology have also produced some changes in demand and supply. They have led to a higher demand for flexible, individualized options. Through new technology and social and economic ratings (e.g., social media platforms like Facebook, Twitter, and blogs), customers are able to share information on destinations, the quality of service in hotels and restaurants, means of transport, etc. A number of hotels have strengthened their brand image and now communicate directly with their customers, promoting a new package through social networks.

In this context, sustainability is becoming part of the key information for customers.

Some web-based resources recommend or disapprove of hotels and restaurants according to their level of commitment to sustainability. Especially in developed countries, customers are increasingly using technology for travel information and making reservations with travel distribution systems.

The problem that arises is that of calculating sustainability in order to render it objectively assessable and avoid deceptive claims that can distort competition.

Regarding this last point, it is worth recalling an important litigation. In 2010, the union of French hoteliers took legal action against user review TripAdvisor and Expedia over "unfair commercial practices".

French hoteliers advocate that people who visit these websites, hotel guests and hospitality professionals were deceived by false information provided on these sites.

In short, Synhorcat (the French national union of hoteliers) said that people who had visited TripAdvisor had been misled because they were often directed to Expedia for more information rather than the hotel's website.

Moreover, the travel-booking site Expedia and its subsidiaries TripAdvisor and Hotels.com were accused of displaying a hotel as "full on requested dates", when in fact rooms were available, and suggesting other nearby available properties that had better commercial terms with Expedia.

The alleged unfair practices included: incorrectly displaying hotel phone numbers so users could not call a hotel directly; announcing special promotional rates when the final price was actually just a standard rate.

The French government and its Directorate General later supported the action for Competition, Consumption and Repression of Fraud (DGCCRF), an intervention seen by some as unprecedented in France.

Expedia has been hit by a Paris Court order to pay a Euro 367,000 ($484,000) fine for "misleading marketing practices".

With regard to B2C contracts, national law combats unfair commercial practices, including unfair advertising, which directly harm consumers' economic interests and thereby indirectly harm the economic interests of legitimate competitors. A commercial practice is commonly considered as unfair in a B2C relationship when it is directly ordered to mislead consumers' transactional decisions in relation to products. As we have seen previously, all commercial communications can influence consumer behavior, but, according to the principle of proportionality, they cannot be considered unfair.

As the European Commission noted since 2005, the laws of the different Member States relating to unfair commercial practices showed differences which can generate mechanisms of distortion of competition and obstacles to the smooth functioning of the internal market. In the field of advertising, Council Directive 84/450/EEC of September 10th, 1984 concerning misleading and comparative advertising established the minimum criteria for harmonizing legislations on misleading advertising, but this Directive does not, in any case, prevent the Member States from

10.2 Best Commercial Practices

retaining or adopting measures which provide more extensive protection for consumers.

For those reasons, the European Parliament and the European Council adopted Directive 2005/29/EC on May 11th, 2005 concerning unfair business-to-consumer commercial practices in the internal market and amending Council Directive 84/450/EEC, Directives 97/7/EC, 98/27/EC and 2002/65/EC of the European Parliament and of the Council and Regulation (EC) No 2006/2004 of the European Parliament and of the Council.

This Directive establishes a single general prohibition of those unfair commercial practices distorting consumers' economic behavior. It also sets rules on aggressive commercial practices.

According to Article 5, "A commercial practice shall be unfair if: (a) it is contrary to the requirements of professional diligence, and (b) it materially distorts or is likely to materially distort the economic behavior with regard to the product of the average consumer whom it reaches or to whom it is addressed, or of the average member of the group when a commercial practice is directed to a particular group of consumers."

Misleading practices, including misleading advertising, deceive or are likely to deceive the consumer, preventing him from making an informed and thus efficient choice. This Directive classifies misleading practices as misleading actions and misleading omissions. Unfair omissions are characterized by the lack of information which the consumer needs to make an efficient transactional decision (such as the main characteristics of the product, the geographical address and the identity of the trader, the price (including taxes), the arrangements for payment, delivery, performance and the complaint handling policy).

According to Article 6, a commercial practice shall be considered misleading "if it contains false information and is therefore untruthful or in any way, including overall presentation, deceives or is likely to deceive the average consumer, even if the information is factually correct", in relation to one or more of the following elements: (a) the existence or nature of the product; (b) the main characteristics of the product; (c) the extent of the trader's commitments; (d) the price or the manner in which the price is calculated, or the existence of a specific price advantage.[6]

A commercial practice shall also be regarded as misleading if, taking into account its factual context and all its features and circumstances, it causes or is likely to cause the average consumer to take a transactional decision that he/she would not have taken otherwise.

According to this Directive, national provisions on aggressive commercial practices should cover those practices which significantly impair the consumer's freedom of choice—practices that use harassment, coercion, including the use of physical force, and undue influence.

According to Article 9, "in determining whether a commercial practice uses harassment, coercion, including the use of physical force, or undue influence,

---

[6]Weatherill and Bernitz (2007); Howells et al. (2006).

account shall be taken of: (a) its timing, location, nature or persistence; (b) the use of threatening or abusive language or behaviour; (c) the exploitation by the trader of any specific misfortune or circumstance of such gravity as to impair the consumer's judgment, of which the trader is aware, to influence the consumer's decision with regard to the product; (d) any onerous or disproportionate non-contractual barriers imposed by the trader where a consumer wishes to exercise rights under the contract, including rights to terminate a contract or to switch to another product or another trader; (e) any threat to take any action that cannot legally be taken."

According to Article 6, 2 of this Directive, "commercial practice shall also be regarded as misleading if, in its factual context, taking account of all its features and circumstances, it causes or is likely to cause the average consumer to take a transactional decision that he would not have taken otherwise, and it involves... non-compliance by the trader with commitments contained in codes of conduct by which the trader has undertaken to be bound, where: (i) the commitment is not aspirational but is firm and is capable of being verified, and (ii) the trader indicates in a commercial practice that he is bound by the code." Moreover, Article 10 highlights that this Directive does not exclude the control of unfair commercial practices by code owners and recourse to such bodies by the persons or organisations regarded under national law as having a legitimate interest in combating unfair commercial practices. Persons or organisations that have a legitimate interest in the matter must have legal remedies for initiating proceedings against unfair commercial practices, either before a court or before an administrative authority which is competent to decide upon complaints or to initiate appropriate legal proceedings.

A particular role has been given to conducts codes, which enable traders to apply the principles of this Directive effectively in specific economic fields. In sectors where there are specific mandatory requirements regulating the behaviour of traders, it is appropriate that these will also provide evidence for the requirements of professional diligence in that sector. The trader or group of traders, who are responsible for the formulation and revision of a code of conduct, should monitor compliance with the code by those who are bound by it. Such control, when exercised at a national or community level, may eliminate unfair commercial practices. This could avoid the need for recourse to administrative or judicial action and therefore should be encouraged. A higher level of consumer protection can be achieved if consumer organisations are informed and involved in the drafting of codes of conduct.

10.2.3 Unfair Commercial Practices and Unfair Commercial Terms

Scholars usually distinguish the legislation and phenomenon of Unfair Commercial Practice from the legislation and phenomenon of Unfair Terms. The latter concerns the contractual phase and, particularly, contracts that contain terms that directly or indirectly limit (or attempt to limit) the rights of the counterparty (such as a consumer) protected under contract law, establishing a significant imbalance, to the consumer's detriment, between the rights and obligations of the contracting parties in opposition to the principle of good faith. These terms are considered unfair and thus not binding.

Unfair commercial practice concerns a different moment of the relationship between parties; it involves the pre-contractual phase during which the trader tries to persuade the consumer in making a certain transactional choice.

On the contrary, it has been noted, with regard to European Union Law, that the unfair terms Directive not only contains provisions relevant to contract law, but it also introduces provisions relevant to unfair commercial practices law.[7]

It is worth recalling the norm that is contained in Article 7 of Directive 93/13/CE on unfair terms, according to which Member States were required to adopt adequate and effective means to prevent the 'use' or 'continued use' of unfair contractual terms by traders. It is evident that the conduct of using unfair terms is an unfair commercial practice according to the definition provided by Directive 2005/29/CE on unfair commercial practice. In fact, Article 5 of this Directive states that "A commercial practice shall be unfair if it is contrary to the requirements of professional diligence..." and, according to Article 2, "professional diligence means the standard of special skill and care which a trader may reasonably be expected to exercise towards consumers, commensurate with honest market practice and/or the general principle of good faith in the trader's field of activity".

Another case of intersection between Unfair Terms and Unfair Practice is the use of unfair, and thus invalid, terms. In fact, the average consumer will not consider whether a clause is binding or not and he/she could have held those terms that are invalid because of their unfairness as part of the contract as well. Therefore, the use of invalid clauses may distort consumers' awareness of their contractual rights or duties and thus their economic behaviour. "The use of invalid terms should also be deemed capable of materially distorting the economic behaviour of the average consumer during the performance of the contract (second element). In this respect, it seems correct to observe that the average consumer, faced with contractual forms drafted by the trader, which do not precisely reflect the legally binding clauses (since they contain some non-binding clauses), would usually be unclear about the parties' rights and obligations arising under the contract, and would normally believe himself to be bound by all clauses. For the same reason, the trader would in practice be able to enforce the rights and powers literally provided in his favour by the unfair contract terms, even if such terms are legally non-binding and in principle unenforceable, thus profiting from the ignorance of the average consumer about the precise legal value (i.e. the non-binding character) of those terms.

---

[7] Orlando (2011), p. 25 ss.

The use of invalid terms is therefore capable in the above circumstances of materially distorting the economic behaviour of the average consumer in relation to the exercise of his 'contractual rights".[8]

Moreover, according to Directive 93/13/CE, terms that are not drafted in plain and intelligible language (non-transparent terms) shall be held as unfair.

According to article 5, "In the case of contracts where all or certain terms offered to the consumer are in writing, these terms must always be drafted in plain, intelligible language. Where there is doubt about the meaning of a term, the interpretation most favourable to the consumer shall prevail". At the same time, lack of transparency can mislead consumer behaviour. Therefore, the use of terms defining the services or goods, or the price or remuneration under the contract not drafted in plain and intelligible language should also be considered as an unfair commercial practice, and particularly a misleading omission pursuant to Article 7 of 2005/29/CE Directive. See article 7 Directive 29/2005/EC on Misleading omissions: "1. A commercial practice shall be regarded as misleading if, in its factual context, taking account of all its features and circumstances and the limitations of the communication medium, it omits material information that the average consumer needs, according to the context, to take an informed transactional decision and thereby causes or is likely to cause the average consumer to take a transactional decision that he would not have taken otherwise.

2. It shall also be regarded as a misleading omission when, taking account of the matters described in paragraph 1, a trader hides or provides in an unclear, unintelligible, ambiguous or untimely manner such material information as referred to in that paragraph or fails to identify the commercial intent of the commercial practice if not already apparent from the context, and where, in either case, this causes or is likely to cause the average consumer to take a transactional decision that he would not have taken otherwise".

As a result of the above considerations, we can say that there is no strict distinction between the rules governing the contractual phase and the rules governing the pre-contractual phase of private relationships. Moreover, it can be misleading to lose sight of the common purpose of consumer protection laws: consumer awareness and freedom of transactional choices.

10.2.4 Some Cases

Let us take a look at some cases regarding unfair commercial practice in B2C relationships to better understand the connection between fairness in B2C contracts and fair completion.

The first one involves a decision on 28.1.2001 held by the President of the Polish Office for Competition and Consumer Protection.

---

[8] Ibidem, p. 30.

10.2 Best Commercial Practices

The decision concerns the use of the term "hotel".

Mrs. Małgorzata Pokrzywnicka conducts commercial activities under the name "Biuro Usług Turystycznych POK-TURIST" and she exploits a hotel-like place of residence.

She recommended the residence through advertisements that created the impression that this residence was a hotel within the four-star category. This qualification was made by using a golden plate placed on the building's façade, through website advertisements, and in distributed leaflets.

In reality, she was not authorized to use the word "hotel" for the place where she provided the accommodation services, and she was well aware of this violation as she had already been held liable by the criminal courts for this activity.

The President ruled that the defendant breached the prohibition on unfair commercial practices by using the word "hotel" for a place of residence that had not been approved as such. In particular, the President assessed that the defendant violated Art. 5 sec. 1 and 2 in connection with Art. 4 sec. 1 and 2 of the Polish Unfair Commercial Practices Act, through which the European Directive 2005/29/CE has been implemented. Article 5(1) of Unfair commercial practices Polish Act says that "A commercial practice shall be regarded as misleading if it in any way causes, or is likely to cause, the average consumer to take a transactional decision that (s)he would not have taken otherwise.

2. In particular, the following practices may be misleading:

(1) disseminating untrue information;
(2) disseminating true information in a way that may mislead;
(3) product launch activities which may be misleading in terms of the products or their packaging, trademarks, trade names or other designations individualising the business or its products, in particular comparative advertising within the meaning of Article 16(3) of the Action to Combat Unfair Competition Act of 16 April 1993 (Journal of Laws 2003/153, item 1503, as amended)".

The President assessed that the fact that a particular place has been qualified as a hotel, within the meaning of the relevant law provisions, guarantees that it is complaint with standards relating to the safety and quality of the services provided to the consumers, amongst others. The qualification is an objective indication for the consumer of what type of services and of what quality may be obtained in a particular place.

The prices offered in the defendant's place of residence were lower than those in other hotels. Hence, the consumer may get the impression that the prices offered by the defendant are attractive in relation to the quality of the services offered if the residence had actually been a four-star hotel.

Since the word "hotel" was used unlawfully, the consumers had a false impression regarding the type of transaction into which they entered.

As a result of the above assessment, the President decided that using the word "hotel" with regard to a place of residence which has not been duly recognized as a hotel in accordance with applicable national legislation, constitutes an unfair commercial practice as it deceives the average consumer and it is likely to affect consumer behavior.

The President ordered the defendant to publish the information about the decision and its content in a local newspaper. No financial penalty was imposed.

Secondly, we can take a look at Case C 435/11 CHS Tour Services GmbH v. Team4 Travel GmbH and the opinion written by NILS WAHL (Advocate General of European Court of Justice) on June 13th, 2013.

This case concerns a B2B relationship, but it has an impact on the distortion of consumer behavior and involves the application of Directive 2005/29/CE.

The Oberster Gerichtshof (Supreme Court of Austria) requested guidance from the European Court of Justice on the following issue: "if a commercial practice turns out to be misleading consumers, does it matter whether the trader has done what he/she could to prevent that from happening?" The Court has only had the opportunity to deal with this issue in an indirect manner. In Case C 453/10 Pereničová and Perenič [2012] ECR I 0000, it held—in response to a question on the impact that a finding of unfair commercial practice would have on the assessment of the fairness and validity of a contractual term under Council Directive 93/13/EEC of 5 April 1993 on unfair terms in consumer contracts (OJ 1993 L 95, p. 29)—that the practice in question was misleading under Article 6 of the Directive, and did not go on to undertake an analysis as to whether there was also a breach of the duty of professional diligence (see paragraphs 40, 41 and 43, and point 2 of the operative part of that judgment). However, Advocate General Trstenjak has expressed such a view on numerous occasions (see her Opinions in VTB-VAB and Galatea, points 78 and 79; in Plus Warenhandelsgesellschaft, points 73 and 74; in Mediaprint Zeitungs- und Zeitschriftenverlag, points 65 and 66; and in Pereničová and Perenič, points 104 to 107).

As we have seen, Article 5 of Directive 2005/29/EC reads:

1. Unfair commercial practices shall be prohibited.

2. A commercial practice shall be unfair if:

(a) it is contrary to the requirements of professional diligence, and (b) it materially distorts or is likely to materially distort the economic behavior with regard to the product of the average consumer whom it reaches or to whom it is addressed, or of the average member of the group when a commercial practice is directed to a particular group of consumers.

In particular, commercial practices shall be unfair which:

(a) are misleading as set out in Articles 6 and 7, or (b) are aggressive as set out in Articles 8 and 9.

Moreover, Annex I contains the list of those commercial practices which shall in all circumstances be regarded as unfair. The same single list shall apply in all Member States and may only be modified by revision of this Directive.

According to Articles 6 and 7 of the Directive, a commercial practice shall be regarded as misleading if it contains false information and is therefore untruthful or in any way, including its overall presentation, deceives or is likely to deceive the average consumer, even if the information is factually correct, in relation to one or

10.2 Best Commercial Practices

more certain elements (and particularly of the main characteristics of the product, such as its availability), and in either case causes or is likely to cause him to take a transactional decision that he/she would not have taken otherwise.

The case concerns two Austrian travel agents, CHS Tour Services GmbH ('CHS') and Team4Travel GmbH ('Team4Travel'), who organise and provide skiing courses and winter holidays in Austria for groups of schoolchildren from the United Kingdom.

In Team4Travel's English sales brochure, a symbol indicating 'exclusive' was placed next to a certain number of the listed accommodation establishments. According to the brochure, the term 'exclusive' is to be understood as meaning 'accomodation that is exclusively available to [Team4Travel] parties at half term or half term and Easter or throughout the whole winter season'. The Austrian court explains that the use of that expression meant that the accommodation establishment had a fixed contractual relationship with Team4Travel and that other tour operators would not be in a position to provide accommodation at that establishment on specified dates. According to the observations submitted by CHS, Team4Travel's price list also stated that '[a]ll prices highlighted...indicate that [Team4Travel] holds all beds exclusively on this date'.

For unspecified dates in the reference order covering certain periods in 2012, Team4Travel concluded contracts for bed quotas with several accommodation providers. Those contracts contained a clause that stated that the specified bedroom quotas would be kept available without restriction for Team4Travel and that the provider could not repudiate that stipulation without Team4Travel's written consent. A booking would become final 28 days before the corresponding arrival date. In order to secure exclusivity, Team4Travel stipulated cancellation rights with the accommodation provider, as well as a contractual penalty.

However, it emerged that, in spite of the abovementioned contracts, CHS reserved bed quotas in the same accommodation establishments as Team4Travel for overlapping booking periods. The Austrian court mentions, moreover, that the reservations were made after Team4Travel had concluded the exclusive contracts. Consequently, the accommodation providers were in breach of their contractual obligations towards Team4Travel.

The accommodation providers informed Team4Travel that no reservations had yet been made by other tour operators. Furthermore, the director of Team4Travel took care to ensure that, because of the lack of available accommodation, no other tour operators would be able to find room in the hotels. She was not aware of the existence of other reservations until legal proceedings were initiated.

As CHS nevertheless also managed to book all or part of the available accommodation for the period of time during which the Team4Travel "exclusivity" operated, it considered the declarations on exclusivity to be incorrect and to constitute an unfair commercial practice. CHS therefore applied for an injunction before the Landesgericht Innsbruck (Innsbruck Regional Court) (Austria) to prevent Team4Travel from stating that Team4Travel offered specific accommodation for a particular arrival date on an exclusive basis.

The Landesgericht Innsbruck refused to grant an injunction, as it held the exclusivity claim to be correct in view of the irrevocable reservation contracts concluded beforehand by Team4Travel.

The Oberlandesgericht Innsbruck (Innsbruck Higher Regional Court of Austria) upheld the decision given at first instance on the grounds that Team4Travel had complied with the requirements of professional diligence and could legitimately expect that its co-contractors would respect their contractual obligations.

CHS subsequently lodged an appeal on a point of law before the Oberster Gerichtshof.

The referring court considers the outcome of the proceedings to depend on the correct interpretation of Article 5(2) of the Directive. The Oberster Gerichtshof submitted two different interpretations for consideration by the European Court of Justice:

1. the effect of the reference to misleading or aggressive practices in Article 5(4) of the Directive, as set out in Articles 6 to 9, is that such practices are, per se, inconsistent with the duty of professional diligence under Article 5(2). In fact, Articles 6 to 9 do not mention the duty of professional diligence under Article 5 (2)(a);
2. if the reference to the distortion of a consumer's economic behavior in Article 5 (2)(b) of the Directive were to be understood as being clarified by the more specific provisions in Articles 6 to 9, Article 5(2)(a) would still be applicable. As a consequence, a misleading practice under Article 6 would require, in addition, a breach of the duty of professional diligence under Article 5(2)(a).

The Advocate General took position on the Relevance of the duty of professional diligence for the concept of 'misleading commercial practice'.

As per the structure of the Directive, it is clear that the notion of 'unfair commercial practices', which are prohibited under Article 5(1), covers three categories of conduct: (i) practices which fulfill the two cumulative requirements set out in Article 5(2); (ii) pursuant to Article 5(4), misleading or aggressive practices as in Articles 6 to 9; and (iii) pursuant to Article 5(5), the practices referred to in Annex I of the Directive (the so-called blacklist) which are automatically considered to be unfair, without any need for an individual appraisal of all the relevant circumstances.

As the Advocate General says, Article 5(4) of the Directive textually clarifies this structure. In accordance with that provision, commercial practices which are misleading (Articles 6 and 7) or aggressive (Articles 8 and 9) are, 'in particular', unfair. The statement 'in particular' shows not only that misleading and aggressive practices are specific sub-categories of unfair commercial practices but, more importantly, that they also constitute unfair commercial practices. Thus, on the basis of a structural and literal analysis, he/she doesn't share the view that Articles 6 and 7 (or Articles 8 and 9) of the Directive merely provide specific examples of distortion of a consumer's economic behavior, with the effect that Article 5(2)(a) remains applicable, as would follow from the second interpretation proposed by the national court.

The same conclusion is confirmed by examining the background and the objective of the Directive. In particular, the observations contained in the Commission

10.2 Best Commercial Practices

proposal regarding misleading and aggressive commercial practices unequivocally point out that the criterion relating to professional diligence under Article 5(2) (a) of the Directive does not play a separate role.

In light of the foregoing considerations, the Advocate General concludes, "the fact that a trader may have complied with the duty of professional diligence under Article 5(2) (a) of the Directive is of no significance in the presence of misleading (or aggressive) commercial practices. CHS and the Austrian, German, Hungarian, Swedish and UK Governments all share this view, as does the Commission; moreover, that view is also consistent with the first interpretation proffered by the national court."

Thus, the Advocate General proposes that the European Court of Justice answer the Oberster Gerichtshof (Austria) as follows:

> Article 5 of Directive 2005/29/EC of the European Parliament and of the Council of 11 May 2005 concerning unfair business-to-consumer commercial practices in the internal market and amending Council Directive 84/450/EEC, Directives 97/7/EC, 98/27/EC and 2002/65/EC and Regulation (EC) No 2006/2004 is to be interpreted as meaning that, where a commercial practice falls within the scope of Article 5(4) of that Directive, it is of no relevance whether the criteria under Article 5(2) a and or Article 5(2)b are also fulfilled.

The CJCE in the judgment 13 september 2013 agreed with such interpretation. In short terms, the issue was the following: in case brochure containing false information, is it possible for a trader to show that the requirements of professional diligence have been complied with in order to prevent a commercial practice from being categorised as 'unfair'?

The CJCE concludes that the Directive would appear to favour a 'top-down approach', that is to say, an assessment which begins with the blacklist of commercial practices, followed by the provisions on misleading or aggressive practices, and ending with the general clause. If one of the first steps indicates the existence of an unfair commercial practice, there will be no need to proceed to the next step, as the contested practice would in any event have to be regarded as unfair. So where a commercial practice falls within the black list, it is of no relevance whether the criteria under Article 5, 2 a) (the practice is contrary to the requirements of professional diligence) and/or Article 5, 2, b) (the practice materially distorts or is likely to materially distort the economic behaviour) are also fulfilled.

The third case concerns an Italian antitrust authority decision.

Some airlines have been sanctioned for unfair commercial practices towards consumers and, in particular, for deceit, weak transparency, inadequacy and even the outright lack of information about ticket prices, which in some cases lack any indication of various predictable and unavoidable fees that are not added in until the moment of credit card payment.

Investigations were launched in response to numerous complaints received from consumers and consumer organisations.

The specific unfair practices are the following:

1. Deceptive advertising distributed in print and via Internet to promote offers that users found to be in fact "unobtainable";

2. Air fares lacking any indication of various add-on fees (e.g., online check-in fees, credit card fees and the VAT applied to national flights) that are added in automatically during the online booking process to result in significantly higher ticket prices;
3. Difficulty or outright impossibility of receiving post-sale assistance for ticket refunds (full or partial) in case of flight abandonment, whether for reasons attributable to the airline or by passenger choice, and specifically the obligation of using a toll number or paying high fees;
4. Publication of the general terms and conditions of transport and general information for Italian consumers in the English language;
5. Unjustified additional charges for making changes in dates, times, passenger names or routes, or reissuing boarding cards at the airport.

The cases considered point out some assessments.

Firstly, it is not possible to establish sector-specific rules by dividing them in rules for B2C relationships and rules for B2B relationships. Unfairness respect to consumers can distort competition and unfair competition can damage consumers interests. Both businesses and consumers are part of the market and their fair interplay aims at reaching common goals in terms of competitiveness, increase of production, and market evolution.

By dividing these areas of interests, we risk losing sight of the purpose of market regulation. It is also important to remember that fair trade does not only mean more competition and production but also market evolution in terms of economic, ecological, and social sustainability.

10.2.5 Environmental Claims and Green Claims

Another important case study on the application of the Directive 29/2005 involves the problem regards environmental claims, which are assertions made by firms about the environmentally beneficial qualities or characteristics of their goods and services. They can refer to the manner in which products are produced, packaged, distributed, used, consumed and/or disposed of. In March 2014, the European Commission published the report "From the commission to the European parliament, the council and the European economic and social committee".

The report also focuses on recent commercial practices, the so-called "environmental claims". The expression 'environmental claims' or 'green claims' refers to the practice of suggesting or otherwise creating the impression that a product or a service is environmentally friendly or is less damaging to the environment than competing goods or services.

The growing use of environmental claims as a marketing and advertising tool is strictly related to the increase in environmental concerns among the population.

Some aspects of the issue are covered by specific EU legislation: Council Regulation (EC) No 834/2007 of June 28th, 2007 on organic production and the

10.2 Best Commercial Practices

labelling of organic products, and repealing Regulation (EEC) No 2092/91. Other examples of specific legislation are Directive 2010/30/EU of the European Parliament and of the Council of May 19th, 2010 on the indication, by labelling and standard product information, of the consumption of energy and other resources by energy-related products; Regulation (EC) No 1222/2009 of the European Parliament and of the Council of November 25th, 2009 on the labelling of tires in terms of fuel efficiency and other essential parameters.

In any case, the Directive UCPD is the main instrument of horizontal legislation for assessing environmental claims.

As the Commission has explained in the Guidance document, the application of the provisions of the Directive to environmental claims can be summarized with regard to two main principles: based on the UCPD Directive's general provisions, traders must, above all, present their green claims in a specific, accurate and unambiguous manner; traders must have scientific evidence to support their claims and be ready to provide it in an understandable way in case the claim is challenged.

In the Guidance on the application/implementation of Directive 2005/29/EC on Unfair Commercial Practices (SEC(2009) 1666, Commission Staff Working Document, December 3rd, 2009) the Commission points out that "The expressions 'environmental claims' or 'green claims' refer to the practice of suggesting or otherwise creating the impression (in the context of a commercial communication, marketing or advertising) that a product or a service, is environmentally friendly (i.e. it has a positive impact on the environment) or is less damaging to the environment than competing goods or services". This may be due to, for example, its composition, the way it has been manufactured or produced, the way it can be disposed of and the reduction in energy or pollution which can be expected from its use. When such claims are not true or cannot be verified this practice can be described as "green washing".

Consumers may weigh up environmental considerations when purchasing products. Increasingly, in planning their advertising and marketing campaigns, traders are taking these factors into account and environmental claims have become a powerful marketing tool. However, in order for environmental claims to be informative for consumers and to be effective in promoting goods and services with lower environmental impacts, it is imperative that they are clear, truthful, accurate and not misleading. They must also not emphasize one environmental issue and hide any trade-offs or negative impacts on the environment. The use of truthful environmental claims is also important in order to protect traders who make genuine claims from unfair competition from those traders who make unfounded environmental claims.

There is no EU legislation that specifically harmonizes environmental marketing. Environmental claims are partly covered by specific community legislation that regulates the environmental performance of a category of products and prohibits the misleading use of the claim, logo or label used in reference to this specific legislation. Beyond those aspects covered by specific EU legislation, the general provisions of the Directive are to be used when assessing environmental claims and establishing whether a claim is misleading either in its content or in the way it is presented to consumers.

This was highlighted when, on December 4th, 2008, the Environment Council adopted conclusions on the Sustainable Consumption and Production and Sustainable Industrial Policy Action Plan. Under point 18 of the conclusions, the Council "INVITES the Member States to fully implement the Directive on unfair commercial practices with regard to environmental claims; INVITES the Commission to include environmental claims in any future guidelines on the Directive on unfair commercial practices".

So, in conclusion, only environmental claims that can be verified are legal, if not they can be considered as unfair commercial practices when they can influence the behaviour of consumers.

Considering the concept of unfair practices outlined so far, it is important to understand when the use of certain declarations relating to the sustainability of the tourist offer or the use of distinctive signs or brands that refer to the ecology or sustainability of one's business can be considered to be an incorrect commercial practice or not.

Of course, claims directly related to quantitative instruments can be considered measurable. It is possible to use sustainability measurement, which is the quantitative basis for informed management according to sustainability principles. The metrics used for the measurement of sustainability (involving the sustainability of environmental, social and economic domains, both individually and in various combinations) are still evolving: they include indicators, benchmarks, audits, indexes and accounting, as well as assessment, appraisal and other reporting systems. We can recall some of the most well-known and widely used sustainability measures: Triple Bottom Line accounting and estimates of the quality of sustainability governance for individual countries using the Global Green Economy Index (GGEI), the Environmental Sustainability Index and Environmental Performance Index. An alternative approach, used by the United Nations Global Compact Cities Program, and explicitly critical of the triple-bottom-line approach, is Circles of Sustainability.[9]

The principal objectives of sustainability indicators are: to inform public policy-making as part of the process of sustainability governance; to provide information on any aspect of the interplay between the environment and socio-economic activities.

In this part of the book, we point out another possible function of sustainability indicators: to distinguish environmental claims that are verifiable from environmental claims that are not verifiable and that can be considered as unfair commercial practices if they can cause the average consumer to take a transactional decision that he/she would not have taken otherwise. In these terms, we can say that, since environmental claims are being shown to influence consumer behavior in general, we can presume that an environmental claim that is not verifiable is misleading and it can therefore be considered to be a form of unfair commercial practice.[10]

---

[9] Hák et al. (2007); Bell and Morse (2008) 2nd ed.; Singh et al. (2012), pp. 281–299.

[10] Orazi and Chan (2020), pp. 107–123.

10.2 Best Commercial Practices

Additionally, the European Union does not see internal markets only as places where economic interests are sole and dominant.

According to Article 2 of the Lisbon Treaty amending the European Union Treaty and the European Community Treaty, signed in Lisbon, on December 13th, 2007: "The Union shall establish an internal market. It shall work for the sustainable development of Europe based on balanced economic growth and price stability, a highly competitive social market economy, aiming at full employment and social progress, and a high level of protection and improvement of the quality of the environment. It shall promote scientific and technological advance."

The subject considered in this last paragraph concerns a matter that is mainly regulated by national law and controlled by national public authority while, as we have seen in the introduction, the principal sources of tourism law are international law, private autonomy and customary law. So, we can say that tourism law, as well as tourism itself, is mainly a product of society. In any case, private autonomy and customary law are not to be left to bear the decisions of individuals and organisations, but they need to conform to some international rights and principles: human rights protection, principles of environmental protection (particularly eco-sustainability), and the principle of hospitality.

Nevertheless, national law regulates some aspects of tourism (like authorization procedures, permits and licenses, etc.). National law also regulates consumer protection regarding contract law (travel packages, time shares, unfair commercial practices, unfair terms, etc.).

The problem arises from the fact that B2C tourism contracts are mostly international. Generally speaking, "with the opening of markets to foreign products and services, with increasing economic integration, regionalization of trade, transportation facilities, mass tourism, growing telecommunications, computer network connections, and electronic commerce, there is no way to deny that consumption already crosses national borders. Foreign goods are on supermarket shelves, services are offered by providers with overseas telemarketing headquarters, using television, the radio, the Internet, and mass advertising in the day-to-day lives of most citizens in the cities of our regional metropolises. One needs no longer travel to be an active consumer, a tourist consumer. One needs no longer go anywhere to be a consumer who contracts internationally or deals with suppliers in other countries. The very methods of production and assembly are now international. International consumer contacts and tourism have become activities of the masses".[11] Thus, it is right to say, consuming internationally is typical of the present time.

The individuation of the national law applicable in international contracts depends on the rule of international private law, which is a set of procedural norms that determine which legal systems and which jurisdictions apply to a given dispute. These rules usually apply when a legal dispute has a "foreign" element, such as in the case of a contract agreed by parties from different jurisdictions.[12]

---

[11] Lima Marques (2001).

[12] Reich (2001), p. 163.

140   10   Unfair Commercial Practices

The determination of the applicable national law it is not a satisfactory solution. The presence of different national laws can cause disparities and uncertainty and create many barriers affecting businesses and consumers, increasing business costs when exercising market freedoms, in particular when businesses wish to engage in cross border marketing, advertising campaigns and sales promotions. Such barriers also make consumers uncertain of their rights and undermine their confidence in the market.

Applying one national legal system instead of another may never be a satisfactory approach. Applying a law conceived within international realities involved in the actual situation better protects the parties' interests. At the European law level, the solution to this problem lies in the harmonization process through European Directives.[13] At the international level, The Hague conference on Private International Law, which is a treaty organisation, oversees conventions designed to develop a uniform system.

As Jan Kropoller stated in 1978, in order to offer effective and adequate protection to the weaker party through Private International Law, this system of norms must evolve towards a set of rules "imbued with social values".[14]

As we have seen, this goal can be achieved entirely just by having interpreters participating actively: both Courts and Legal Scholars.

References

Bell, S., & Morse, S. (2008). *Sustainability indicators. Measuring the immeasurable?* (2nd ed.). Routledge.

Colley, R. H. (1961). *Defining advertising goals for measured advertising results.* Association of National Advertisers.

De Leon Arce, A. (2007). *Conflict law and the harmonization of substantive private law in the European Union. Liber Amicorum Guido Alpa, private law beyond the national systems.* British Institute of International and Comparative Law.

Hák, T., Moldan, B., & Lyon, A. (Eds.). (2007). *Sustainability indicators: A scientific assessment.* Island Press.

Holloway, J. C., & Plant, R. V. (1992). *Marketing for tourism* (2nd ed.). Longman.

Howells, G., Micklitz, H. W., & Wilhelmsson, T. (Eds.). (2006). *European fair trading law. The unfair commercial practices directive.* Ashgate.

Kropholler, J. (1978). Das kollisionsrechtliche System des Schutzes der schwächeren Vertragspartei. *Rabels Zeitschrift, 47,* 634.

Marques, C. L. (2001). *Insufficient Consumer Protection in the Provisions of Private International Law – The Need for an Inter-American Convention (CIDIP) on the Law Applicable to Certain Contracts and Consumer Relations.* http://www.oas.org

Micklitz, H. W. (2009). Unfair commercial practices and misleading advertising. In H. W. Micklitz, N. Reich, & P. Rott (Eds.), *Understanding EU consumer law.* Intersentia.

---

[13] De Leon Arce (2007); Pongelli (2013), p. 24.

[14] Kropholler (1978), p. 634.

References

Micklitz, H. W. (2010). Unfair commercial practices and European private law. In C. Twigg-Flesner (Ed.), *The Cambridge companion to European Union private law* (p. 229). Cambridge University Press.

Middleton, T. C., Fyall, A., & Morgan, M. (2009). *Marketing in travel and tourism* (4th ed., p. 242). Butterworth-Heinemann.

Moutinho, L. (2011). *Strategic management in tourism* (p. 2). Wallingford, Oxfordshire.

Orazi, D. C., & Chan, E. Y. (2020). They did not walk the green talk!: How information specificity influences consumer evaluations of disconfirmed environmental claims. *Journal of Business Ethics, 163*, 107.

Orlando, S. (2011). The use of unfair contractual terms as an unfair commercial practice. *European Review of Contract Law, 7*, 25.

Pongelli, G. (2013). The proposal for a regulation on a common European sales law (CESL) and its gradual evolution. *Comparative Law Review, 4*, 24.

Reich, N. (2001). Consumerism and citizenship in the information society-the case of electronic contracting. In T. Wilhelsson (Ed.), *Consumer law in the information society* (p. 163). Elgar.

Singh, R. K., Murty, H. R., Gupta, S. K., & Dikshit, A. K. (2012). An overview of sustainability assessment methodologies. *Ecological Indicators, 15*, 281.

Weatherill, S., & Bernitz, U. (Eds.). (2007). *The Regulation of Unfair Commercial Practices under EC Directive 2005/29/CE. New Rules and New Techniques*. Hart.

Part III
Tourism Industry Business Contracts and Sustainability Policies

Chapter 11
Tourism Industry Business Contracts

Contents

11.1	Tourism Industry Business Contracts 145
	11.1.1 B2B Contracts in Tourism Market 145
	11.1.2 Long Term Contracts and Resilience Clauses 147
	11.1.3 Long Term Contracts and Business Interruption 149
11.2	Business Contract Law and Competition Law 151
	11.2.1 Unfair Competition, Unfair Terms in Case of B2B Contracts 151
	11.2.2 Some Cases 153
References 156

11.1 Tourism Industry Business Contracts

11.1.1 B2B Contracts in Tourism Market

Business contracts play an essential role in building relationships between companies and business partners. Contracts specify the terms of agreements, the services or products to be exchanged, and any deadlines associated with the partnership.

It is worth examining contracts of the so-called "passive cycle" of the company (i.e., supply contracts, service contracts, tender contracts), distribution agreements and the organization of competitive management structure contracts (i.e., management contracts and franchising contracts) within the tourism industry.

These contracts are typically B2B contracts that can range from a simple one-page purchase order for the sale of goods useful for tourism activity, to an extremely complex hundred-page document for a trade level agreement between international companies such as an international franchising contract.

A B2B contract is commonly characterized by the following phases:

Pre-contractual phase: one party identifies the products or services and possible sources necessary for the commercial activity.

Contractual phase: the creation of a formal relationship between parties, covering contract negotiations and validation operations;

© The Author(s), under exclusive license to Springer Nature Switzerland AG 2021
S. Landini, *Sustainable Tourism Contracts*,
https://doi.org/10.1007/978-3-030-83140-0_11

Logistics phase: this phase is important for supply contracts in particular, and it consists of placing purchase orders and delivering goods and services;

Settlement phase: invoicing, payment authorization and payment, execution of contractual obligations;

Post-processing phase: gathering information for management reports, i.e., statistical research.

During the pre-contractual phase, there usually is a preliminary agreement, letters of intent, and agreement in principle. This agreement is called "umbrella agreement". "Umbrella agreements between parties are private arrangements that provide a framework of clauses which regulate future contracts. Generally, they are not concerned with immediate contractual decisions but rather they explicitly spell out the principles that guide future contractual decisions. There are two "tests" that we can use in order decide whether a private arrangement is an "umbrella agreement" or not. The first test concerns the "selection processes". Umbrella agreements are arrangements that do not predetermine future selection processes".[1]

Also, according to Article 2.1 of the UNIDROIT principle [principles of international commercial contracts], a contract may be considered as concluded either by the acceptance of an offer or by the conduct of the parties that is sufficient to show agreement.

UNIDROIT Principles (the Principles) were published in 1994 and they were considered to be "soft law" and hence not binding on the courts. Indeed, the intention of the UNIDROIT Working Groups was to develop a set of norms suited to accommodate the needs of the international commercial community.[2]

When negotiating complex and high-value transactions, negotiations generally proceed in stages and the agreement is reached only step by step, as the parties exchange writings known by a variety of names, such as "letters of intent", "agreements in principle", "memoranda of understanding", "heads of agreement" etc... While the preliminary writings do not represent the final agreement, their precise nature and legal effects remain unclear.

What if, for instance, the parties sign an informal "Preliminary agreement", containing the terms of the agreement so far reached, during the negotiations, and declare their intention to sign a definitive contract at a later stage, by including expressions such as "Subject to contract" or "Formal agreement to follow"?

What is the nature and the legal effects of such an agreement? A general principle of contract law, provided in the UNIDROIT principle as well (Article 2.1.15), is the parties' duty to negotiate in good faith. A party which negotiates or breaks off negotiations in bad faith is liable for the losses caused to the other party, who may recover the expenses incurred in the negotiations and may also be compensated for the lost opportunity to conclude another contract with a third party.

---

[1] Mouza and Furmston (2008), pp. 37–50.

[2] Lando (2003), p. 123.

11.1.2 Long Term Contracts and Resilience Clauses

The contractual phase is characterized by clauses that govern the life of the contractual relationship. B2B contracts are usually long-term contracts, also known as "relational contracts". The term 'relational contracts' signifies a contract based upon a relationship of trust between parties and an on-going duty to cooperate in order to allow each party to perform its obligations properly.[3]

As some authors say "Firms are riddled with relational contracts: informal agreements and unwritten codes of conduct that powerfully affect the behaviors of individuals within firms. There are often informal quid pro quos between co-workers, as well as unwritten understandings between bosses and subordinates about task-assignment, promotion, and termination decisions. Even ostensibly formal processes such as compensation, transfer pricing, internal auditing, and capital budgeting often cannot be understood without consideration of their associated informal agreements. Business dealings are also riddled with relational contracts. Supply chains often involve long-run, hand-in-glove supplier relationships through which the parties reach accommodations when unforeseen or uncontracted-for events occur. Similar relationships also exist horizontally, as in the networks of firms in the fashion industry or the diamond trade, and in strategic alliances, joint ventures, and business groups. Whether vertical or horizontal, these relational contracts influence the behaviours of firms in their dealings with other firms".[4]

All explicit contractual terms are just an outline as there are implicit terms and understandings.

As a consequence, these contracts are subject not only to the usual risks of a breach by one of the parties, or of supervening events making performance impossible or excessively more onerous, but also to the risk of an irreparable breakdown of the parties' mutual trust and confidence, making the continuation of their relationship unsustainable. In practice, these contracts frequently include so-called termination clauses that define the contingencies in which the contract may be terminated and specify how the right to terminate may be exercised: by mere notice to the other party or by a court decision; whether termination takes effect immediately or only after a certain period of time; whether the terminating party or the other party is entitled to damages, etc.

We can recall the application of the clause of force majeure that in short term essentially frees both parties from liability or obligation when an extraordinary event or circumstance beyond the control of the parties (e.g. acts of God like a Pandemic, war). The term "force majeure" comes from French but with regard to the present meaning it is important to remember the German concept of "höhere Gewalt". According to German jurisprudence, there is a höhere Gewalt if the event causing the damage has an external effect and the harm caused cannot be averted or rendered harmless by the extremely reasonable care. However, it must be noted that the

---

[3]McNeil (1978), p. 854.

[4]Baker et al. (2001), p. 1.

French force majeure is not identical with the German höhere Gewalt. Andreas Blaschczok Gefährdungshaftung und Risikozuweisung [1998 Heymanns]; Nils Jansen Die Struktur des Haftungsrechts [Mohr Siebeck 2003]. See also: BGH X ZR 146/11; LG Frankfurt a. M., lexetius.com/2012, 4178. See in common law, Carslogie steamship Co Ltd vs. Royal Norwegian Government [1952] AC 292. The complaint's vessel was damaged by a collision with the defendant. After the collision the complaint repaired the vessel that was certified to sail for NY. On the way the vessel suffered other damage from stormy weather at sea. The Court held that the defendant from the collision, not for further damage sustained by the natural events at the sea.

In the settlement phase, there are payment clauses or a separate payment agreement, which are written agreements, commonly called promissory notes, between a promisor and a payee. The promisor is the party paying a specific amount of money to another party known as the payee. The payment agreements or clauses usually include information about terms and means of payment, repayment, and any penalties for defaulting on the agreement.

In commercial agreements, parties may agree that, should one party fail to perform in accordance with the terms of the agreement, the other party should be entitled to receive a specified penalty or measure of damages. A stipulation of this nature in an agreement is commonly known as a penalty clause. The agreement usually states that damages are claimable in addition to the penalty where the penalty is insufficient to compensate for the damages suffered by the non-breaching party.[5]

Another important clause that is usually included in this part of the contract is the arbitration or multi step clause.

In case of arbitration clauses, the parties agree not to sue each other, and instead will resolve their disputes through arbitration. Arbitration is a process that allows a third-party arbitrator to help with discussions between the parties. It is increasingly common for parties who agree to include an arbitration clause in a contract to establish an obligation to negotiate before commencing arbitration proceedings. In essence, if a party wishes to start arbitration proceedings, it must first negotiate with the other party in order to try to reach an amicable solution to the dispute. It is clear that the time, expenses and reputational burdens associated with arbitration far exceed the costs of negotiation. These clauses are referred to as "escalation clauses," "multi-tier clauses," or "multi-step alternative dispute resolution clauses.".[6]

In general, essential elements of the contract will appear in a business contract as clauses covering:

- the description of the parties involved, including: names, addresses, roles etc.;
- the definition and interpretation of terms used in the contract;
- in the case of an international contract, the law and the jurisdiction under which the validity, correctness, and enforcement of the contract will operate;

---

[5]Dimatteo (2001), p. 633.
[6]Berger (2006), p. 5.

- the duration and the territory of the contract, which determines the times and places in which the contract is in force;
- the nature of obligations fees, services rendered, goods exchanged, rights granted, etc. This part includes terms and conditions for invoicing and payment such as warranties, delivery, liability, rejection, termination and accounting provisions.

The typical contract model is composed as follows:

- a preamble that outlines the parties involved in the contract and the nature of the consideration;
- a list of contract clauses, organized in logical groups (such as duration, terms of payment etc.);
- an approval section that enumerates whom from each party approved the contract.

In some business environments, it would be very difficult and costly if the terms of every contract had to be newly settled for each transaction. A significant amount can be saved by using general standard form contracts for newly established contract agreements. As we have previously mentioned, regarding consumer contracts, one party can dictate the terms of such standard contracts.

11.1.3 Long Term Contracts and Business Interruption

The 2020 pandemic situation put in evidence the importance to provide for clauses and conventional tools to face occurrences that can cause business interruption and the resulting losses. Let's think to the hotel lease contract and the problem for the lessee to pay the price in case of business interruption. Let's think to the difficulty to respect the terms of the agreements of franchising contracts or management contracts due to the business interruption losses. We've already considered how the pandemic changed the travel packages. Now we can consider how pandemic changed the terms of B2B contracts in order to permit their socio-economic sustainability in the long duration of the bargain.

A possible solution can be found in the renegotiation clause that can benefit both parties in its application. It takes into account the fact that things often change over the life of a contract and in the event that the contract proves to be uneconomical for one of the parties, this clause formalizes the process by which parties can come to the table to create a more equitable situation. The following is a sample of renegotiation clause: "In the event, and not more than once during any twelve (12) month period, that company believes that the compensation or requirements of the agreement no longer represents an appropriate cost for the services rendered or the scope of services, company may request in writing a meeting to be held within 30 days of the request to enter into good faith negotiations to resolve such beliefs. In the event that these negotiations do not result in a mutually agreeable resolution within 90 days of the counterparty receipt of a written request for renegotiations, either party may terminate this agreement for convenience with a 30 day notice".

The force majeure and hardship clauses have been thrown into relief in the wake of the COVID-19 pandemic, where they have provided relief to commercial counterparties unable to perform their contractual obligations because of events outside their control. In March 2020, as a result of the uncertainty created by COVID-19, the ICC (International chamber of commerce) updated the standard form of the Force Majeure and Hardship clauses as following:

1. Force Majeure means the occurrence of an event or circumstance that prevents or impedes a party from performing one or more of its contractual obligations under the contract, if and to the extent that that party proves: [a] that such impediment is beyond its reasonable control; and [b] that it could not reasonably have been foreseen at the time of the conclusion of the contract; and [c] that the effects of the impediment could not reasonably have been avoided or overcome by the affected party.

2. In the absence of proof to the contrary, the following events affecting a party shall be presumed to fulfil conditions (a) and (b) under paragraph 1 of this Clause: (i) war (whether declared or not), hostilities, invasion, act of foreign enemies, extensive military mobilisation; (ii) civil war, riot, rebellion and revolution, military or usurped power, insurrection, act of terrorism, sabotage or piracy;

(iii) currency and trade restriction, embargo, sanction; (iv) act of authority whether lawful or unlawful, compliance with any law or governmental order, expropriation, seizure of works, requisition, nationalisation; (v) plague, epidemic, natural disaster or extreme natural event; (vi) explosion, fire, destruction of equipment, prolonged break-down of transport, telecommunication, information system or energy; (vii) general labour disturbance such as boycott, strike and lock-out, go-slow, occupation of factories and premises.

3. A party successfully invoking this Clause is relieved from its duty to perform its obligations under the contract and from any liability in damages or from any other contractual remedy for breach of contract, from the time at which the impediment causes inability to perform, provided that the notice thereof is given without delay. If notice thereof is not given without delay, the relief is effective from the time at which notice thereof reaches the other party. Where the effect of the impediment or event invoked is temporary, the above consequences shall apply only as long as the impediment invoked impedes performance by the affected party. Where the duration of the impediment invoked has the effect of substantially depriving the contracting parties of what they were reasonably entitled to expect under the contract, either party has the right to terminate the contract by notification within a reasonable period to the other party. Unless otherwise agreed, the parties expressly agree that the contract may be terminated by either party if the duration of the impediment exceeds 120 days.

The ICC standard for Hardship Clause is the following:

1. A party to a contract is bound to perform its contractual duties even if events have rendered performance more onerous than could reasonably have been anticipated at the time of the conclusion of the contract.
2. Notwithstanding paragraph 1 of this Clause, where a party to a contract proves that: (a) the continued performance of its contractual duties has become excessively onerous due to an event beyond its reasonable control which it could not reasonably have been expected to have taken into account at the time of the conclusion of the contract; and that (b) it could not reasonably have avoided or overcome the event or its consequences, the parties are bound, within a reasonable time of the invocation of this Clause, to negotiate alternative contractual terms which reasonably allow to overcome the consequences of the event.

Since one of the most disputed issues is whether it is appropriate to have the contract adapted by a third party (judge, arbitrator) in case the parties are unable to agree on a negotiated solutions, the clause, proposed by ICC, provides two options between which the parties must choose: adaptation or termination. The same issue needs to be faced in case or renegotiation clauses, in case the parties are not able to reach a renegotiation agreement.

Maybe it is possible to consider also the adaptation of the terms of the agreement thanks to artificial intelligence intervention according to predetermined algorithms. This solution can help also to adapt the terms of the agreement to the changing reality. For example, in case of green clauses (see in case of green franchising[7]), to adapt the terms of the contract to new green standards.

Another possible conventional tool could be insurance: business interruption insurance is a type of insurance that covers the loss of income that a business suffers after a disaster causing the interruption of the business and the loss of income. The income loss covered may be due to disaster-related closing of the business facility or due to the redeveloping process after a disaster. It differs from property insurance that covers only the physical damage to the business.

In this case, since the loss is difficult to prove and to quantify, parametric insurance can help. Parametric insurance is an insurance product that offers pre-specified pay-outs linked to a trigger event. Trigger events depend on the nature of the parametric policy and can include environmental triggers, epidemic triggers, etc. This contract is characterised by an index or metric that is intrinsically related to the costs or revenues of the insured. These policies will pay out upon confirmation of the index threshold being overcome.[8]

11.2 Business Contract Law and Competition Law

11.2.1 Unfair Competition, Unfair Terms in Case of B2B Contracts

Also, in the case of B2B contracts, it is possible to have a strong party that determines the content of the contract, and a weak party, who can just "take or leave it". Hesselink takes into account the main possible reasoning for judicial control of unfair contract terms (unequal bargaining, distributive justice, market failure, paternalism, the ethos of the market, comparative law, and the nature of an optional instrument) and concludes that none of them requires a distinction between business to consumer (B2C) and business to business (B2B) contracts.

---

[7] See Sect. 12.3.2.

[8] Turner (2020).

He concludes "None of the policy reasons for the control of standard terms requires a limitation to B2C contracts or a different test for B2B contracts. In this respect, we could speak here of an 'overlapping consensus".[9]

Some national laws provide norms to prevent companies with a dominant position in their economic sector from abusing this position and from distorting competition. This aim requires preventive intervention to investigate company mergers, since these may create dominant positions.

Special dispositions are provided in European Union Law in art. 82 of Eu Treaty. The Court of Justice of the European Community defined the concept of the dominant position in the United Brands case (27/76 of February 1978). A dominant position is "a position of economic strength enjoyed by an undertaking which enables it to prevent effective competition being maintained in the relevant market by giving it the power to behave to an appreciable extent independently of its competitors, customers and ultimately of consumers". The main indicators of dominance are: a large market share; the economic weakness of competitors; the absence of latent competition and control of resources and technology. Moreover, in judgment on the Hoffmann-LA Roche case (85/76 of February 13th, 1979), the Court of Justice of the European Community stated that abusive exploitation of a dominant position is "an objective concept". It is "recourse to methods different from those which condition normal competition in products and services on the basis of the transactions of commercial operators", with the effect of further reducing competition in a market already weakened by the presence of the company concerned.

Art. 82 (now art. 102 of the consolidated version of the treaty on the functioning of the European Union) establishes that "any abuse by one or more undertakings of a dominant position within the internal market or in a substantial part of it shall be prohibited as incompatible with the internal market in so far as it may affect trade between Member States".

Article 82 of the Treaty does not define dominance, but merely gives examples of "abusive practice":

(a) directly or indirectly imposing unfair purchase or selling prices or other unfair trading conditions;
(b) limiting production, markets or technical development to the prejudice of consumers;
(c) applying dissimilar conditions to equivalent transactions with other trading parties, thereby placing them at a competitive disadvantage;
(d) making the conclusion of contracts subject to acceptance by the other parties of supplementary obligations which, by their nature or according to commercial usage, have no connection with the subject of such contracts.

Abusive practices may take various forms. In addition to those mentioned in the Treaty, the Commission and the Court have identified others:

---

[9]Hesselink (2011).

11.2 Business Contract Law and Competition Law   153

- geographical price discrimination,
- loyalty rebates which discourage customers from using competing suppliers,
- low pricing with the object of eliminating a competitor,
- unjustified refusal to supply,
- refusal to grant licenses.

As recently noted, "it is clear that anti-competitive practices within globalized industries have a clear and damaging impact on developed as well as developing countries and that appropriate analysis and instruments should be designed to reduce these practices.

If such damaging anti-competitive activities occur in sectors where operators are global, they are likely to affect negatively the tourism industry since this industry is typically a globalized industry. Here, the global tourism industry should be understood in a broad sense, considering the different stages of its added-value chain. The tourism industry is a major source of the creation of wealth with many high-skilled jobs both in developed and developing countries. This industry can in fact be considered in its vertical dimension, associating very different specialties as will be seen in the next section".[10]

11.2.2 Some Cases

In order to understand the peculiar reasoning of Courts and National Competition Authorities in case of a violation of rules on the abuse of dominant market positions, we can consider an interesting Decision of the Irish Competition Authority O. E/02/ 001 on the Reduction in Travel Agents' Commissions by Aer Lingus plc (Case: COM/15/02).

The Competition Authority received a complaint in January 2002 with regard to Aer Lingus plc ("Aer Lingus").

The activities of Aer Lingus include the provision of passenger operations and cargo air transportation services to the UK, mainland Europe, and the US, as well as within Ireland. Aer Lingus distributes its tickets through its website, travel agents and reservations staff. The closure of all Aer Lingus Travel Shops was announced on January 15th, 2002. Aer Lingus was trying to move towards booking over the Internet.

The complaint alleges that Aer Lingus plc ("Aer Lingus") had abused its dominant position in the full-service airline market in the State by unilaterally reducing the commission on ticket sales from 9% to 5%, effective February 1st, 2002. It was claimed that this would reduce the number of travel agents in the State, leading to reduced competition among travel agents.

---

[10] Souty (2004).

The unilateral reduction in profit margins by Aer Lingus would result in travel agents going out of business and consumers would therefore lose an important source of impartial advice and information.

Because of the reduction in travel agent numbers, it would be difficult for new full-service airlines to enter the Irish market.

From the consumers' point of view, the reduction of travel agents would adversely affect elderly persons who tend not to have credit cards.

The subject is covered by Section 5 of the Irish Competition Act 2002 and reads as follows, according to art. 82 of the EU Treaty:

(1) Any abuse by one or more undertakings of a dominant position in trade for any goods or services in the State or in any part of the State is prohibited.

(2) Without prejudice to the generality of subsection 1, such abuse may, in particular, consist in-

(a) directly or indirectly imposing unfair purchase or selling prices or other unfair trading conditions,

(b) limiting production, markets or technical development to the prejudice of consumers,

(c) applying dissimilar conditions to equivalent transactions with other trading parties, thereby placing them at a competitive disadvantage,

(d) making the conclusion of contracts subject to the acceptance by other parties of supplementary obligations which by their nature or according to commercial usage have no connection with the subject of such contracts.

In order to establish that there is a breach of Section 5 of the Act, the Authority must demonstrate that the undertaking in question: holds a dominant position in a relevant market; and has abused that dominant position.

The creation or existence of a dominant position does not breach the Act; rather it is the abuse of that position that constitutes the breach.

In assessing dominance, the Authority takes into account if and to what extent an undertaking encounters constraint on its ability to behave independently. Those constraints might, for example, be entry barriers that make it difficult for potential competitors to compete effectively.

Based on the data provided in the complaint, the market share of Aer Lingus would appear to be between 40% and 50%. In the Virgin/British Airways case, BA was found to be dominant with a market share of 39.7% in 1998.

The market share of Aer Lingus, based on the information in the complaint, is well above BA's 39.7%. However, it appears that the market share of Aer Lingus is only four (not eight) times that of its closest rival.

There would appear to be sufficient competitive constraints on Aer Lingus that would prevent it from acting independently of its rivals by, for example, raising prices above the competitive level. Regarding the market position abuse, it could be argued that Aer Lingus is using its buyer power to dictate excessively low commissions. In a commission levels survey, Aer Lingus' levels did not seem out of line with other national flag carriers. Thus, there is insufficient evidence to suggest that Aer Lingus is exerting any market power it has to set excessively low commissions.

11.2 Business Contract Law and Competition Law

Regarding a possible reduction in competition, the complaint argued that there would be less competition due to the decline in the number of travel agents. However, a decline in the number of outlets does not necessarily lead to a decline in competition.

It is also worth remembering an American case, which has certain aspects that are similar to the Aer Lingus case, decided by the Barbados Fair Trading Commission. The Commission received a report from the Travel Agents Association of Barbados (TAAB) alleging that LIAT (1974) Ltd. had engaged in anti-competitive practices with respect to the sale of airline tickets. LIAT was enabling its own retail ticket outlets to offer certain benefits and privileges to customers while not permitting travel agents the opportunity to offer the same.

In January 2009, the Commission completed its investigation into this matter and found that: the airline could not be defined as a direct competitor of the travel agents, and so could not be said to have acquired market share at the expense of travel agents as alleged. Moreover, LIAT's conduct was directly aimed at enhancing the production of the product, and consumers were allowed a fair share of the benefits in the form of lower ticket prices.

In this case however, LIAT's market position is significant, no distortion of competition arises from the conduct of the air company with respect to the travel agents, because travel agents are not direct competitors of the company and because the company conduct is complaint with consumer interests.

According to the Fair Competition Act of the State of Barbados, there was no abuse of a dominant position.

Another typical problem in B2B relationships is that of delayed payments to suppliers by big firms such as big hotel companies, for which national laws try to provide solutions. In European Union countries, this issue is ruled by Directive 7/2011 of February 16th, 2011 on combating late payment in commercial transactions. A number of substantive changes are to be made to the previous Directive 2000/35/EC of the European Parliament and of the Council of June 29th, 2000 on combating late payment in commercial transaction. As noted by the European Commission, even though a supplier delivers the goods or performs the services on time, many corresponding invoices are paid well after the deadline. It is a matter of fact that late payments negatively affect liquidity and the financial management of undertakings, undermining their competitiveness and profitability when the creditor needs to obtain external financing because of late payment. It is obvious that the risk of these negative effects strongly increases in periods of economic downturn. According to paragraph 13 of this Directive, "provision should be made for business-to-business contractual payment periods to be limited, as a general rule, to 60 calendar days. However, there may be circumstances in which undertakings require more extensive payment periods, for example when undertakings wish to grant trade credit to their customers. It should therefore remain possible for the parties to expressly agree on payment periods longer than 60 calendar days, provided, however, that such extension is not grossly unfair to the creditor".

Another characteristic of B2B contracts in the tourism sector is that they are usually incomplete contracts because of some peculiarities of market demand in this sector: seasonality and uncertainty.

The term 'incomplete contract' indicates the limitations of contracts that fail to specify not only investment levels, but also many of the other contingencies that a complete contract might include. The reason for this failure is usually due to the fact that some contingencies cannot be imagined, or due to the costs of writing complex contracts.[11] With regard to the tourism sector, we also have to consider that, as economists have noted, the tourism market demand is stochastic because it depends on stochastic and exogenous variables (natural resources, institutional aspects, social and cultural elements, economic and political conditions, psychological factors). Other goods in this industry are typical experience goods and the consumption is time intensive. As result of the above considerations, it is correct to say that the demand, the reservation price, the frequency and the duration of holidays are all stochastic variables. Another important characteristic of the tourism sector is that the tourist product is a non-storable good because the product supplied to the customer is not a physical good, but an immaterial service-good.

Some authors observe that "in the tourism sector it is very difficult to observe complete contracts. The typical tourism incomplete contracts regulating the business relationship between the Tour Operator and the Hotel are the Free Sale and the Allotment contracts. In this paper we analyze these incomplete contracts into a microeconomic perspective and within an optimal contract design approach. In particular, through optimal contract design and incomplete contract approaches we analyze the design and efficiency consequences of imperfections resulting from contractual incompleteness".[12]

References

Baker, G., Gibbons, R., & Murphy, K. J. (2001). Relational contracts and the theory of the firm. *Quarterly Journal of Economics, 117*, 1.

Berger, K. P. (2006). Law and practice of escalation clauses. *Arbitration International, 22*, 5.

Castellani, M., & Mussoni, M. (2007). An economic analysis of the tourism contracts: Allotment and free sale. In Á. Matias, P. Nijkamp, & P. Neto (Eds.), *Advances in modern tourism research* (pp. 51–85). Physica-Verlag HD.

Dimatteo, L. A. (2001). A theory of efficient penalty: Eliminating the law of liquidated damages. *American Business Law Journal, 38*, 633.

Hart, O., & Moore, J. (1988). Incomplete contracts and renegotiation. *Econometrica, 56*, 755.

Hart, O., & Moore, J. (1999). Foundations of incomplete contracts. *Review of Economic Studies, 66*, 115.

Hesselink, M. W. (2011). Unfair terms in contracts between businesses. *Center for the Study of European Contract Law*, 6.

---

[11] Hart and Moore (1988), pp. 755–778; Id., (1999), pp. 115–138.

[12] Castellani and Mussoni (2007), pp. 51–85.

References

Lando, O. (2003). Principles of European contract law and UNIDROIT principles: Moving form harmonisation to unification? *Uniform Law Review, 8*, 123.

McNeil, R. (1978). Contracts: Adjustment of long-term economic relations under classical, neo-classical, and relational contract law. *Northwestern University Law Review, 72*, 854.

Mouza, S., & Furmston, M. (2008). From contract to Umbrella agreement. *The Cambridge Law Journal, 67*, 37.

Souty, F. (2004). *Passport to Progress: Competition Challenges for World Tourism and Global Anti-Competitive Practices in the Tourism Industry.* http://www3.dogus.edu.tr

Turner, S. (2020). *Parametric insurance policies: Do they have to be weather-related?* www.airmic.com

Chapter 12
Tourism Industry Contracts and Structural Formulas: Management and Ownership

Contents

12.1	Business's Legal Structures	159
	12.1.1 Business Ownership, Partnership, Corporation	159
12.2	Hotel Lease	160
	12.2.1 Contents of Hotel Lease	160
	12.2.2 Lease, Management, Franchising	162
12.3	Hotel Franchising	163
	12.3.1 Franchising Contents	163
	12.3.2 Green Franchising	166
12.4	Hotel Management Contract	167
	12.4.1 Contents of Management Contracts	167
	12.4.2 Management Contract as Example of Collaborative Contracting	171
References		175

12.1 Business's Legal Structures

12.1.1 Business Ownership, Partnership, Corporation

Business ownership forms are a business's legal structures. The most common forms of business ownership are: sole proprietorship, partnership and corporation, cooperatives and societies.

It is important not to confuse business ownership forms with business types, such as retail, service, etc.

Business ownership form choice is one of the most important decisions that one will make when starting a business because each form of business ownership has its own liabilities and responsibilities. If a corporation is more expensive to form and maintain, it provides the business owner with more personal liability protection than sole proprietorship or common partnership forms of business ownership.

Moreover, the form of business ownership will affect many aspects of business operations, including attracting potential clients.

© The Author(s), under exclusive license to Springer Nature Switzerland AG 2021
S. Landini, *Sustainable Tourism Contracts*,
https://doi.org/10.1007/978-3-030-83140-0_12

It should also be noted that it is not necessary to keep the same form of business for the entire life of a business. For example, many small businesses start out as sole proprietorships and then become corporations later on.

The sole proprietorship form is a business that is owned and operated by one individual who is personally responsible for all the liabilities and obligations his business incurs. This means that if the business fails, any of his assets can be seized to discharge the liabilities that are owed. On the positive side, a sole proprietorship is the easiest form of business to set up.

A general partnership is defined as a business arrangement between two or more individuals who share the profits and liabilities of the business. However, general partnerships are not the only types of partnership arrangements that can be formed. In many countries, Limited Liability Partnership are an option.

Corporations create a distinct legal entity separate from its owners (shareholders). The extended liability protection is one of the main reasons that businesses choose the corporation form: in general, no member of the company can be held personally liable for the debts, obligations, or acts of the company. A shareholder is only liable for the unpaid portion of the shares owned.

It is also possible to separate ownership from management through contracts such as lease contracts and management contracts.

12.2 Hotel Lease

12.2.1 Contents of Hotel Lease

A lease contract is an agreement for leasing real estate and apartments, manufacturing and farming equipment, and consumer goods such as automobiles, televisions, stereos, and appliances.

A lease is a contract between the property lessor (owner) and a lessee (or tenant) who obtains the right to possess and use the property owned by the lessor for a certain period of time without gaining ownership. The lessee agrees to pay rent and a deposit. Upon regaining possession of the property, the lessor shall refund the lessee the total amount of the deposit, minus any damages to the property, normal wear and tear expected, and minus any unpaid rent.

It is important to distinguish rental of a hotel business and lease of property for hotel use.

The agreement contains special provisions on contract renewals regarding contract duration. Generally, it is provided that at the expiration date, the lease will automatically be renewed for a certain period of time unless either party notifies the other of its intention to terminate the lease at least, usually, one month before its expiration date.

Usually lease contracts provide that:

12.2 Hotel Lease

- the lessee shall not sublease nor assign the premises without the written consent of the lessor;
- the lessor may not enter the premises without having given the lessee at least 24 hours' notice, except for in case of an emergency. The lessor may enter to inspect, repair, or show the premises to prospective buyers or lessees if notice has been given;
- the lessee agrees to occupy the premises and shall keep them in the same good conditions and shall not make any alternations without the written consent of the lessor;
- the lessor agrees to regularly maintain the building and grounds.

In all countries, lease contracts dealing with commercial goods and services (such as a hotel lease) are strictly regulated by statute. Commercial lease laws govern the rights and duties of lessors and lessees in lease contracts that involve commercial goods. In USA most states have enacted, with regard to commercial lease contracts as well, the Uniform Commercial Code (UCC), which is a set of suggested laws relating to commercial transactions. The UCC was one of many uniform codes enacted by the late nineteenth-century movement towards uniformity among state laws. The National Conference of Commissioner on Uniform State Laws (NCUSL) is a non-governmental body formed in 1892 upon the recommendation of the American Bar Association for the purpose of promoting "uniformity in state laws on all subjects where uniformity is deemed desirable and practicable." Made up of lawyers chosen by the states, the Conference oversees the preparation of proposed laws, "Uniform Laws" which the states are encouraged to adopt. For over a century this process, carried out through committees that prepare successive drafts for review and ultimate approval by the full Conference has continued to function. By the moment the Commissioners have approved more than two hundred uniform laws, of which more than 100 have been adopted by at least one state. A few have been widely adopted and have, as a consequence, approached the hoped for uniform national law on their subject. Commercial lease contract is regulated by article 2A of the UCC.

Regarding commercial leases, it is important to distinguish the bare rent of real estate use by the lessee for a certain commercial activity specified in the lease contract from the lease of a business or of the branch of a business. One can own a business without having to do the initial start-up work by leasing a business from an established business owner.

A lease agreement is almost like ownership and is frequently used in the hotel business. The hotel company rents a building and runs the entire operation, paying rent every month or every year.

Lease agreements are not particularly popular among big operators because they are quite risky and costly. Ownership and leasing are an "asset heavy" way to develop a business. In fact, hotel companies cannot develop a large number of properties with lease agreements; otherwise the balance sheet becomes too heavy and risky. In the 2008 financial crisis, for instance, companies that were heavily leveraged with lease and ownership were on the edge of bankruptcy because they had to keep on paying the rent.

Moreover, it is important to consider the owner's costs and responsibilities. Often the lessee is responsible for general repairs and maintenance, but structural repairs and capital items are generally excluded from the lessee's obligations. These are the specific items for which the owner is responsible: the roof, gutters, downpipes, walls, air-conditioning and any other plant and equipment that is, or becomes, the property of the lessor. Other costs include: underground power, sewerage works, and fixtures and fittings related to services such as gas, electricity, water or drainage.

Lease contracts sometimes include redevelopment clauses or early termination clauses. Such clauses entitle the owner to terminate a lease before the end of the lease in order to carry out major works to renovate or redevelop the building (in the case of the redevelopment clause). It is a matter of fact that without premises, a business may be forced to close or suffer a loss in sales and unforeseen expenses if it is required to relocate.

If a lessee decides to agree to a redevelopment clause, it is strongly advised that the clause should provide for compensation for the loss of goodwill.

In commercial leases, the institution of compensation for the loss of commercial goodwill is of fundamental importance in relation to the company's ability to generate profits in those places through past and on-going contacts with the public and leading to recognize the company's assets taken as a whole, higher value. In Italy, for instance, according to art. 34 of the Italian Act of 1978 n. 392, a lease agreement termination that does not involve termination for breach, termination or withdrawal of the lessee, gives rise to the lessee's right to compensation for the loss of goodwill, consisting of a sum to be equal to eighteen month's paid rent (and twenty-one months in the case of the hotel business).

12.2.2 Lease, Management, Franchising

Lease contracts need to be distinguished from other contracts adopted to manage hospitality industry.

Management contracts are other contractual instruments that are used to separate ownership from management.

A management contract is an agreement between a hotel owner and a hotel management company under which, for a fee, the management company operates the hotel in the hospitality industry.

A management agreement is substantially an agency agreement: the hotel management company operates the hotel, making all the day-to-day decisions on behalf of the owner. The hotel management company appoints a general manager, who will generally come from its own system. The general manager will hire the staff and will control costs and revenue and food costs, will apply brand standards, and will generally supervise the management of the hotel.

A franchise agreement will cost an owner less than a management agreement, but at the same time, he/she will receive fewer services, because a franchise agreement usually provides only sales services, as well as purchasing, sales tools, a brand, a reservation system, a network, international advertising and exposure for the hotel operator. Essentially, the franchisor is a supplier who allows an operator, or a franchisee, to use the supplier's trademark and distribute the supplier's goods. In return, the operator pays the supplier a fee.

Most groups attempt to have a balanced portfolio with the right amount of lease agreements, the right amount of ownership, the right amount of management agreements and the right amount of franchise agreements. In this way, a business should be sustainable during difficult periods and profitable during good periods.

12.3 Hotel Franchising

12.3.1 Franchising Contents

A franchise contract is an agreement under which one party (the franchisor) grants another party (the franchisee) the right to carry on a business, supplying goods or services under a specific system or marketing plan. The business is associated with a particular trademark, advertising or commercial symbol owned, used, licensed or specified by the franchisor.

The franchisee is required to pay or agree to pay a fee to the franchisor before starting or continuing the business.

The term 'franchise' consists of the rights granted by a party (the franchisor) that authorize and require another party (the franchisee), in exchange for direct or indirect financial compensation, to engage in the business of selling goods or services on its own behalf under a system designated by the franchisor which includes know-how and assistance, prescribes in substantial part the manner in which the franchised business is to be operated, includes significant and continuing operational control by the franchisor, and is substantially associated with a trademark, service mark, trade name or logotype designated by the franchisor.

The term franchisee includes a sub-franchisee in its relationship with the sub-franchisor, and the sub-franchisor in its relationship with the franchisor. At the same time, the term franchisor includes the sub-franchisor in its relationship with its sub-franchisees.

In the pre-contractual phase, the franchisor is obliged to send the franchisee a disclosure document (a document containing the information required under the national law, see, for instance, Article 3 of the Italian Franchise Law (Act May 6th, 2004, n. 129), the franchise agreement, and a copy of the franchising conduct code adopted. In Europe, one of the most important franchising conduct codes is that of the European Franchise Federation (EFF), which is an international non-profit Association constituted in 1972 (1). Its members are national Franchise Associations or Federations established in Europe.

Regarding the pre-contractual duty of disclosure, it is important to determine the information that is required to be disclosed, i.e., all data that can be reasonably expected to have a significant effect on the prospective franchisee's decision to acquire the franchise.

In order to establish the franchisor's obligations, it is fundamental to define the concept of know-how, which is part of the franchisor's obligations.

According to the European Franchise Federation (EFF) the term know-how in a franchising contract: "means a body of non-patented practical information, resulting from experience and testing by the Franchisor, which is secret, substantial and identified.

Secret means that the know-how, as a body or in the precise configuration and assembly of its components, is not generally known or easily accessible; it is not limited in the narrow sense that each individual component of the know-how should be totally unknown or unobtainable outside the Franchisor's business.

Substantial means that the know-how includes information which is indispensable to the franchisee for the use, sale or resale of the contract goods or services, in particular for the presentation of goods for sale, the processing of goods in connection with the provision of services, methods of dealing with customers, and administration and financial management; the know-how must be useful for the Franchisee by being capable, at the date of conclusion of the agreement, of improving the competitive position of the Franchisee, in particular by improving the Franchisee's performance or helping it to enter a new market .

Identified means that the know-how must be described in a sufficiently comprehensive manner so as to make it possible to verify that it fulfils the criteria of secrecy and substantiality; the description of the know-how can either be set out in the franchise agreement or in a separate document or recorded in any other appropriate form".

The obligations of the franchisor shall be:

- to have operated a business concept with success, for a reasonable time and in at least one pilot unit before starting a franchise network;
- to own, or have legal rights to the use, of the network's trade name, trademark or other distinguishing identification;
- to provide the individual franchisee with initial training and continuing commercial and/or technical assistance during the entire life of the agreement.

On the other side, the obligations of the franchisee are:

- to devote its best endeavours to the growth of the franchise business and to the maintenance of the common identity and reputation of the franchise network;
- to supply the franchisor with verifiable operating data in order to facilitate the determination of performance and the financial statements necessary for effective management guidance, and allow the franchisor, and/or its agents, to have access to the individual franchisee's premises and records at the franchisor's request and at reasonable times;

12.3 Hotel Franchising

- not to disclose to third parties the know-how provided by the franchisor, neither during nor after the termination of the agreement.

The minimum content of a franchising contract shall contain: the rights granted to the franchisor; the rights granted to the individual franchisee; the goods and/or services to be provided to the individual franchisee; the obligations of the franchisor; the obligations of the individual franchisee; the terms of payment by the individual franchisee; the duration of the agreement, which should be long enough to allow individual franchisees to amortize their initial investments specific to the franchise; the basis for any renewal of the agreement; the terms upon which the individual franchisee may sell or transfer the franchised business and the franchisor's possible pre-emption rights in this respect; provisions relevant to the use of the franchisor's distinctive signs, trade name, trademark, service mark, store sign, logo or other distinguishing identification by the individual franchisee; the franchisor's right to adapt the franchise system to new or changed methods; provisions for the termination of the agreement; provisions for surrendering promptly upon termination of the franchise agreement any tangible and intangible property belonging to the franchisor or other owner thereof.[1]

As someone underlines "Franchising contracts are designed to bring together two kinds of entrepreneurs, the franchiser and the franchisee, and to maintain their relationship in the long run. In contrast to standard exchange contracts in law, which are specifically designed to bring about the completion of an exchange efficiently, franchise contracts are designed to make it possible for the entrepreneurs to initiate, to maintain, and to eventually terminate their relationship without dispute (. . .)Every franchise contract includes a set of provisions that define the commencement, termination, and ongoing operations of franchise relations. The internal organisation of franchise contracts specifies what kinds of rights and obligations are distributed to the parties and the nature of this allocation within each domain of provisions. We argue that the commencement and termination aspects of franchise contracts are usually written in order to make the relationship between the parties clear, and the contingencies specific. In these provisions, the contract is written in discrete terms in which each party's rights and duties are specifically delineated. The contractual provisions dealing with the ongoing operations and the conduct of the parties, on the other hand, cannot be made specific because it is impossible to define all the future contingencies and possible business opportunities. Under these conditions, the contract is usually written in relational terms in which each party's rights and obligations are defined in terms of powers and liabilities towards each other rather than in terms of specific duties and rights".[2]

---

[1] Lafontaine and Blair (2008–2009), p. 381.

[2] Leblebici (1996), pp. 403–418.

12.3.2 Green Franchising

What has been said so far becomes important for drawing up a green franchising i.e., a franchising contract ordered to reach eco-sustainable goals.[3]

The green approach can be applied to both products and services and takes place in very different areas: from clothing to food, from tourism to services for companies. Each of the eco-sustainable franchising activities focuses on a particular behavior that is essential for living a more eco-sustainable and eco-responsible life, which, as previously mentioned, are: reduction, reuse and recycling.

Ecological franchises dedicated to REDUCTION respond to the needs of companies and individuals regarding energy efficiency or the sale of products that reduce the production of waste, such as organic food sold in bulk or ecological products obtained from recycling. In this case, the franchisor normally guarantees all the necessary technical training, especially for renewable energy and plant services. The franchisee is obliged to respect the training obligations and to respect the rules of conduct, which are normally contained in a conducts code, to which the contract refers to as an integral part of the contractual content. In this way, the provision of the franchisor's rights to carry out periodic checks and the provision of terms for adjustment in the event that the checks result in breaches and penalties for cases of late adjustment are also important. Prolonged failure to adapt may lead to the termination of the contract. This too may be expressly provided for in the contract.

Ecological franchises that focus on REUSE invest in a growing sector, such as the second-hand market, taking advantage of all the opportunities provided by e-commerce. Eco-responsible behaviors, such as the regeneration of cartridges or the reuse of children's clothing and accessories, are an established and consolidated trend in purchasing habits. Something similar can be applied to the hospitality industry. Hotels need to compel their guests to reuse or recycle their towels during their stay. Washing towels every day uses too much water, too many detergents and too much energy. The hotel usually tries to persuade their guests to recycle or reuse with a simple card in the room which requests guests to reuse towels or linen. In this case, the franchisor has to provide the franchisee with its know-how regarding communication to guests, even though there are uniform practices in the sector.

Ecological franchises specialized in RECYCLING enhance recycling and monetize the separate collection of waste, which not only reduces the impact on the environment, but also offers tools of loyalty and additional income for those who already own a business. Some hotels and resorts try to minimize the direct impact of tourist activity on the environment through various initiatives: water usage and recycling, reducing the impact on the environment.

However, sustainability also includes social sustainability. Sustainable Franchising balances its business needs with the impact on health, and the quality and equity goals of social franchising for health. The franchisor and franchisee have to face trade-offs as they select financing strategies: increasing cost recovery from

---

[3] Bellone and Matla (2012).

franchisees may impact the program's ability to serve the poor; focusing on high margin products rather than service delivery may reduce the impact on health; and programs often struggle to find a balance between prioritizing cost savings and training or quality assurance activities.

We can list several advantages of investing in green/sustainable franchises:

- high loyalty business opportunities;
- sensitive consumers looking for reliable products;
- accurate attention to cutting-edge marketing strategies;
- high rate of innovation and creativity;
- good ease of access, economics and logistics;
- cost reduction.

In this respect, the know-how acquired by the franchisor in "green communication" with consumers becomes important. Special training and the delivery of distinctive signs, brochures etc. must be provided by the franchisor. Provisions must also be made to reduce the risk of injury to the intellectual property of the franchisor.

Of course, green franchising also presents challenges for the franchisee: technological capability because some green activities can be facilitated by technology; careful evaluation of the investment and the necessary commitment.

12.4 Hotel Management Contract

12.4.1 Contents of Management Contracts

The terms of a sustainable franchise find a mirror application in the case of a management contract where the manager undertakes to respect specific sustainability obligations.

A management contract is an agreement under which a company (called operator or provider) runs a business on behalf of a third party (called owner) in return for a fee. In this arrangement, the responsibilities and rewards of owning and operating are divided in accordance with the contract drawn up between the parties. In this case, the know-how on how to manage the activity in a sustainable way is the responsibility of the operator and specific obligations can be inserted against him.

In short, we can say that a management contract is an onerous agreement under which a company assigns its management (and its know-how) to another company.

It is well known that the method of management contracts was developed in the British Empire during the nineteenth century as a form of managing enterprises in overseas territories on behalf of domestic British enterprises.[4]

---

[4]Schlüter (1987), p. 18.

The nature of the relationship is that the operator is responsible for the day-to-day running of the business, including hiring and firing employees. As well as providing accommodation, and additional functions such as conference facilities, the operator will take reservations and conduct the marketing and promotion of the business. The operator will be responsible for routine maintenance and will procure other capital projects needed for the business, although these will typically be authorized and paid for by the owner.

The owner may be an individual or a company (such as a Bank or an Insurance Company) that wishes to own a business, usually as a long-term property investment. The owner typically benefits from the management expertise, skills, know-how and often, the commercial structure of the operator, which would otherwise not be available to an owner attempting to operate the business himself.

The main benefits for the operator are:

- to have the possibility to expand its scope of operations and brand diffusion with little or no capital outlay.
- to cover marketing and central management costs by way of a management charge through the 'base fee' paid by the owner and other charges.

The large variety of these contract arrangements is continuously evolving. In the early days of management contracts, the remuneration of the operator consisted of a base fee and an incentive fee generally based on gross operating profit (GOP).[5] GOP is calculated by deducting operating costs from gross revenue. Owners began to realize that this remuneration substantially left them with all the risk. In many cases, other measures of performance are taken into account such as RevPAR (revenue per available room) or ROR (room occupancy rate). In some cases, the operator may be required to guarantee a minimum return to the owner on the invested capital.

Capital improvements are divided into:

- routine capital improvements, required to maintain revenues and profits at their present levels;
- discretionary capital improvements, to generate more revenue.

If the owner elects to postpone a required repair, this will not eliminate or save the expenditure but merely defer the payment. For instance, if a hotel has operated with a maintenance budget that is lower than normal, it is likely to have accumulated a considerable amount of deferred maintenance. An insufficient reserve will eventually undermine the standard of the property and may also lead to a decline in the hotel's performance and its value.

The negotiation of the management agreement, which focuses on the respective rights and obligations of the owner and the operator, is critical to the financial success of the business and the return on the owner's investment. The first draft of the agreement will usually be offered from the prospective of the operator. The

---

[5] Pizam (2005), p. 290.

12.4 Hotel Management Contract

operator will usually seek a long-term right to operate the business under its brand, according to standards commonly used across the operator's firm or group.

The owner will try to negotiate the terms of the agreement, introducing some balance and giving the owner rights and remedies.

The main obligations of the owner are: fee payment and the obligation to integrate the operator into the owner's structure.

Above, we have seen the two main kinds of fees: base fee and incentive fee.

In addition to these, other fees are usually provided:

- a commitment fee, to be paid in case of special pre-agreements or when the agreement includes construction clauses. This fee generally operates as an advance payment;
- a termination fee paid when the agreement is terminated or when the construction period is terminated. It usually acts as a safety clause, in case the management company does not comply with its obligations;
- a special services fee, for additional services provided within the agreement framework, such as construction work, leasing of specific rights of industrial property, maintenance services provisions and technical support, public relation services and advertising, mediation for loan credits, etc;
- fees paid for expenses and costs to the management company during the agreement period and due to the business management services provision.

The obligation to integrate the operator into the owner's structure arises from the goal of management relationship itself. As we have already mentioned, the purpose of a management contract is to undertake the management of another company. To achieve this, the management company needs to become part of the owner's structure. This means that the owner has to allow the operator to intervene within the structure. In this way, the operator obtains control from the owner but, according to the mutual obligation of cooperation and collaboration (see infra), such control should be based on the owner's initial and continuous consent.

The main obligations of the operator are related to its fiduciary duties. Other obligations refer to the exact goal assumed by the provider or represent the implicit means to achieve the scope of the relationship:

- assignment of management staff and staff training. After signing the agreement, the management company selects, detects and places competent managerial and administrative staff in the assigning company. Managerial skills and know-how improvements are expected. Staff training is also part of the provider's obligation. Management agreements usually include a special appendix about the terms and procedures for know-how transfer and staff training;
- respect for the managed company's policy. Any action from the management company needs to comply with the philosophy and the scope of the managed company. For instance, in the case of a tourism enterprise, the management company has to respect its local and/or ecological character;
- obligation to integrate the managed company in the provider's business network. The provider normally assumes the obligation to incorporate the managed

company into its business network, comprehensive of its strategic alliances and partnerships.

Management agreements are usually long and sometimes complex, but often it is many of the same issues that arise.

In particular, the owner should be careful not to accidentally create a tenancy under which the operator will enjoy the rights of a business lessee. This risk arises because the management agreement, if it is not correctly drafted, can have the basic features of a lease: exclusive possession of the premises for a defined period of time.

Moreover, operators typically prefer long initial terms and several long renewal periods that can be exercised by the operator. The owner may prefer a shorter duration without specific renewal rights.

It should be noted that the relationship between owner and operator is usually governed not only by the traditional management agreement but also by parallel arrangements such as a license, royalty or service agreements.

In practice, differences emerge between the terms of management agreements which are entered into as part of a 'sale and manage back' transaction and those management agreements which are entered into by operators on a standalone basis, in relation to a new development, for example.

The management agreement should clearly distinguish between the responsibilities to be assumed by the owner and those to be assumed by the operator and should specify what each party needs to provide to enable the other to perform its part of the agreement.

Apart from the typical obligations of the owner (fee payment, integration of the operator into the structure) and of the operator (transfer of management, staff training, etc.) mentioned above, other terms and conditions are usually negotiated in management relationships.

The owner should limit the operator's ability to be involved in other businesses that compete in the same business sector as that of the owner.

The owner will not want to have the necessity of managing the operations but should have the ability to oversee and, in appropriate circumstances, manage the incurrence of costs and expenses so as to preserve the return on its investment. The operator should prepare, deliver and keep on operating capital expenditures and budgets approved by the owner. Flexibility to adjust these budgets to meet changing circumstances should be considered.

Operators who run the business under their own brand will likely demand the right to incur expenditure in order to preserve the brand reputation associated with its goodwill and common operating standards. These agreements can be onerous for the owner. Where such a right is provided for the operator, the owner could incur unpreventable costs. For instance, if the operator's hotel group decides to introduce a swimming pool in all its branded hotels, the owner could be forced to agree to the building of a new pool complex at his hotel.

The operator should provide complete, detailed and accurate financial data to the owner, who may reserve the right to audit the books from time to time. The oversight of accounting books should be in accordance with accepted accounting standards.

12.4 Hotel Management Contract

The owner should have the right to terminate if the operator defaults under the agreement. The owner may also have the right to terminate if the operator fails to meet the defined performance measures detailed in the management agreement, or if the operator experiences change.

He may also reserve the right to terminate without cause, but in this case the operator usually requires the payment of a termination fee equivalent to the anticipated return over the unexpired duration of the contract.

Business continuity on termination is important and the management agreement should provide for a smooth transition on termination or expiry.

Ownership of intellectual property rights in the management processes, computer systems and branded materials should be addressed in the management agreement. If the operator retains these rights, there should be adequate protection for the owner in terms of business continuity in the case of termination or expiry of the agreement.

Taking the above into consideration in order to determine the characteristics of such contracts, we can say that management contracts are mainly used as a means of cooperative development between companies. In fact, the goal of a management contract is the transfer of the management of an enterprise, corporation, business unit or facility from the owner to the management company, known as the operator or provider.

Therefore, management contracts, along with franchising contracts, are types of business governance structures and part or all of the managing activities of the collaborating parties are performed according to a common objective achievement.

Since the operator runs the management under its name and on behalf of the owner, the profits, damages, rights and liabilities emanating from the operator's activity are upon the owner, who also takes the risk for the success or failure of management. At the same time, it is normally stated in the contract that the manager's payment will be determined according to management results. As we have seen, an incentive fee calculated on the profits is usually provided.

12.4.2 Management Contract as Example of Collaborative Contracting

It is a matter of fact that the above conditions determine a strong interplay between the position of the owner and the position of the operator.

Not only is the operator controlled by the owner, but the operator's interests become attached to the owner's interests as well. This is not only because of the management fees, which are usually partially determined by the management's results, but also because of the owner's integration into the business networks of the provider. The parties therefore share common goals and a common structure.

In this way, it is possible to highlight another key element of management contracts: their fiduciary content. A fiduciary duty arises from the management contract. It can be defined as the duty of the operator to adopt the objectives of the owner. The fiduciary element obviously varies depending on the obligations provided in the contract, the duration and the significance of the specific relation.[6] Due to such fiduciary duties, a continuous dialog and a constant negotiation between parties about important management choices is required. Some authors say "Therefore, there is an obligation for collaboration of both parties and especially for preparing the recipient to include the provider in the legal and business structure of business management provision. However, the meaning of collaboration obligation does not only consist of the obligation for provider's inclusion in the recipient's structure. It also includes provision of information from one party to the other. As stated above information must be provided both by the management company to the recipient and by the recipient to the management company; this is a compulsory term for their collaboration and for the success of the agreement. Moreover, according to the duty of care, which characterizes the parties' fiduciary relation, especially as an assignment of such an important responsibility like management and as a means for a company to fully invest in another, it is obvious that even if such an obligation is not mentioned in the agreement, both parties are obliged to consult each other before performing any action provided by the agreement and make any possible effort for a continuous collaboration with each other, in order to take the best possible decision".[7]

A constant negotiation is also required in order to solve conflicts, conventionally avoiding the termination of the contract, which is not an easy process and may involve high risks and losses for both parties. At the same time, the agreement's benefits are usually only evident after years of cooperation. Another key element of management agreement is its long duration.

Moreover, a management contract is a typically incomplete agreement because it is not possible to determine all aspects of the relationship in advance, rather many aspects need to be constantly negotiated because of the above considerations. "This relation is determined by the special role and function of corporate management. Management not only is the controlling and major activity of every corporation, always linked with its institutional self-existence, but it also constitutes a very complex activity related to every aspect of a corporation and affecting every matter of it. The relation between the parties involves issues concerning asset control, separation of control and ownership, roles in decision making, allocation of risk, link of provider's fees and recipient's results, careful planning, transfer of know-how and intangible assets, integration of provider's staff in the recipient's structure, allocation of responsibilities, obligations and liability. Thence, every management contract is characterized by a controversy: it can never be complete enough as the management's object cannot be fully determined in advance, while it must have a detailed content that should try to cover as much as possible aspects of the relation. Nevertheless, in every case, the object of transfer should be limited to a more or less extensive degree, as it cannot reach the full separation of the recipient from its own

---

[6]Hynes (1997), p. 443.

[7]Diathesopoulos (2010), p. 90.

12.4 Hotel Management Contract

management. Furthermore, the actual value of the exchanges that the relation involves cannot be easily quantified and measured. The measurement and evaluation of the provider's performance is a very difficult task and it is usually approximately conducted; that is a matter directly affecting the need for detailed initial planning of the relation as it could evolve to a source of future conflict".[8]

Because of the parties' interdependent cooperation, trust, reliance, mutuality, and the resolution of problems by consent represent the real foundations for the relationship between the owner and the operator.

Fiduciary duties can be specified in several bilateral obligations.

The element of trust created by the management contract imposes upon both parties, and particularly on the operator, the obligation of confidentiality, which requires the operator to keep any confidential information known due to the management relationship secret.

This obligation is normally explicit in most management contracts. In any case, this obligation derives from the fact that the operator acts as a manager for the owner.

The fiduciary nature of the management agreement also determines a bilateral duty of disclosure: the operator has to inform the owner about management development and other issues arising from management. On the other hand, the owner has to inform the operator about the financial, managerial and structural status of the enterprise.

One of the most typical terms of the agreement is the prohibition of the transfer of rights and liabilities, which means that parties are not allowed to transfer a right or liability arising from the management relationship to a third party.

Some authors also talk about the existence of a bilateral obligation of collaboration composed of single obligations (duty of disclosure, duty of integration of the provider into the owner's structure, constant negotiation, etc.) arising from the fiduciary nature of the management relationship. A peculiarity of the obligation of collaboration as a duty of constant negotiation is that it is usually not clearly predefined.

It is an open term that needs to be defined according to the concrete circumstances and needs of each case. Such a duty is determined only with regard to its purpose: its aim is always the effective performance of the duties by the contracting party and the best possible implementation of the agreement scope.

Such an obligation may not be specified in text in the contract. In many cases it simply arises from the interpretation of the agreement as an implied term. Moreover, social mores may favor behavior of collaboration.

A duty of non-competition is part of the above obligation of collaboration.

In the management agreement, the company undertaking the management is informed about any strengths and weaknesses of the owner because of the managerial merge between the parties.

---

[8]Ibidem, p. 40.

It is obvious that the management company, by acquiring full access to such details concerning the managed company, may find itself in an extremely favorable and advantageous position in terms of competition.

The obligation of non-competition constitutes the major restraint of the parties' powers and of their business freedom.

According to that duty, they are obliged to avoid any financial or commercial activity that could cause competition between them, thus limiting their business freedom. But the reason for this restraint represents the foundation of the management relationship, which is "the preservation of the relation, the enhancement of mutuality, the achievement of the relational goals and the emphasis on long-term mutual interest rather than on short-term individual profit.

Therefore, contractual solidarity/preservation of the relation, creation and restrain of power, harmonization of the relational conflict, harmonization with the social matrix, reciprocity and contract norms are related to this kind of bilateral obligation" (9).

As we have previously mentioned, what was said about green franchising can be repeated for the management contact. However, the contents of the two contracts are very different.

In the case of a management contract, it is possible for the operator to offer his know-how in green management in a similar way to what was seen for the franchise where the management is left to the franchisee, but it is the franchisor who, thanks to his own green know-how, has identified particular management rules, codes of conduct and training for the franchisee.

In the case of franchising, compliance with the green management rules is the responsibility of the franchisee, while in the case of a management contract it is up to the operator.

In the case of green franchising, the problem in applying green policies concerns the possible breach of contract by the franchisee and the determination of compensation obligations.

In the case of management, in the event that green policies result ineffective (in terms of energy saving) or incorrect (e.g., in cases of green washing by the operator), the owner will act for the breach of the contract and for compensation for the damage.

Therefore, having considered these issues, we have highlighted how important it is to draft the contract correctly, with adequate specification of the obligations incumbent on the parties and with the provision of penalties, which can quantify and give a value to green policies in case of a lack of pecuniary losses, and out-of-court conflict resolution tools to allow the attempted contract.

References

Bellone, V., & Matla, V. (2012). *Green Franchising*. Münchner Verlagsgruppe GmbH.

Diathesopoulos, M. (2010). *Relational contract theory and management contracts: A paradigm for the application of the Theory of the Norms*. Cambridge University Press.

Hynes, J. D. (1997). Freedom of contract, fiduciary duties and partnerships: The Bargain principle and the law of agency. *Washington Law Review, 54*, 443.

Lafontaine, F., & Blair, R. D. (2008–2009). The evolution of franchising and franchise contracts: Evidence from the United States. *Entrepreneurial Business Law Journal, 3*, 381.

Leblebici, H. (1996). The organization of relational contracts: The allocation of rights in franchising. *Journal of Business Venturing, 11*, 403–418.

Pizam, A. (2005). *International Enciclopedia of hospitality management*. Butterworth-Heinemann.

Schlüter, A. (1987). *Management und Consulting Vertrage*. De Gruyter.

Chapter 13
Conclusions

Contents

13.1 Contract as a Source of Tourism Law 177
    13.1.1 Private Autonomy and Regulation of Tourism Activity 177
    13.1.2 The Distinction Between B2B and B2C Contracts 178
13.2 Tourism Contracts and Levers to Sustainability 179
    13.2.1 Contracts as Levers 179
13.3 Contracts 2.0 Towards Sustainable Tourism 181
    13.3.1 Smart Contracts 181
    13.3.2 Smart Contracts in Tourism Sector 182
    13.3.3 Smart Contracts and Sustainable Tourism 182
References 183

13.1 Contract as a Source of Tourism Law

13.1.1 Private Autonomy and Regulation of Tourism Activity

As widely stressed in the book, tourism activity (products of hospitality industry, travel contracts, combinations of both) is regulated not only at level of national and international law. It is a matter of fact that, the most part of rules governing conducts of tourism operators and their customers can be found in contracts. This consideration doesn't show anything of anomalous from the point of view of the sources of law, but it is perfectly consistent with the application of the principle of subsidiarity in private law.

According to the principle of subsidiarity nothing should be done by a larger and more complex organization which can be done as well by a smaller and simpler organization closer to the matter. In other words, any activity which can be performed by a more decentralized entity, should be done by this. The principle of subsidiarity is a common principle of European union. In this regard, the principle of subsidiarity seeks to safeguard the ability of the Member States to take decisions and action and authorises intervention by the Union when the objectives of an action

---

© The Author(s), under exclusive license to Springer Nature Switzerland AG 2021   177
S. Landini, *Sustainable Tourism Contracts*,
https://doi.org/10.1007/978-3-030-83140-0_13

cannot be sufficiently achieved by the Member States, but can be better achieved at Union level and vice versa.[1]

The word subsidiarity comes from the Latin term *subsidium* that means help. Commonly there are two levels of subsidiarity: vertical subsidiarity (so called institutional subsidiarity), acting among public authorities, and horizontal subsidiarity (so called social subsidiarity), acting between public institutions and individuals.

In case of horizontal subsidiarity, the law subsidizes the private autonomy, that could be considered as an important instrument for the completion of the scale of values at national and international law level.

As underlined in the first chapter, tourism is also a phenomenon in continuous evolutions. Thus, it is difficult to regulate it with top down rules; massive and detailed national laws can become a burden for the tourism industry. For these reasons many governments decide against strongly regulating the private law of tourism according to a policy of minimal regulation.

Therefore, the main sources of tourism private law are customary law and private autonomy, which are clearly limited by national law (i.e., consumer's protection law, environmental protection law, etc.) and fundamental international principles.

13.1.2 The Distinction Between B2B and B2C Contracts

Private autonomy finds a different level of application in B2B contracts and in B2C contracts. In case of consumers contracts several threats and constraints impact on the freedom of consumers' choice (information asymmetry, unbalanced economic power in negotiation, pressure to sign, etc.).

The freedom of choice of consumers is important in order to improve fair competition in the market. Moreover, the consumers' freedom of choice is an aspect of major importance in a consumer society. In fact, as stressed in the book, consumers can contribute to a better society, as they result to be mainly attracted by sustainability at different level: socio-economic sustainability, environmental sustainability and lately health sustainability. According to the European directives on consumers, the term "consumer" means any natural person who is dealing for purposes that are outside his trade, business, or profession.

With regard to the tourism market, customers sometimes deal for purposes that are both outside and inside their trade, business, or profession. Business travellers are a good example of this. The tourism industry can be divided into leisure tourism and business tourism, characterized by the provision of facilities and services to delegates who attend meetings, congresses, exhibitions, and business events. In any case, also business travellers like to, during some brief moments of their trip, break routines and try out new activities.

---

[1] Nuzzo (2014); Jarvad (1994), pp. 797–803.

13.2 Tourism Contracts and Levers to Sustainability

For these reasons with regards to tourism sector, it is more correct to use the word traveller than consumer. The traveller is the counterparty of the tourism business and needs the same protection as the consumers with some specific rights and duties concerning the characteristics of tourism contracts. On first, tourism contracts are usually international contracts, as tourism is a global phenomenon. Many people choose to travel to learn about different cultures. It is not only cultural travellers that visit historic and culturally significant sites. On second, tourism can affect environmental sustainability. Natural attractions might themselves be destroyed by the multitude of tourists visiting them. Thus Governments must raise awareness about the natural environment needing protection from pollution caused by economic activity which allows for the environment to be enjoyed by many people. Governments have also to help and incentivize the private autonomy interventions in a sustainable perspective. Therefore, sustainability is a key word in tourism. So individuals or associations, acting independently according to the principle of subsidiarity, could active solutions of public interest and the States, regions, metropolitan cities, provinces and municipalities shall promote citizens' autonomous initiatives.

It is a priority to combine the development of the tourism sector with the preservation of cultural properties: both the so-called cultural property (museums, archaeological sites, etc.), and environmental heritage (natural beauty, parks, etc.). On third tourism and travel can be affected by occurrences (wars, terrorism attacks, natural phenomena, etc.). Thus, it is important to govern such occurrences and protect travellers that can find modifications in the execution of the contract.

Business contracts (B2B contracts) play a fundamental role in building relationships between companies and business partners. Contracts include the terms of agreements, the services or products to be exchanged.

With regard to B2B contracts we must underline the importance of maintaining conditions of fair competition in the market and collaboration in the negotiation and execution of contracts in a win-win attitude that can motivate firms to conduct environmental protection from the perspective of enhancing firm value. Win–Win is a situation, game, negotiation, or strategy in which all the parties benefit one way or another, so there are no losers. Win–win strategies can increase climate resilience and simultaneously improve air quality, and consequently health and wellbeing, while implement the economic development.

13.2 Tourism Contracts and Levers to Sustainability

13.2.1 Contracts as Levers

According to the principles of Physics, a lever is a mechanism that can be used to exert a large force over a small distance at one end of the lever by exerting a small force over a greater distance at the other end.

Generally speaking, a lever is an instrument to achieve a result higher than the strength applied.

In metaphoric terms, contracts could represent a lever when the effects produced by the contracts are of greater importance respect to the individual interests of the parties as they can reach socio-economic results of high value.

As said, consumers usually make environmental friendly choices and companies try to attract consumers' choices demonstrating that their products respect environmental friendly standard, so they have to build the governance of the production in that way. This implies special conduct codes governing the conduct of all participants to the production. Such conduct codes will be included in contracts governing the production chain.

We made the example of green franchising where the franchisor has to draw franchising contracts towards high environmental standards in term of energy saving, reduction of carbon foot print, etc.

Another example can be made with regard to the statutes of associations of tourism operators. As we have previously seen, tourism operator organisations contribute to sustainability through strategy and policy development. For instance, the IHRA (International Hotel and Restaurant Association) aims at developing eco-tourism by promoting sustainability among their members, fighting the various issues of climate change and by promoting measures in place to reduce CO_2 emissions.

IHRA statute include clause ensuring that all members, or all of those members who want to cover a particular position, are compliant with predetermined targets of sustainable development.

Moreover, IHRA has created the Emeraude Hotelier Certification.

The IHRA estimates that almost 80% of all hotels are small and medium enterprises (SMEs) at different stages of organisational development, and only 20% consist of large enterprises. There are only few international standards for the hospitality industry, and national regulations differ greatly from one nation to another. It seems to be necessary to find universally recognized standards that meet the different needs of hotels worldwide.

The creation of the Emeraude Hotelier Certification addresses this issue. Hotels will be awarded with the Emeraude Hotelier recognition if they successfully implement the guidelines stipulated to enhance sustainable tourism.

This certification should serve to motivate hotel management as well as staff to continuously develop sustainable practices.

The Emeraude Hotelier certification is based on a three-level scale. Depending on the number of criteria the hotel fulfils, it will be awarded with one, two or three Emeraudes.

The design of the association contract, of the Statute of the association, of the rules of the Certificate Competition the result of private autonomy moving the parties toward sustainable choices.

All these terms and conditions need be adequate to the changing reality and to the evolution in the qualification and determination of sustainability standards.

13.3 Contracts 2.0 Towards Sustainable Tourism

The technology can represent an important tool in building sustainable tourism contracts.

13.3 Contracts 2.0 Towards Sustainable Tourism

13.3.1 Smart Contracts

Smart contracts can be defined as an incorporation of contractual clauses encoded in computer language, in software or computer protocols, which are used for the conclusion and the execution of contractual relationships by conferring autonomous implementation of the programmed terms upon the occurrence of certain conditions defined.

Smart contracts usually take advantages from the Block chain technology. Block chain is a digital record of transactions: individual records, called blocks, are linked together in single list, called a chain. Each transaction added to a Block chain is validated by multiple computers on the Internet.[2]

A Block chain is a database that stores encrypted blocks of data then chains them together to form a chronological single-source-of-truth for the data.

Digital assets are distributed instead of copied or transferred, creating an immutable record of an asset, that is decentralized, allowing full real-time access and transparency to the public.

A transparent ledger of changes preserves integrity of the document, which creates trust in the asset.

Block chain's inherent security measures and public ledger make it a prime technology for almost every single sector.

This technology exploits a complex algorithm capable of estimating the interests of the counterparties, defining the content of the contract and, evaluating the moment in which the predefined conditions in the protocol are realized, proceeding to the conclusion and execution of the contract, obviously according to the law of default programming in the algorithm.

The construction of the algorithm itself is equipped with a self-learning function that allows it to modify the variables based on previous "experiences", making the result, that is the definition of the contractual regulation, unpredictable even for the developer.

Therefore, if in the abstract it could be affirmed that the algorithm executes a program and that it respects a predefined will, in the concrete case the construction of the function itself makes the system autonomous from the same instructions given from the beginning.

---

[2] Savelyev (2016); Szvabo (2010); Cuccuru (2017), p. 107 ss.; Perugini and Dal Checco (2018); Di Maio and Rinaldi (2016); De Caria (2019), p. 731 ss.

After an initial phase of application confined to the monetary and financial sector only, the technology is now applicable to any type of contract.

13.3.2 Smart Contracts in Tourism Sector

We have already considered the impact of technology in the tourism sector at level of distribution and consumer participation in the design of the tourist package thanks to the use of platforms or of Apps. We have seen how technology has also innovated the tourism production with regard to the use of virtual reality in tourist offers as well as in the promotion and distribution of travel packages.

Also with regard to tourism sector, we can list the greatest benefit of the Block chain—Smart Contract combination in terms of considerable increase in efficiency:

- Automation and legal certainty of the execution of contractual obligations visible to all network participants and not only to the parties involved.
- Transparency of contractual obligations and their results and implications such as to be presented and therefore "pre-understood" by all participants of the Block chain.
- Immutability of recorded transactions and therefore the inability to modify or cancel the contract.
- Possibility of finding an agreement in the absence of trust.

These characteristics, in terms of efficiency, allow to:

- save a considerable amount of resources in the negotiation and contract execution phases;
- accelerate performance; significantly reduce the likelihood of disputes and disputes between the parties.

13.3.3 Smart Contracts and Sustainable Tourism

The benefits of the Block chain applied to the tourism sector become of particular importance in the present moment due to the need to have a more flexible tourist offer with the possibility of last-minute changes taking into account the variations of the moment.

Moreover, smart contracts can be part of Smart Tourism phenomenon, that have emerged few years ago as a novel approach to new realities in tourism caused by the impact of the innovative information and communication technologies (ICTs) over the destinations, travellers, and businesses (including travel agencies, tour operators, hotels, carriers etc.). Within the smart tourism research domain, the Smart Tourism Destinations have received the most attention. The framework for Smart Tourism Destinations is based on the development of smart cities (municipalities that use information and communication technologies (ICT) to increase operational efficiency) and it is addressed to enhance tourists' satisfaction thanks to personalized services, development of a conceptual model for smart destination competitiveness, and analysis of the effects of smart destination strategy and solutions on the destination management processes and tourism experience. Smart Tourism Destinations use information and communication technologies (ICTs) and promise market advantage contributing to sustainable tourism development by implementing sustainability initiatives.[3] Smart tourism is reliant on technologies such as ICT, mobile communication, cloud computing, artificial intelligence, and virtual reality. It supports integrated efforts at a destination to find innovative ways to collect and use data derived from physical infrastructure, social connectedness and organizational sources (both government and non-government), and users to increase efficiency and also sustainability (let's think to the possibility to improve the use of public means of transport and to inform tourist about not conventional tourist destinations).

Advantages in the application of smart contract to tourism are:

- Regional assets, new market trends (eco-friendlier solutions) and the advantage of big data analysis.
- Better data management, diversification of tourism offers, more networking and cooperation between tourism operators.
- Sustainability dimension (circular economy and climate changes issues) in the tourism sector, that is one of the main themes of interest for future events.

These are the main opportunities and market needs identified, that put sustainability and economic development on the same wave recalling a famous quotation of Kofin Annan "Our biggest challenge in this new century is to take an idea that seems abstract - sustainable development - and turn it into a reality for all the world's people".

References

Cuccuru, P. (2017). Blockchain ed automazione contrattuale. Riflessioni sugli smart contract. *Nuova giur. civ. comm.*, p. 107 ss.

De Caria, R. (2019). The legal meaning of smart contracts. *European Review of Private Law, 6*, 731 ss.

Di Maio, D., & Rinaldi, G. (2016). Blockchain e la rivoluzione legale degli Smart Contracts. *Riv. dir. bancario, Attualità*, www.dirittobancario.it

Jarvad, I. M. (1994). Subsidiarity and autonomy. *History of European Ideas, 19*(4–6), 797–803.

Laranja, M., Marques Santos, A., Edwards, J., & Foray, D. (2021, January). From digital innovation to "smart tourism destination": Stakeholders' reflections in times of a pandemic. *Territorial Development Briefs Series.*

---

[3]Laranja et al. (2021).

Nuzzo, M. (Ed.). (2014). *Il principio di sussidiarieta nel diritto privato*. Giappichelli.

Perugini, M. L., & Dal Checco, P. (2018). *Introduzione agli* Smart Contract, in *www.papers.ssrn. com*

Savelyev, A. (2016). Contract law 2.0: "smart" contracts as the beginning of the end of classic contract law. *Higher School of Economics Research* (Paper No. WP BRP 71/LAW/2016).

Szvabo, N. (2010). *Smart contracts*, https://www.fon.hum.uva.nl